ARTISTS of the

CANYONS & CAMINOS

ARTISTS of the CANYONS & CAMINOS

SANTA FE: EARLY TWENTIETH CENTURY

Edna Robertson
and
Sarah Nestor

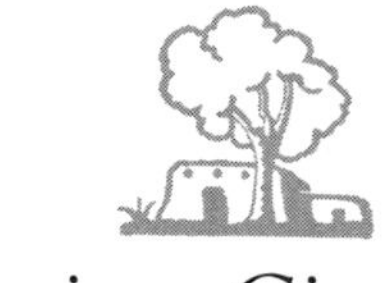

Ancient City Press

AN IMPRINT OF GIBBS SMITH, PUBLISHER

Salt Lake City | Charleston | Santa Fe | Santa Barbara

10 09 08 07 06 5 4 3 2 1

Published by
Ancient City Press
An imprint of Gibbs Smith, Publisher
P.O. Box 667
Layton, Utah 84041

Orders: 1.800.835.4993
www.gibbs-smith.com

Cover designed by Gabriella Hunter
Interior designed by TTA Design
Printed and bound in the United States of America

Library of Congress Cataloging-in-Publication Data

Robertson, Edna, 1919–
Artists of the canyons and caminos : Santa Fe, the early years / Edna Robertson and Sarah Nestor. — 1st ed.
p. cm.
Originally published: P. Smith, 1976.
Includes index.

ISBN 1-4236-0114-9

1. Art, American—New Mexico—Santa Fe—20th century. 2. Artists—New Mexico—Santa Fe—Biography. I. Nestor, Sarah, 1943– II. Title.

N6535.S33R62 2006
759.189'56—dc22

2006011560

Contents

Foreword

I am happy to have the opportunity to celebrate the thirtieth-anniversary edition of this special book. My wife, Catherine, and I first went to Santa Fe over thirty years ago, at a time when the town was smaller and the roads were mostly unpaved. Yet the spirit of the place, as singular then as it is today, was evident.

I came with an open heart and wide-open eyes to discover for myself what I had read by John Sloan and others—that Santa Fe was a unique place of creativity and community for artists, especially painters, and possessed a quality of light that inspired their efforts. I had learned that for years Sloan and his wife had taken the long road trip from Manhattan to Santa Fe, leaving his Chelsea Hotel studio for the summer. I had also read about how Sloan's friends Will Shuster, Jozef Bakos, William Penhallow Henderson, and many others produced wonderful works of art and experienced a camaraderie seemingly analogous to that shared by Henri Matisse and André Derain, after summers spent in the south of France early in the twentieth century. There they created a way of looking at the world that came to be known as Fauvism.

When we arrived in Santa Fe in late September 1972, we did not know where to stay, but, having read Willa Cather's *Death Comes for the Archbishop*, we decided to stay at the Bishops Lodge. The chamisa was golden, glowing in the autumn light, and the skies were the bluest I have ever seen. In the fireplace in our room we made a piñon fire one night and a juniper fire the next, both perfuming the air with a mesmerizing aroma. We were prepared for something magical to happen.

And magic did happen. At the Fine Arts Museum on the Santa Fe Plaza we met Edna Robertson, curator of paintings, who immediately befriended us and took us under her wing. She had a special affinity for the early generation of Santa Fe artists and their work. Over the years, the museum had nurtured its local painters and consequently had a marvelous collection of paintings from this generation. Edna let me roam through the bowels of the museum and look at the paintings, including those on the walls, in the storage rooms, and recorded in the archives via old photographs and letters.

We also went on excursions around town, visiting members of the early generation of artists who were still alive. We called on Jozef Bakos, out on Tano Road, who even as an old man painted at an easel set up in his house. He told me stories about life on Camino del Monte Sol, where impoverished artists had built adobe houses themselves, renting them to tourists in the summer while they lived in tents and then reoccupying them in the winter.

Following that, I spent many enjoyable afternoons with Fremont Ellis in his studio on Canyon Road, discussing his life in that earlier period. I also heard tales from Jane Baumann about going with her husband, Gustave Baumann, to Indian ceremonial dances on freezing winter nights, as well as about stimulating conversations the artists had about music, painting, and literature, all contributing to the rich cultural life which was a blend of rusticity, sophistication, and cosmopolitanism. The artists realized they were very fortunate to live in that time and place, and we realized we were fortunate to be there learning about them.

Other individuals who helped me understand the era were Alice Rossin ("Little Alice"), the daughter of William Penhallow Henderson, and his wife, Alice, who was the editor of *Poetry Magazine*. Alice related anecdotes about her father, who was a painter and also the architect and developer of Sena Plaza in downtown Santa Fe. She told us about riding her horse up Camino del Monte Sol to the end of town and into hills. When I come to Santa Fe now, I still see it through eyes transformed by such recollections.

This book originated in the spirit that permeated my first grand adventure in Santa Fe. During that visit and many subsequent ones, Edna Robertson, her daughter Sarah Nestor, Catherine, and I collaborated in its creation. Edna and Sarah were great allies in setting words to vision, and I am delighted the book is now back with us so that new readers can appreciate and draw inspiration from the creative atmosphere in early-twentieth-century Santa Fe.

Gibbs Smith
September 2006

Preface

Artists of the Canyons & Caminos had its beginning at a meeting in the basement of the Fine Arts Museum in Santa Fe. As Curator of Collections, I was always delighted when interested and interesting people asked me to show them the works in storage. Cathy and Gibbs Smith of Peregrine Smith, Inc. first visited me asking to see prints by John Sloan, but by a couple of happy hours later, I had managed to show them many of my other favorite works as well and to tell them some of the stories handed on to me by the artists through the years. Before they left, Gibbs suggested that a book could develop based on my "tales from the basement." We agreed that while a great deal had been written about Taos, there was a need for a running account of Santa Fe's artists and their relationship with the museum during its early years. I hesitated for a long time before starting, as I did not feel that I had known the artists early enough or well enough, but when I finally undertook the project, I was lucky enough to have the help of many who had a longer and closer connection. The artists themselves and their families and friends all helped. The museum's long and lovingly kept artists' files, old exhibit catalogues, and the photo archives were all of tremendous value. Most importantly, I had the sensitive collaboration of my daughter, Sarah Nestor, a writer and editor. I couldn't have worked on the book without her expert and generous help. I am also most grateful to David Noble, who made a splendid contribution as photographic editor.

Anyone reading the book undoubtedly will become aware of the fact that the Art Museum is the real protagonist. In the early years of the century there were almost no commercial galleries in Santa Fe, and the artists sold their work directly from their homes and studios. After it was built, the museum became their gathering place and almost their club. Since the guiding spirits of the museum in those early days were mainly anthropologists, they often saw art in relationship to the whole culture and had a tendency to prefer for the permanent collection those works whose subject matter reflected the land and the Spanish and Indian cultures of the Southwest. They hoped to make Santa Fe a center for study and interpretation of the people of the area, as well as a center for all the arts. Dr. Hewett, the director of the School of American Research (the museum's parent organization) and the Museum of New Mexico, was sympathetic to the arts, and encouraged Indian painters and other artists as well. It was he who asked Robert Henri to come to the city in 1916 and advise as to the policies and character of the new museum. Into this friendly atmosphere the artists who gathered in Santa Fe brought their own excitement and vision of the land and people.

In writing about them I depended heavily on the stories the artists told me. This, I think and hope, gave an immediacy and honest feeling of their lives and times to the book. Only a few of the many fine painters and sculptors who lived and worked in Santa Fe before World War II are included. Leaning as I did on records of the exhibitions held at the museum, and on direct conversation with those whom I knew, my information was somewhat limited. Many interesting early artists had already died when I started working at the museum in 1959, and others I knew had not yet become very active in the arts during the time of which I was writing.

When the book was first published, in 1976, Betty and Zeb Conley, owners of Jamison Galleries, held an autograph party which brought together an amazing number of the artists. It was a fine party, with old friends autographing their pictures in each others' copies, laughing and talking over old times. Many younger artists, too, were listening to the jokes and stories of this earlier time. It was a moving afternoon, and perhaps the last time many of these old friends came together.

For omissions and mistakes in the writing, I apologize. To the artists, the museum, and the many friends who helped, I give most hearty thanks. I enjoyed telling these tales and am glad that people have asked to have them reprinted.

Edna Robertson
November 1981

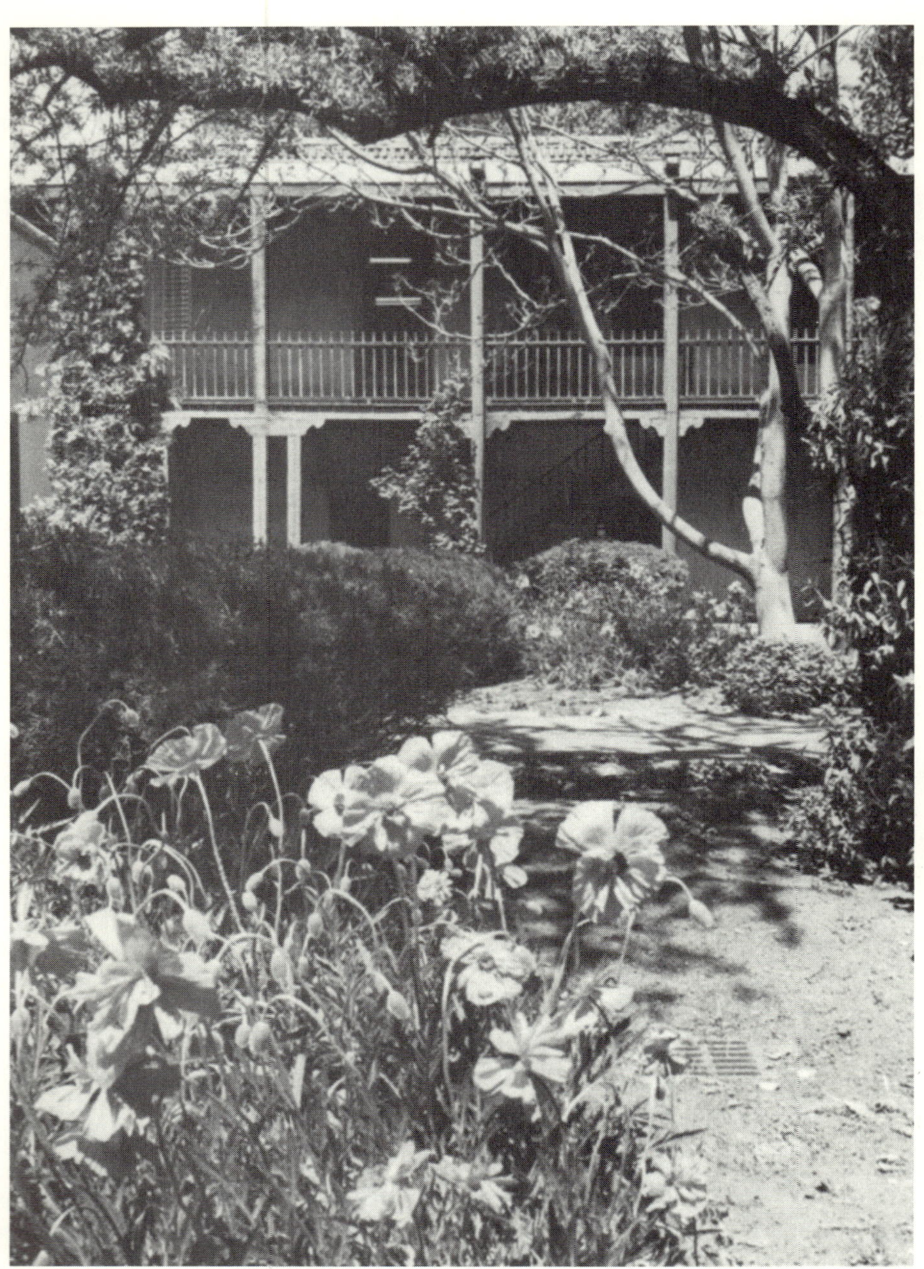

Santa Fe's Sena Plaza in the 1970s.

1
A Good Place to Paint

Some places in the world have a particular atmosphere, a sense of romance that artists respond to, which they call "good places to paint." Santa Fe, New Mexico, is one of these places. It is in the air itself, so clear and sharp in the high altitude that shapes and colors come through with startling intensity; brilliant primary colors of the daytime soften to pastels at twilight. The weather is capricious—natives may see all four seasons in the course of twenty-four hours—but seldom extreme. The plant and animal life of desert, dry riverbeds, and hills, pine and aspen forests, and lichen-covered alpine rocks offers an unusual richness of natural subject matter. Dominating the landscape are the sculptural landforms of mesas and mountains, and over them a sky so blue that it seems downright unnatural to visitors.

People have lived in the area for a long time, clustering near precious water sources. A number of cultures have managed, each in its own way yet blending with what came before, to live in harmony with the environment. Visitors often say Santa Fe has a European feel; artists claim they are more welcomed into the community here than in other American cities. Then there is the fact that it is more gracious, somehow, to be poor in an adobe house. Perhaps, too, the area's long tricultural background (Spanish, Indian, and Anglo) contributes to the tolerant atmosphere in which the arts flourish.

Santa Fe is the state capital, and the Palace of the Governors, which is now a museum, is the oldest public building

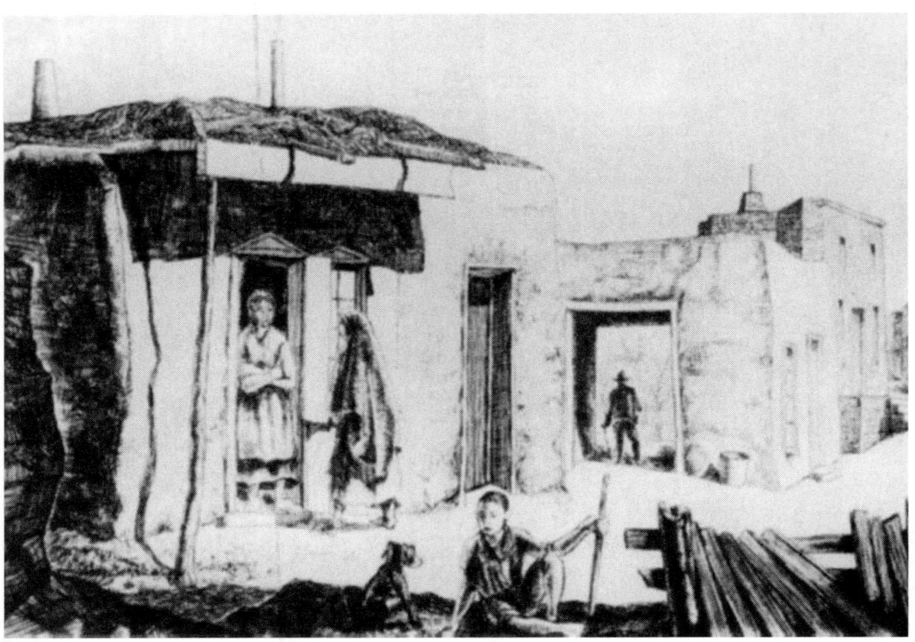

B.J.O. Nordfeldt, Boy, Pup, *n.d. Etching, 7 x 8 7/8 in. Museum of New Mexico.*

in the United States. It faces the plaza which has been the center of the town's life since the Spaniards established Santa Fe as a Royal City in 1610. The town sprawls at the base of the Sangre de Cristo Mountains, named for the rosy tint they take on at twilight. Santa Fe is officially recorded at 6,900 feet; the mountains rise another 5,000 feet above it. A number of the houses and other buildings (especially the older ones) are made of sunbaked adobe bricks, and since adobe must be built thick and not too high, the buildings have heavy proportions. This and the mud plaster with which they are generally coated make them appear to grow from the soil on which they rest. Many of the narrow, sometimes unpaved streets still follow old patterns—straight and parallel, like most royal cities, in the downtown area, more rambling in the residential areas to the south, and cut by the historic trading trails which end at the plaza. In the summer's rainy season, the Acequia Madre (Mother Ditch) still sends its quiet murmur along the street named for it, irrigating the massive cottonwoods and many of the gardens along its sides.

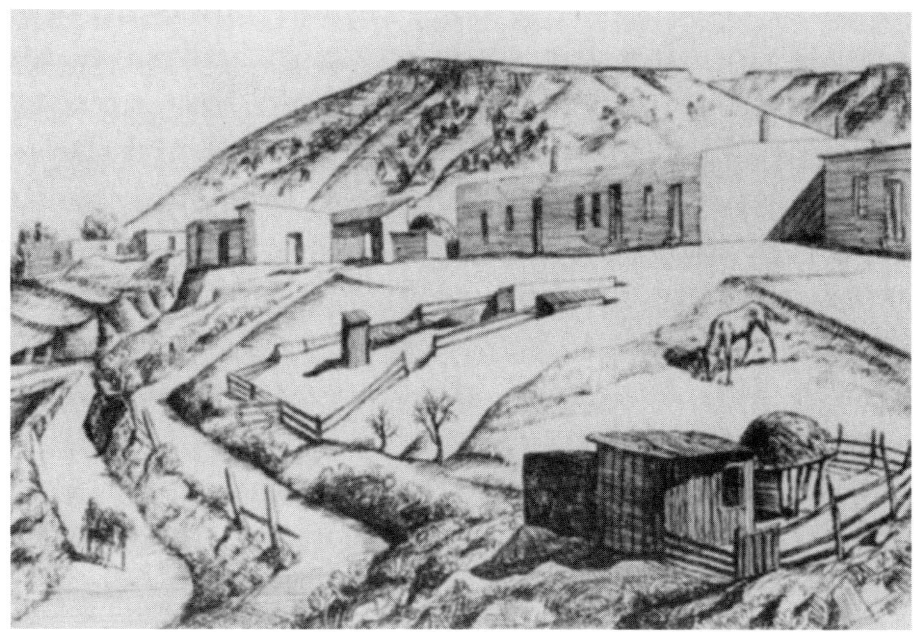

B.J.O. Nordfeldt, Placita Attalaya, *n.d. Etching, 6 x 9 in. Museum of New Mexico.*

Several hundred years before the arrival of the Spaniards, the Tano Indians inhabited a village in the same spot. And sometimes, even now, people putting down foundations for new walls come upon their silent traces—pieces of pottery and, occasionally, the remains of burials. The modern descendants of these long-gone inhabitants, who still live in surrounding pueblos, come in to Santa Fe to stroll the streets or sit under the portal of the Palace of the Governors, selling their jewelry and the bread they have baked in outdoor ovens.

The mountains are never out of one's consciousness; different in each variation of weather and time of day, but always covered with the army of small round trees called by their Spanish name, piñons. Above them, as one's eyes climb, come taller evergreens and the aspens which make whole mountainsides shine in the autumn like the legendary gold of the conquistadores.

Coronado and his men were the first of these conquerors in 1540–1542. They followed the ancient trails from Chihuahua, stopping at Indian villages along the northward way, always hoping to find the seven golden cities of Cibola. With them came Franciscan brothers and priests, looking for souls to claim and save. Mexico was held firmly for the King of Spain, but men are seldom content. They moved on restlessly toward the mysterious north. In 1598, General Oñate established the first capital of New Mexico at San Juan del Junque. Shortly afterward, the capital was moved about 30 miles south to the place which Oñate named La Villa Real de la Santa Fé de San Francisco de Asís—and the Spanish city of Santa Fe was born.

In 1609, work started on the great fortress and palace which was to be the center of government and house the governor and his troops. The plan was the same as that used for all of the royal cities. Facing the front of the palace, then as now, was the plaza. Across the plaza to the south, a chapel for the soldiers was built. Later, when more settlers came following the army, the *paroquia* (or parish church) was built at the east side of the plaza. Little by little, roads crept out from this center.

San Miguel Church, said to be the oldest church in the United States, was built in 1626 to accommodate the Christianized Indians who lived in the area known as the "Barrio de Analco." The *barrio* (or neighborhood) was south of the Santa Fe River, which rushed with water in those days, when the spring sun melted the deep mountain snows.

In 1680, the Indians rose in fury against the European intruders and after severe fighting drove the Spanish back down the trail to Mexico. At first, the besieged settlers barricaded themselves in the fortress-palace, but they finally escaped to the south when the Indians dammed the ditch which brought water into it courtyard. It was a dreadful journey—the old and very young in lumbering wooden carts drawn by oxen, the others walking. There were the Indians, and further along there were the perils of exhaustion and heat, and the terrible desert country to be crossed before the survivors could reach El Paso del Norte. They called it the "Jornada del Muerte"—the Journey of Death.

Twelve years later, in 1692, General Diego de Vargas led a group of soldiers and settlers again up the Rio Grande to the north. It is said that when they arrived just northwest of Santa Fe they camped at the site of present-day Rosario Chapel. That night, General de Vargas prayed before the figure of the Virgin Mary, later affectionately called "La Conquistadora," which had come with the first Spaniards. She had been carried back to Mexico in their flight, and came north again when De Vargas and his people returned. He vowed that if the reentry into Santa Fe were peaceful, he would hold a mass and fiesta each year. During the years of the Spaniards' absence, the Indians had moved into the town and established a pueblo and government in the Palace of the Governors, but, miraculously, when De Vargas and a group of the Franciscans entered the town the next morning, they were greeted with courtesy, and the Indians agreed to let the settlers stay. Since that time, Santa Fe has held the annual fiesta, as De Vargas promised. It remained principally a religious festival, with masses and processions, until 1917. More recently, although the religious aspect is still present, a large number of secular events have developed, such as parades, pageants, and the burning of a figure of Old Man Gloom, called Zozobra.

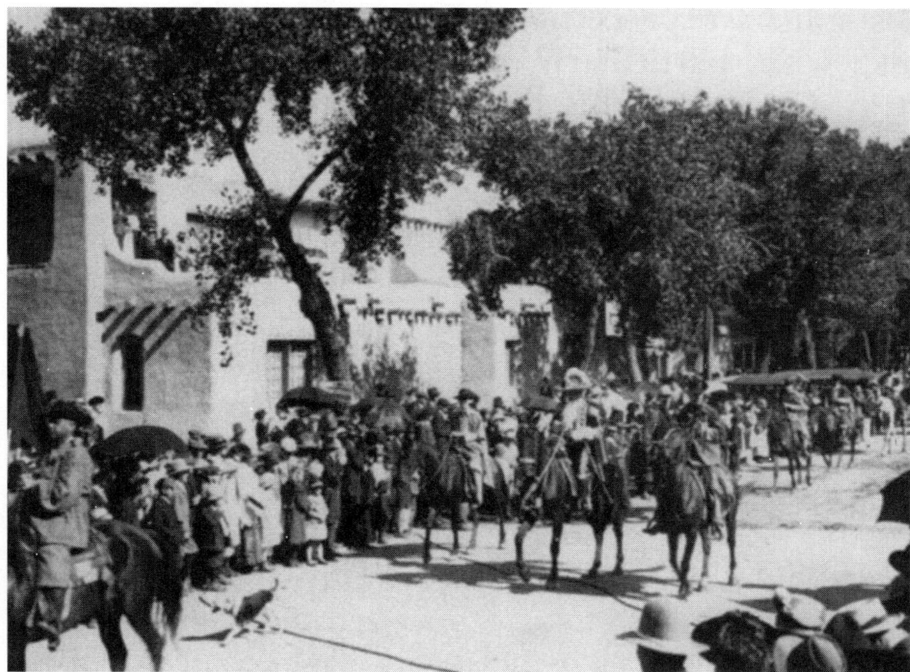

An early fiesta parade passing the Art Museum.

In spite of the Indians' admirable restraint at the time of the peaceful reentry of the Spanish, the years following were marked by many violent clashes between the military and the Indians. The Franciscans did all they could to protect their pueblo congregations, and the King of Spain had pronounced them his subjects, to be treated as such; but the soldiers viewed them as a threat. Despite the skirmishes and uprisings, however, the settlement grew.

When Mexico broke away from Spain in 1821, New Mexico became part of the new country; then when Mexico forbade the priesthood, most of the priests and monks left the area. It was during this time that the Penitente Brotherhood grew, becoming the only source of religious observances in many of the villages in northern New Mexico. Starting as a lay brotherhood of the order of St. Francis, the Penitentes began carving and painting their own religious figures, or *santos.* They also developed their own rituals, some of which drew the disapproval of the Catholic Church. In modern times they have modified their practices, but during Holy Week, and especially on Good Friday, some of the small towns still have processions reenacting the Way of the Cross, with particularly devout members chosen to portray Christ and his disciples. Many families in the villages still carry on the tradition of carving santos today. The figures made in earlier times are cherished by the families who have handed them down for generations, as well as by museums and other collectors.

Unlike the isolated villages, Santa Fe was exposed to many influences. During the years following De Vargas's reentry in 1692, it grew into a thriving center for trade, with regular wagon trains coming up the Camino Real (the Royal Road) from El Paso, and by the mid-nineteenth century, over the Santa Fe Trail from Missouri. French trappers and traders came too, and mountain men wandered down from Taos and the north. There was a customs station at Arroyo Hondo, where a heavy tax was levied on the wagons coming in from the East. After they had passed through the station, the drivers traditionally stopped to wash and dress in their best and brightest clothes and then swept into the town down what is still called the Old Santa Fe Trail, circling the plaza, whooping and cracking their whips. A celebration was certainly in order after the weeks or months on the trail. A monument

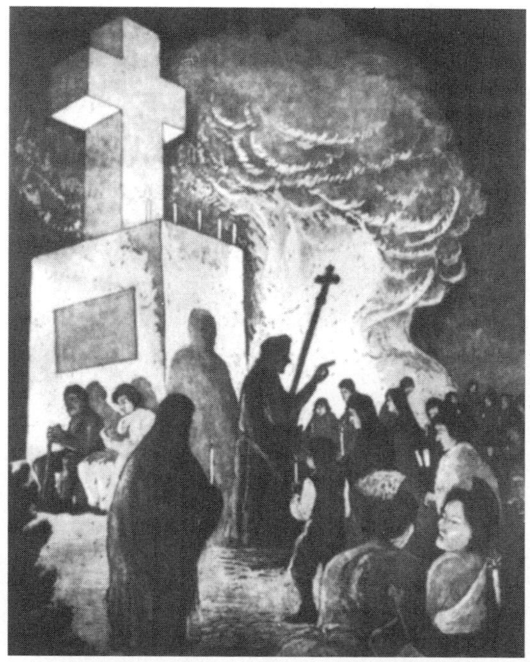

Will Shuster, Cross of the Martyrs, *n.d. Aquatint, 12 x 9 in. Museum of New Mexico. The candlelight procession to the Cross of the Martyrs is a surviving religious event of the fiesta and a memorial to twenty-one priests who died nearby in the late seventeenth century.*

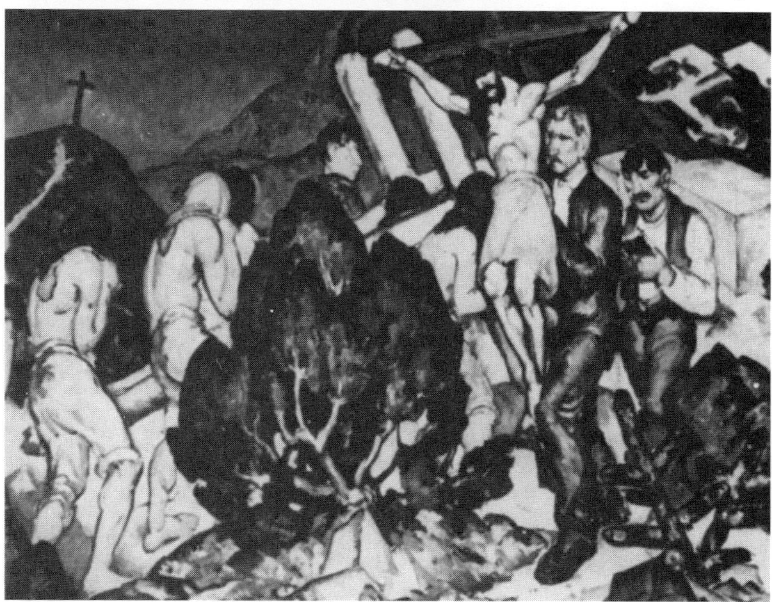

William Penhallow Henderson, Holy Week in New Mexico, *1920. Oil, ca., 32 x 40 in. Museum of New Mexico. Penitente processions like this may still be seen in northern New Mexico on Good Friday, with the roles of Christ and his disciples enacted by the most devout villagers.*

in the present-day plaza designates the end of the Santa Fe Trail, and some of the town's shops are still located around it.

The early merchants were important and often colorful citizens, and many interesting stories are still told about them. One of the large nineteenth-century trading companies was Spiegelberg Brothers. Solomon Jacob Spiegelberg was the oldest of the brothers, and the first to leave Germany. He followed the Santa Fe Trail in an ox-train and, joining the command of Colonel Doniphan, accompanied him to Chihuahua, Mexico. He then returned with the regiment to Santa Fe, where he was appointed sutler, and went on to establish a wholesale and retail general merchandise business. Younger members of the family followed, and for many years their store was a landmark on the south side of the plaza. An appealing story about one of Solomon's sons was recorded and is retold in the *New Mexico Historical Review* of January 1928:

> *A gorgeous gilded circus wagon was left in Santa Fe by a traveling circus. The Spiegelberg brothers purchased it and put Abe in charge as their field representative. Its interior was remodeled to transport a full stock of dry-goods, clothing, hats, caps, bacon, ham, jewelry, watches,*

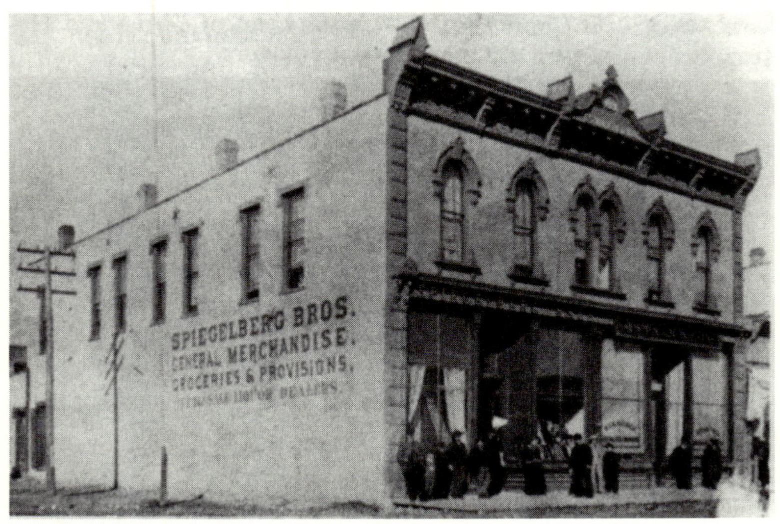

Spiegelberg Brothers' store.

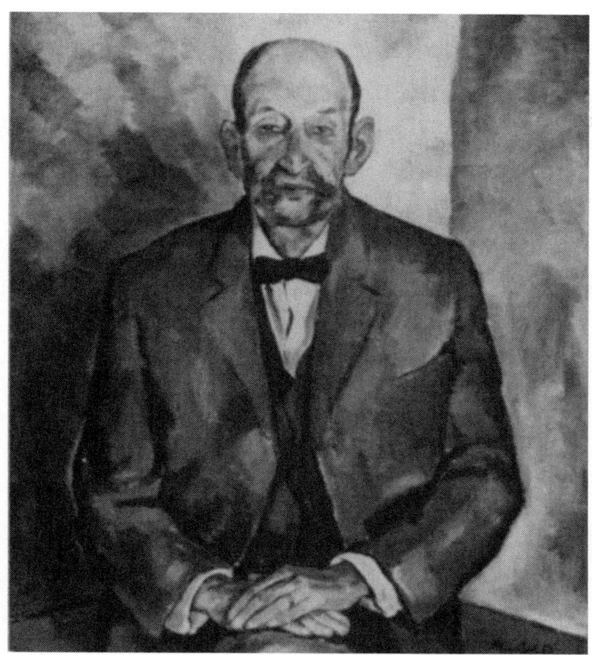

B.J.O. Nordfeldt, Portrait of Abe Spiegelberg, Old-Timer, *1919. Oil, 32 x 29 in. Museum of New Mexico.*

> *shoes, rifles, pistols, powder, and bullets. This golden chariot was a blaze of light as the sun reflected from its mirrors and gilding. It created excitement among Indians and natives everywhere. This glamorous vehicle even made a trip into Chihuahua.*

Not only did these early merchants impress their customers, they were often impressed with what *they* saw, and hence became some of the first patrons of the arts in the area. Abraham Spiegelberg, of the gilded circus wagon, was regarded as an authority on Indian, Mexican, and Spanish Colonial handicrafts.

Meanwhile, Santa Fe was increasingly affected by events in the outside world. In 1846 the last Spanish governor, Manuel Armijo, fled from New Mexico; the American army entered the town and claimed New Mexico for the United States. In 1862, Santa Fe was briefly occupied by Confederate troops en route to

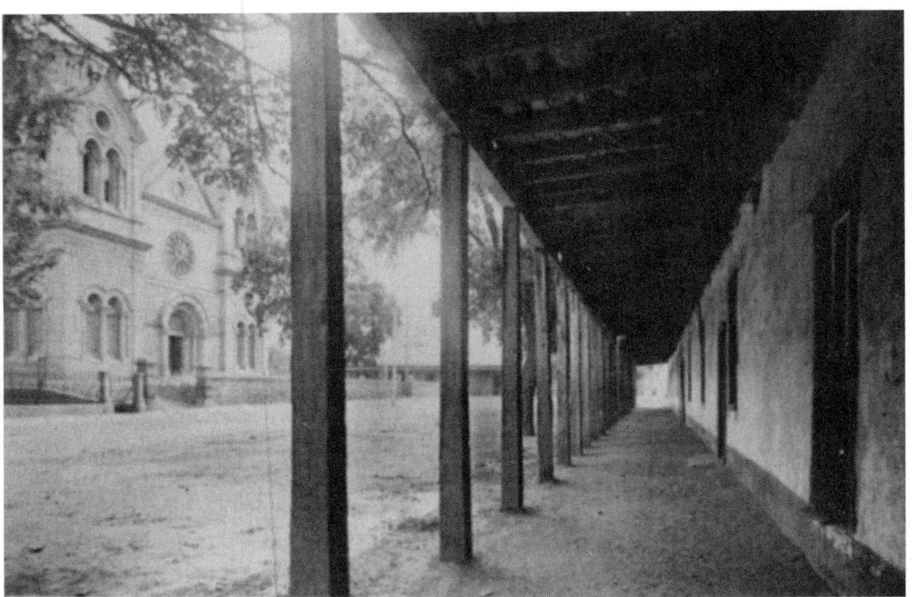

St. Francis Cathedral.

the Colorado silver mines; but with the help of Colorado troops, the New Mexicans won the Battle of Glorieta Pass and pushed back the intruders, freeing the capital city once again. New Mexico remained a territory until 1912, when, along with Arizona, it entered statehood and, in a sense, the twentieth century.

An event of greatest importance to the life of the town, and the whole area, was the arrival in 1851 of Jean Baptiste Lamy, first as bishop and then, in 1875, as archbishop of an area including present-day Utah, Colorado, Arizona, and New Mexico. Among many other accomplishments, this tireless man brought the Sisters of Light to Santa Fe to establish Loretto Academy as a boarding school for girls, and started St. Michael's School for boys. In 1869, he began building the present cathedral over and around the old *paroquia* at the east end of the plaza, using stone quarried at the nearby town of Cerrillos, but having the building designed in the Romanesque style of his native France. Under his direction St. Vincent Hospital was established in 1865. It is impossible to list all of his many loving concerns, but one was his planting a number of trees in the downtown area, some of which still shade the streets in their old age.

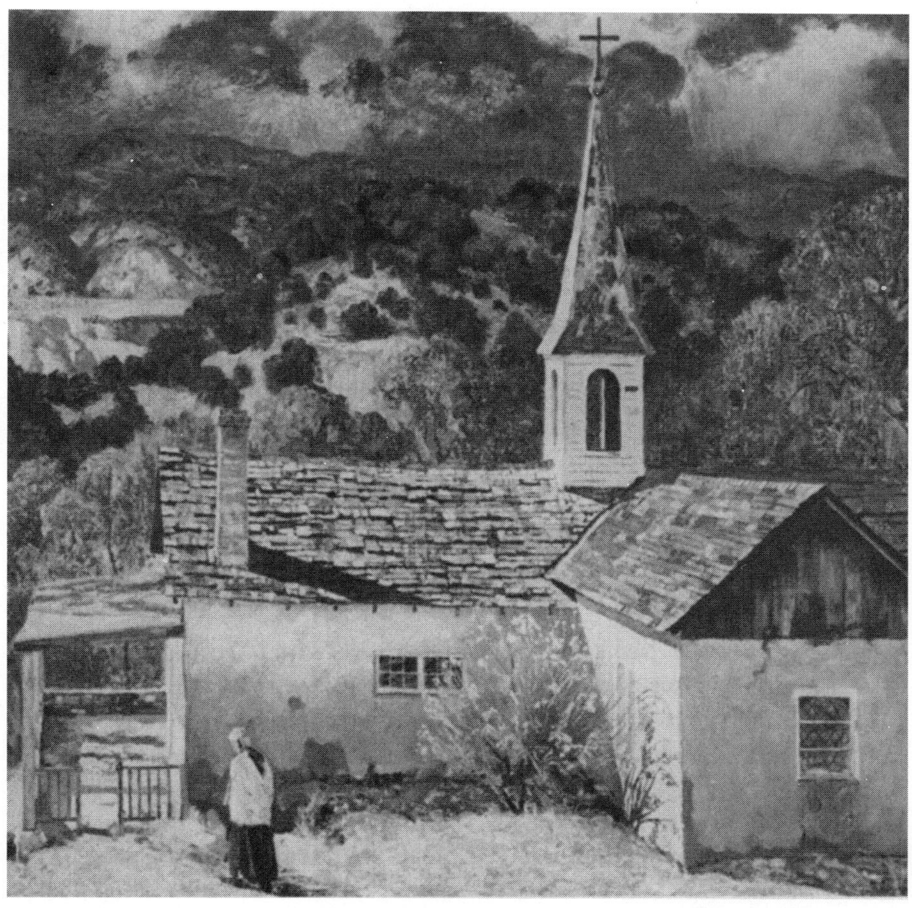

Theodore Van Soelen. The Bishop's Chapel, *ca. 1928. Oil, 36 x 40 in. Museum of New Mexico. Archbishop Lamy loved this little chapel north of town on the road to Tesuque and often went there to be alone. The chapel is preserved at the guest ranch called the Bishop's Lodge.*

During the territorial years, the plaza remained the center of all activity in the town; the Palace on its north side was the seat of government until 1886 and again, when the new building was destroyed by fire, from 1892 to 1900. But as the American influence grew, more and more people built stores and houses which would have looked at home in Illinois or New Jersey. By the early twentieth century, many of the old Spanish buildings had fallen into decay, or were "modernized" by having their shady portals removed. The Palace itself changed its appearance

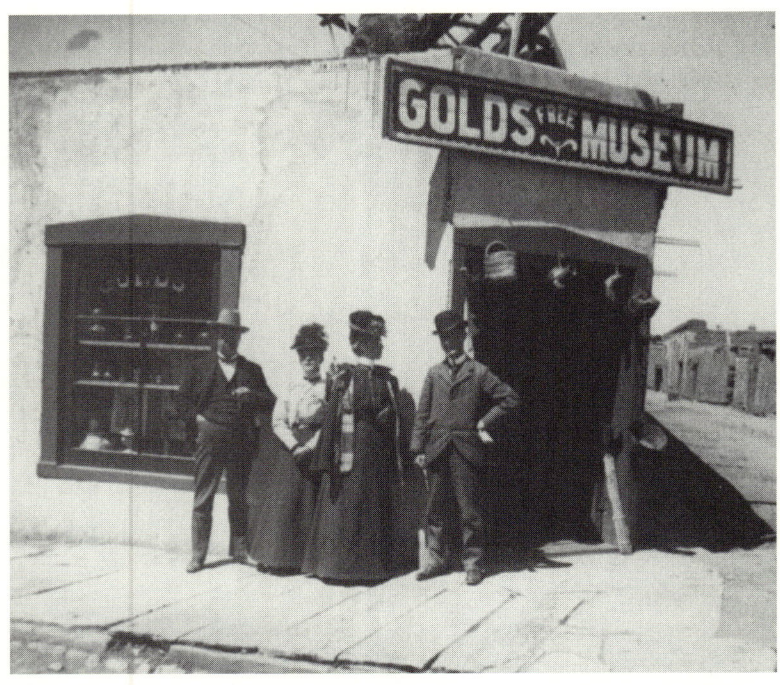

The corner of San Francisco Street and Burro Alley, one block west of the plaza.

several times to suit prevailing styles. It was the School of American Research (first called the School of American Archaeology), in 1907, banded together with the New Mexico Historical Society to form the Museum of New Mexico and save the old Palace. No longer used for government purposes after the new domed capitol was built in 1900, it was about to be torn down to make room for new stores.

When the first American artists started coming west to Santa Fe before the turn of the twentieth century, they found a part-Americanized, part-Spanish town. During the sessions of the Territorial Legislature, there was a great bustle, but the rest of the year it was a small, leisurely, and, to the Easterners, very remote village. Although there was already a small group of painters established seventy miles north in Taos, Santa Fe was not yet an art center. Many of the earliest artists came to the city as health seekers suffering from respiratory ailments. We may be grateful to the dry fine air which brought so many of these talented and renowned people to New Mexico, many of them arriving on stretchers to stay at Sunmount Sanitorium. The air worked such magic that some of them are still living at a hearty and healthy old age today, providing a link between the beginnings of the art colony and the present flourishing group. Besides the power of the land and the richness of its history, it is undoubtedly the presence of artists that has drawn more artists to Santa Fe.

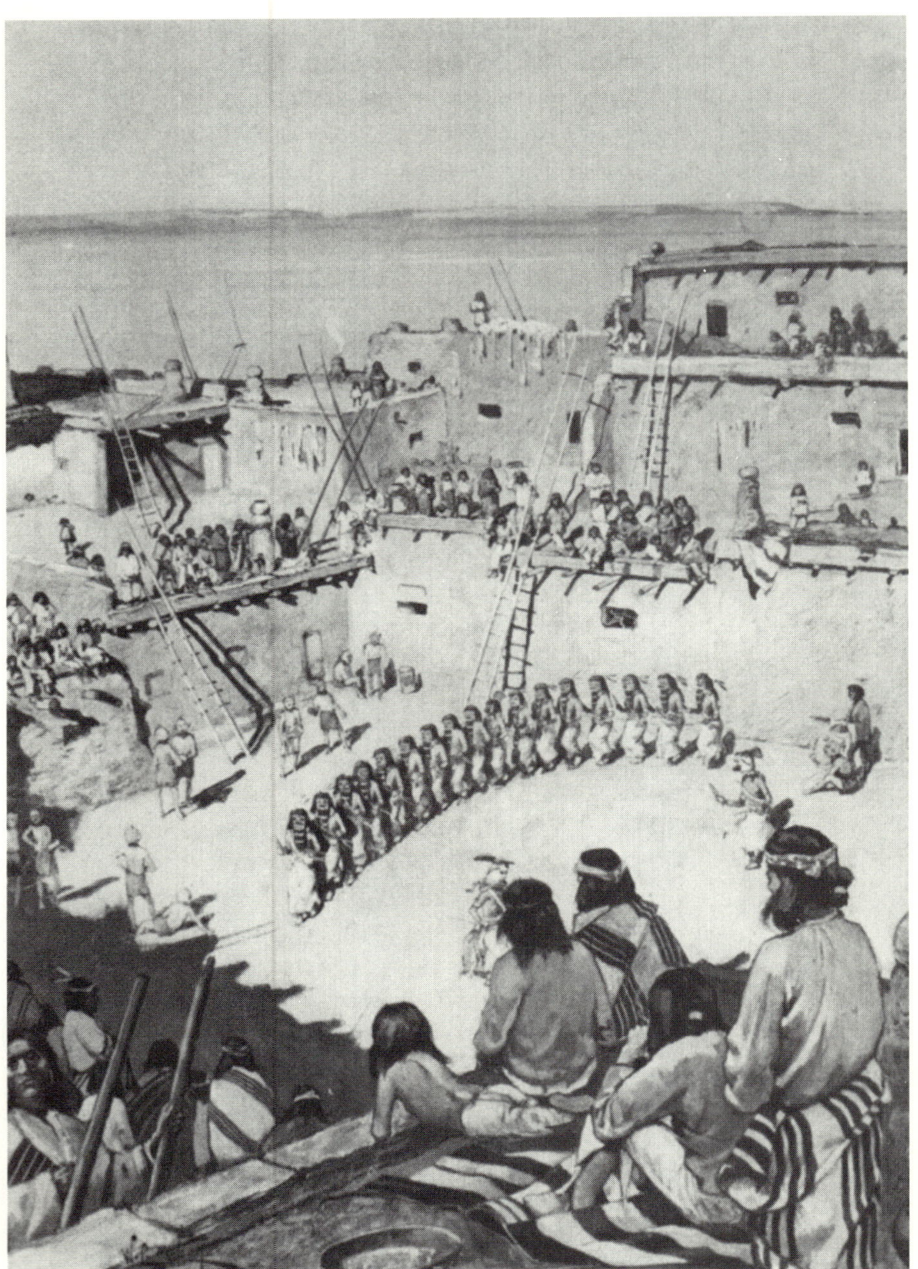

Willard L. Metcalf, Dance of the Great Knife, *1881–82. Gouache, 19 3/4 x 15 3/4 in. Museum of New Mexico. Metcalf was in Zuni Pueblo when he recorded this dance, also called Dance of the Homatchi.*

2
Early Artists

From the first days of Western exploration, artists had occasionally wandered through Santa Fe. Some accompanied expeditions, such as those that did surveys for the projected railroads. Others came with the census takers. Peter Moran, who was with the group that did the first census of the southwestern Indian pueblos, has left us a collection of chalk sketches which are wonderful as a record of the Indian villages and people of his time. Also, after the entry of United States troops in 1846, there was a steady stream of army mapmakers and artists. Some of these young soldier-artists had received training in drawing and watercolor painting at West Point, and many of their sketches are still in existence. The collections of the Museum of New Mexico contain a delightful painting which may have been produced by one of these soldiers. Painted in the 1880s, it shows the Santa Fe plaza with a picket fence around it and a military band playing on a stand under the trees. It also pays tribute to the Spiegelberg Brothers' store.

One of the earliest artists actually known to have worked in Santa Fe was George Stanley, who was called "Professor," after the fashion of the time for piano players and painters. He apparently came from Colorado and set up a studio in Santa Fe for a short time. An advertisement in the daily newspaper, the *Santa Fe New Mexican*, on November 20, 1897, stated that "Mr. George Stanley, the artist, has removed from the south side and has taken rooms at Mrs. Goodwin's boardinghouse on lower Palace Avenue. He will be pleased to see his friends at his new studio and

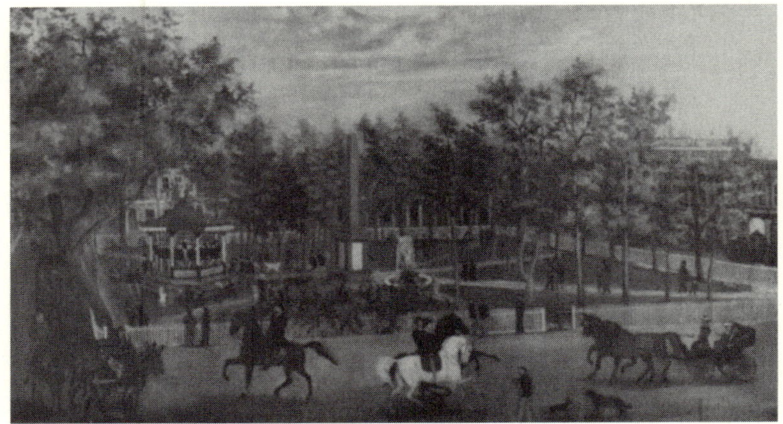

Unknown artist, Santa Fe Plaza in the 1880s, *n.d. Oil, 36 1/2 x 60 1/2 in. Museum of New Mexico. Notice that the artist, forgetting to put in an entrance to the plaza, painted over the fence and added a turnstile.*

is ready to fill orders for watercolors or oil paintings at his present studio." On December 22, 1897, the newspaper announced an "Art exhibition at Seligman's" (Seligman was one of the leading merchants of the town at the time, and for many years an interested patron of the artists):

> *Prof. George Stanley, the artist, who came to Santa Fe about a year ago, has on exhibition at Seligman Bros. store, a fine collection of watercolor pictures of New Mexico life and scenery which cannot fail to please the lovers of art. Prof. Stanley is an artist of much ability, and his sketches of Indians and Mexican life, because of their trueness to nature and perfectness in coloring have gained him more than a local reputation.*

He may have had a considerable reputation at the time, but it has been difficult to trace any more about him or his stay in Santa Fe. The only further clue which has turned up is that there was a "dashing and debonair" Englishman named Charles St. George Stanley who arrived in the Denver area in 1867, where he did numerous illustrations for Frank Leslie's *Illustrated Weekly*

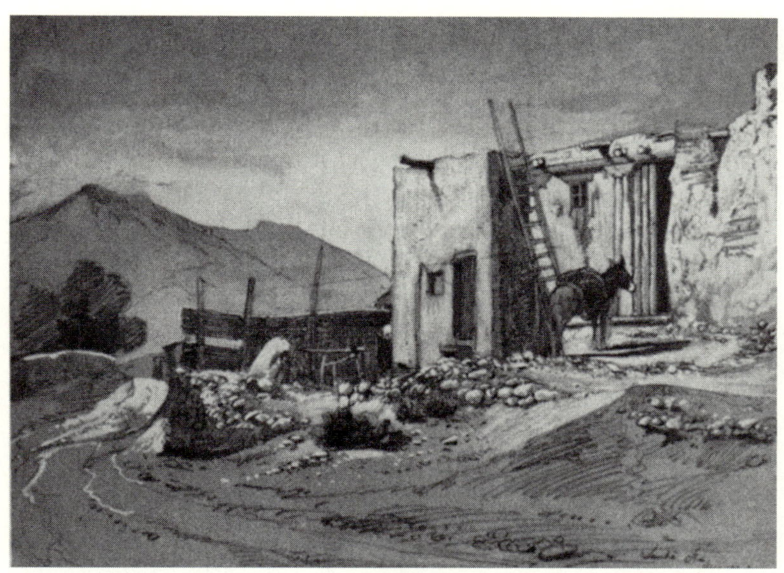

Peter Moran, Santa Fe, *ca. 1880–1882. Pencil and Chinese white drawing Roswell Museum and Art Center.*

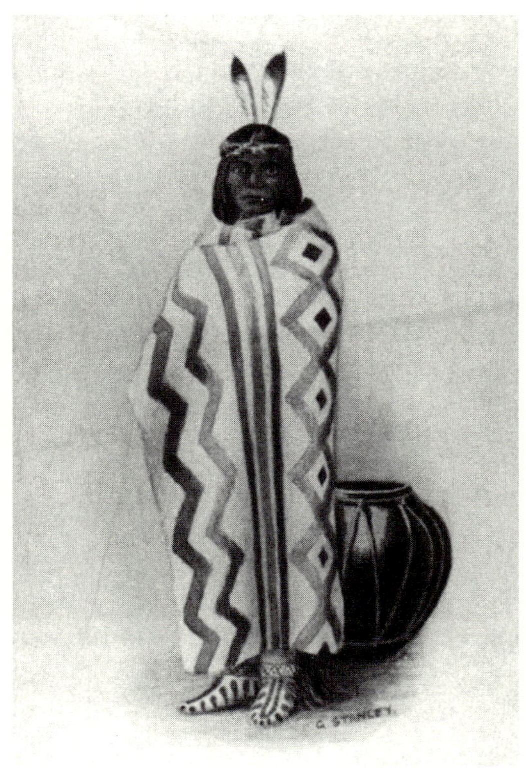

George Stanley, Untitled, *ca. 1898. Watercolor, 12 x 9 in. Museum of New Mexico.*

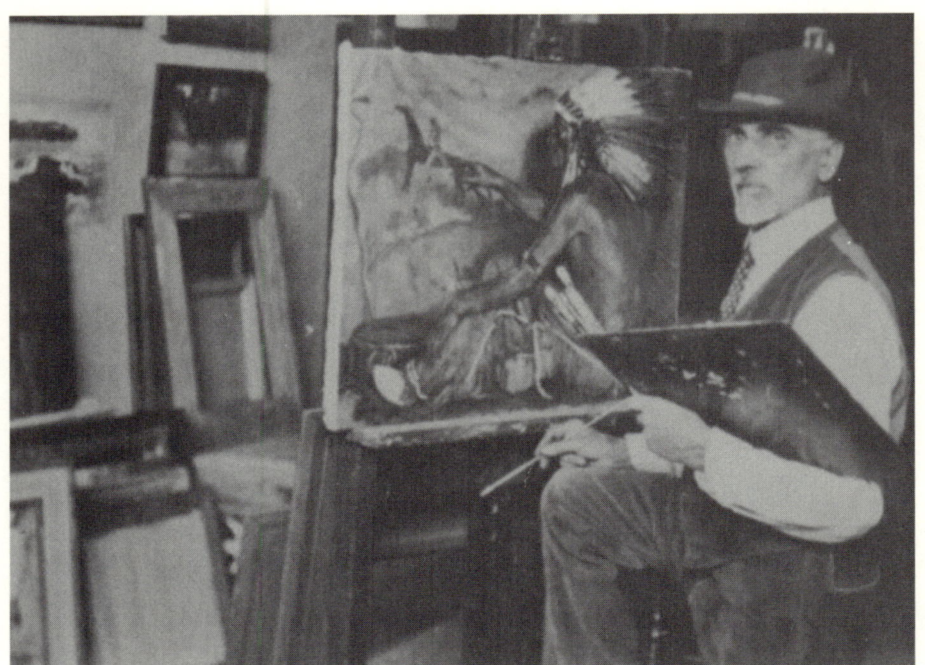

Joseph Henry Sharp.

and for *Harper's Weekly*, as well as some landscape paintings for the Colorado Central Railroad. (The railroads were to become major patrons of artists who were painting in the West.) Whether Santa Fe's "Prof." Stanley was the same artist or even a relative of Colorado's Stanley remains in doubt. Neither is it known how long he stayed in the ancient city nor how successful he was in acquiring commissions in his studio on Palace Avenue.

Joseph Henry Sharp, later a founding member of the Taos Society of Artists, was one of the first painters to visit Santa Fe whose work was already known and highly regarded in the East. He spent the summer of 1883 painting in the area, but was drawn to Taos, and after that year his western trips from his home in Cincinnati took him either there or to the Crow Indian Reservation in Montana, where President Theodore Roosevelt had a cabin built for him. His stories of New Mexico enticed many other artists west, either to visit or to stay, most notably Bert G. Phillips and Ernest L. Blumenschein, who visited Taos in 1893. In an interview in August 1932 with Ina Sizer Cassidy,

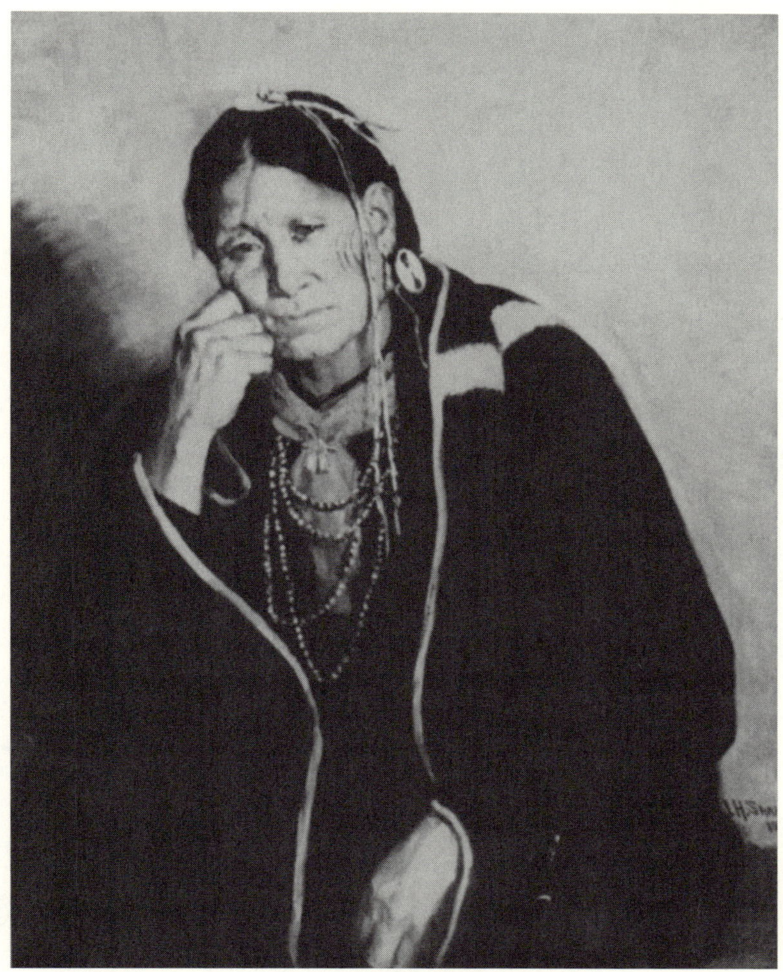

Joseph Henry Sharp, Taos Indian Portrait, *1914. Oil, 30 x 24 in. Museum of New Mexico. This painting was given to the Art Museum by the artist, for the opening exhibition in 1917.*

Sharp was asked, "How did you become interested in the Indians?" His answer expressed an attitude which was popular with many people besides the artists at that time:

> *I was always interested, even as a small boy. I guess it was Fenimore Cooper who first attracted me to the Indian. It was the romance of youth, of boyhood I suppose. But boys always did like Indians. Then when I came to*

know them I liked them for themselves. Perhaps they attracted me as subjects to paint because of their important historical value as First Americans. There is something very intriguing about "First Americans." Then the color of their costumes and dances, this no less attracted me. Their color is glorious, and so belongs to them and to their country.

This statement could have applied to many of the artists painting in the Southwest at the turn of the century, and reflects the fact that the country had now come to a point in history when the Indians were no longer regarded as a threat to Manifest Destiny and the push of western expansion by the United States. People rebounded from the image of the Indians as bloodthirsty savages to the often exaggerated idea of them as romantic Hiawatha figures. In his painting of Indians, however, Sharp always retained a reserve and truthful dignity, which caused some of his fellow painters to dub him "that ethnologist."

Another early visitor, and one who returned again and again throughout his hundred-year-long life, was Warren Rollins. He is credited with having had the first one-man exhibition of art in the Palace of the Governors in 1909. He was painting in Taos at the time, along with Bert G. Phillips, Ernest L. Blumenschein, and Frank Sauerwein; the four were the town's only artists. Santa Fe had almost no artists, so Rollins decided that this would be a fertile area for him to show his work. His friends tried to discourage him, saying, "Don't go to Santa Fe; they have no appreciation of art and never will have"; but Rollins gathered his work together and, armed with a letter of introduction from Bert G. Phillips, made his request to former territorial governor Bradford Prince, an official of the New Mexico Historical Society. Not overly encouraging, Governor Prince is reported to have said, "I can't see what good an art exhibit will do; on the other hand, I can't see that it could possibly do any harm." So the show was hung. In spite of the gloomy predictions, Rollins's show was a great success. He stayed on to found and become the first president of the Santa

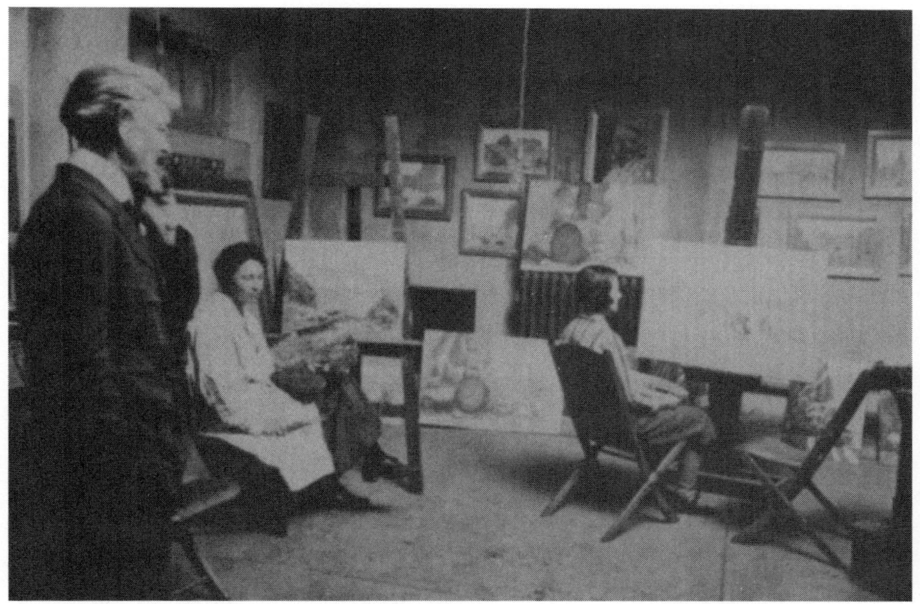

Warren E. Rollins teaching an art class in his studio at the Palace of the Governors, ca. 1910.

Fe Art Club, and to teach art classes in a studio at the Palace—although he felt that "great art is precisely that which never was nor will be taught."

Rollins, who had been born in Carson City, Nevada, in 1861 in the early months of the Civil War, saw the country change during his lifetime from a land of vast isolated spaces, with many areas holding to their own cultures and ways of life, into the complex society of the modern age. He lived in San Francisco as a boy, and received his art training at the San Francisco School of Design. As a young man he painted the sea and the ships which sailed to this Pacific port, working in a lighthouse which he used as a studio. Later, he travelled throughout the West, as far east as the Dakotas, through New Mexico and Arizona, and northwest to Oregon, earning a precarious living at a trade which has long since vanished. He was an itinerant sign painter, creating slogans and designs to sell products ranging from soap to tobacco, painted on billboards, freight cars, and barns.

For many years, he occasionally visited and lived with the Hopi Indians in Arizona, staying in their homes, where he

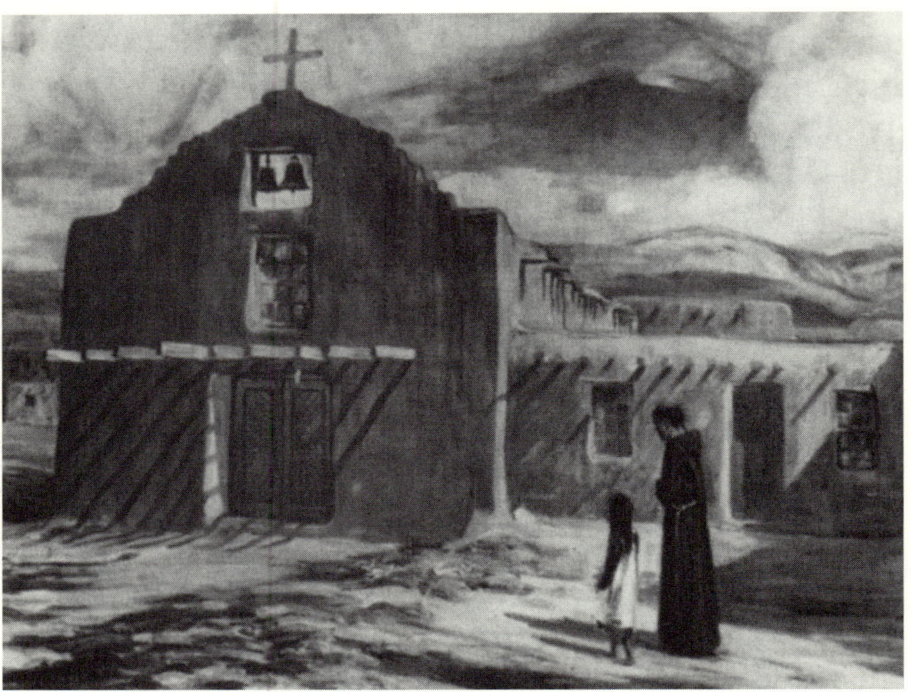

Carlos Vierra, Jemez Pueblo Mission, *ca. 1920. Oil, 28 x 36 in. Museum of New Mexico.*

observed and recorded many of their ceremonies and rituals while absorbing the rhythm of their daily lives. His paintings of the Hopis won him great acclaim, and were acquired by leading museums. Rollins did many of his most admired paintings for the Santa Fe Railroad, which had built him a cabin in Paradise Valley, near the south rim of Arizona's Grand Canyon. Between trips he returned often to Santa Fe, where, in later years, he came to be regarded as the dean of Santa Fe painters. For the last twenty-five years of his life, he suffered from palsy, but when painting became impossible for him the indomitable old man turned to crayon, and continued to share his vision of the Indian lands and people until his death in 1962 at the age of a hundred and one.

By the early 1900s, people were becoming aware of New Mexico not only through the work sent back east by the few artists working there, but also through its growing acclaim as a health resort. Carlos Vierra was the first of many artists to come

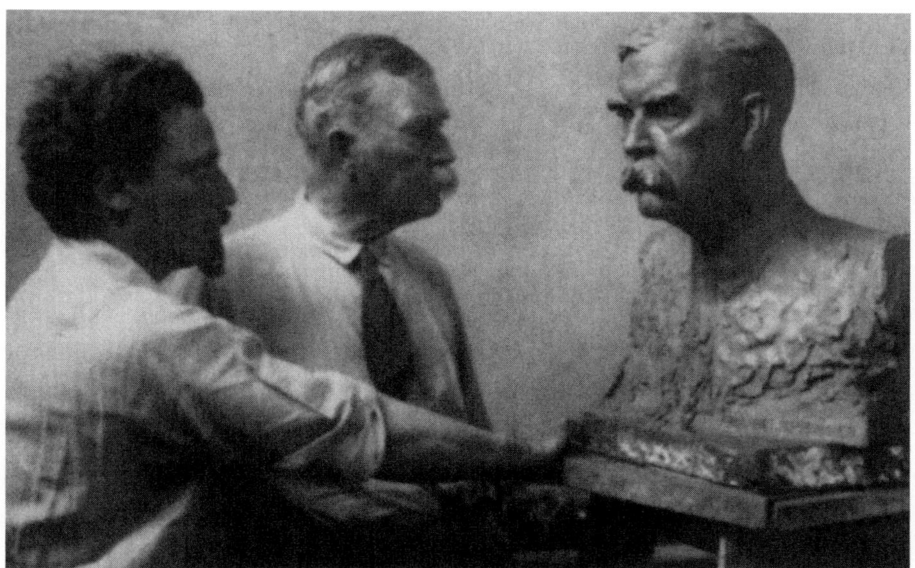

Sculptor Cartaino Scarpitta and the Hon. Frank Springer view the sculptor's bust of Springer, 1922.

for his health, and also the first to make Santa Fe his permanent home. He was a Californian of Portuguese descent. Vierra's family had immigrated to America from the Azores, where the men of the family all followed the sea. His father hoped that none of his sons would turn to the hard life he had left, but young Carlos was pulled by his two great loves: painting and the ocean. Before he was twenty-one he left home and sailed around the Horn in a wooden ship to New York, where he studied art and achieved some success as a cartoonist. But in 1904, lung trouble brought on by overwork led him to New Mexico. What must have seemed a terrifying disaster opened the way for the vital part he played in Santa Fe's cultural development.

His first stop in New Mexico was a little cabin on the Pecos River, where he led a rugged outdoor life until he contracted a severe cold which brought him to the sanitorium in Santa Fe. When he recovered, he opened a photographic studio on the plaza, and soon became established as a sensitive, artistic photographer as well as a painter.

When the School of American Archaeology established its headquarters in Santa Fe in 1907, Vierra became acquainted with that group, especially the director, Dr. Edgar L. Hewett, artist-archaeologist Kenneth Chapman, and the Hon. Frank Springer, territorial senator, lawyer, scientist, and patron of the arts. Vierra loved the early pueblo and mission styles of building and eagerly entered into plans for the restoration of the Palace and, later, for the construction of the new Fine Arts building.

Vierra was one of the major contributors to development of the so-called "Santa Fe" style of architecture, which is a blend of Spanish and Pueblo Indian styles. He was able to design and build his own house, still considered one of the most beautiful examples of this style, through the generosity of Springer. Knowing of Vierra's slender means and delicate health, Springer offered him the use of a large piece of land on the Old Santa Fe Trail at the south edge of town, proposing that if Vierra would design and build a house there, his wife and he could live in it during their lifetimes; at their deaths it would revert to the Springer family. Vierra worked on the house for three years, including in it a two-story studio with a Zuni Indian-style fireplace and a balcony. The adobe house is decorated with hand-carved beams and has modelling around its doors and windows. While it was still under construction, Vierra used to chuckle at hearing the house referred to by tourists as "the ruins near Cutting's" (a more acceptable house nearby), as his intention was to make the building look "old and expressive."

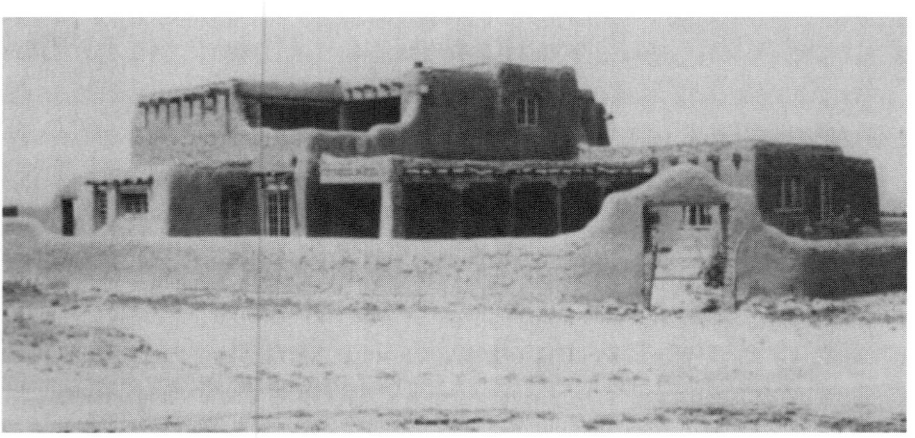

Carlos Vierra's house—"the ruins near Cutting's."

As a member of the School of American Research (the new name for the School of American Archaeology), Vierra studied the architecture of the ruined Mayan cities, then developed his notes into murals showing the cities as they appeared in their prime. They were installed in 1915 and still hang in the Hall of Man at Balboa Park in San Diego, California. But the murals for which he is best known in Santa Fe are those in the St. Francis Auditorium of the Art Museum. They were painted by Vierra and Chapman following the death of the designer, their close friend, painter Donald Beauregard. The three panels painted by Vierra show Columbus at the Franciscan monastery of Rabat in Portugal, with a vision of great ships in the sky; the Franciscans pleading for the Mayas with the Spanish soldiers; and the building of the New Mexican missions. (The figure of Columbus, by the way, is a self-portrait of Carlos Vierra.)

In talking to people who knew Vierra, one gets an impression of an exciting, dynamic, and charming man. They describe him as small, very handsome, always in later years wearing a World War I battle jacket and carefully wrapped puttees. He drove a huge open Packard touring car, and each autumn made a grand pilgrimage on the terrifying single-lane road down La Bajada Hill to Bernalillo, where the best grapes in the area were grown, to get the materials for his homemade wine. People note that the wine was sometimes a little peculiar, but the process of making it was a tremendous spectacle. He also loved cats, and usually had five or six—all named either Muff, Puff, or Fluff. Witnesses insist that he trained several of them, one to do back flips, and another to play as though on a fiddle.

Very few people know that Vierra was also a pioneer in aerial photography; in fact, he flew over and photographed Chaco Canyon shortly before Charles Lindbergh made his own photographic flight over the same area. As architect, artist, photographer, archaeologist, and a passionate advocate of maintaining the character and appearance of old Santa Fe, Vierra made contributions to the city that are felt to this day.

Sara Mack, artist daughter of artist Sheldon Parsons, regards her father as the second member of the art colony in Santa Fe. In

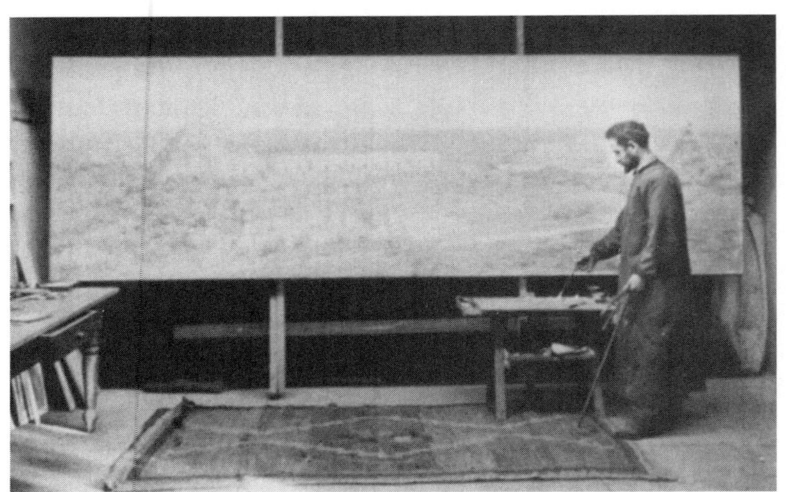

Carlos Vierra working on one of his murals of the pre-Columbian cities of the Yucatan. Painted for the Panama–California Exposition, these murals still hang at Balboa Park in San Diego, California.

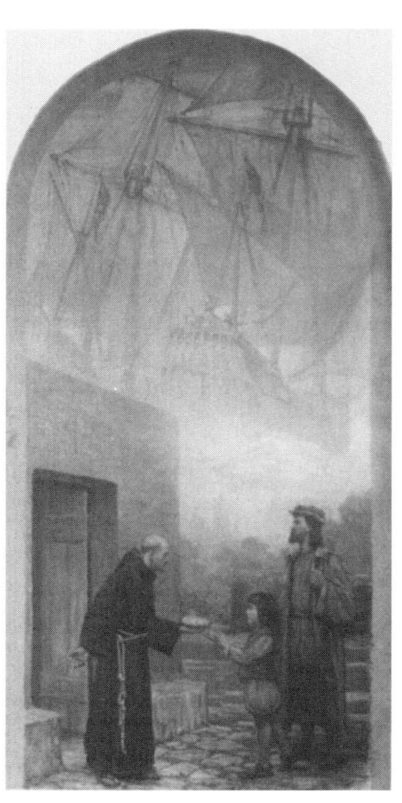

A Beauregard mural in St. Francis Auditorium of the Art Museum, which was completed by Vierra. This panel shows Columbus at the Franciscan monastery in Portugal with his dream of ships above him. The head of Columbus is a self-portrait by Vierra, 1912–1915.

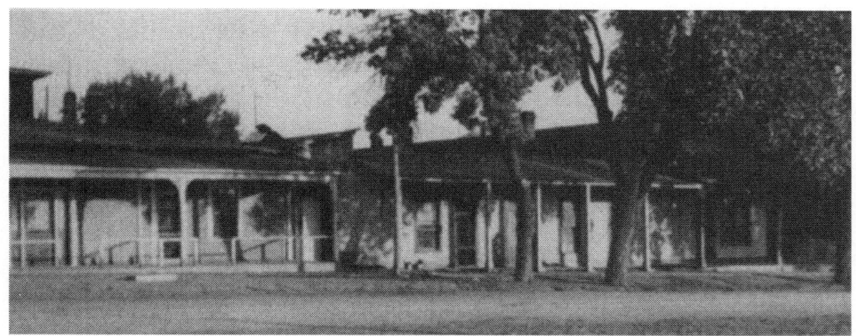

Padre Gallegos house around 1914 when Sara and Sheldon Parsons lived there.

an exhibition catalog for the work of her husband, painter Victor Higgins, she writes:

> *My father [Sheldon Parsons] was the second painter to make Santa Fe his home, and he was the first to become director of Fine Arts of the Museum of New Mexico. Carlos Vierra was the first to settle here. But soon after our arrival in 1913 many more and many famous painters came to Santa Fe, some to take up residence but most of them to come only for a summer or so, or for occasional visits.*

Sheldon Parsons came to Santa Fe from New York to rebuild his health. His wife, noted photographer Caroline Reed Parsons, had died on January 10, 1913, and when Parsons received a commission to paint murals for the exposition being planned in San Francisco, he and his twelve-year-old daughter set out for the West. They sold everything they owned before leaving, and travelled the Santa Fe Railroad. The railroad was always happy to let painters travel in exchange for their pictures, which were hung in hotels and railroad offices to promote western travel.

Arriving in Denver, Parsons suffered a severe relapse of an earlier arrested case of tuberculosis. Doctors recommended New Mexico's climate, and so after two months the father and daughter took the train to New Mexico. Interested citizens found the little girl and her father a place to live and bought some paintings which Parsons had brought with him. Their first home was a two-room apartment in the northeast corner of the James Norment house on Washington Avenue. The big rambling adobe, which had been converted into a number of apartments, was in good repair, and had a long history, having been owned originally by Padre Gallegos. Recently it has been restored and carries a plaque denoting its historical importance.

Parsons was desperately ill for several months after he and Sara moved into the little apartment, so ill that at one point the doctor warned Sara that he would not live. He also told her that her father must have nourishing food such as beefsteak each day. This was a terrible burden for a twelve-year-old. She has said that she could hardly find money for shredded wheat, let alone the sustaining food he needed so badly. It is incredible that they managed at all, but a number of people cared tremendously about making Santa Fe a cultural center and helped artists in any way they could. Sara has said that the doctors and storekeepers often exchanged their services for paintings.

As Parsons gradually regained strength, commissions were given him by Springer and others, and his house became a meeting place for whatever artists came to town. In 1914, Sara and her father gave a Thanksgiving feast and invited all of their friends. Later, Sara wrote:

> *I believe that my painter father, Sheldon Parsons, and I . . . were the first to welcome Victor Higgins. [He had stopped off in Santa Fe on his way to Taos, where he became a member of the Taos Society of Artists, having been financed by Chicago's mayor, Carter Harrison.] I am positive I was the first child of thirteen to cook him a five-course Thanksgiving dinner on a two-burner oil stove that smoked and sputtered in a small adobe room overlooking piñon-dotted foothills and the handsome snow-capped peaks of the Sangre de Cristo Range. It was on this same Thanksgiving Day that Victor first proposed to me. . . .*

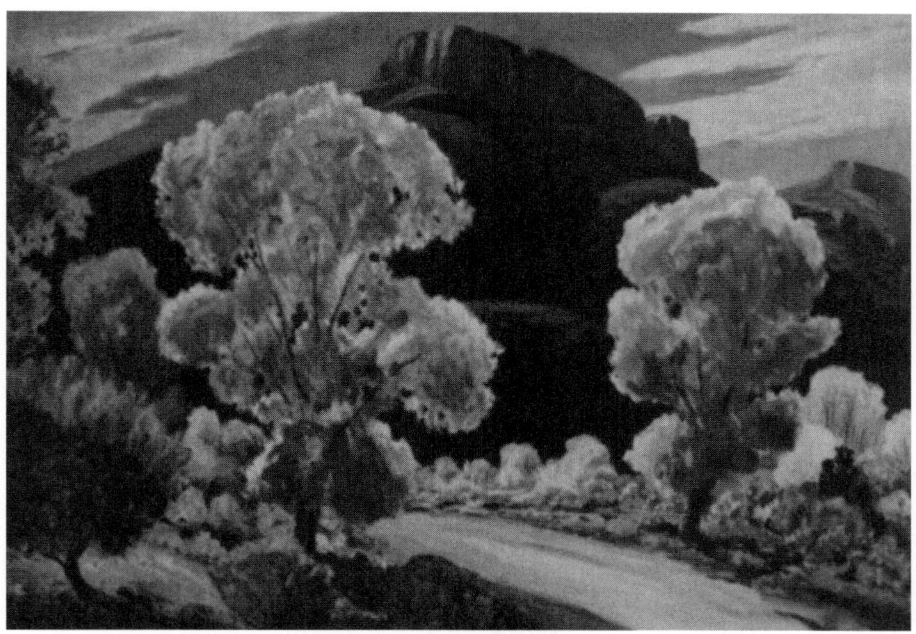

Sheldon Parsons, View Near Otowi, *ca. 1936. Oil, 24 x 36 in. Museum of New Mexico.*

Five years later, Sara and Victor Higgins were married, and she moved to Taos where the close-knit art group was in full swing. Between ages twelve and eighteen, while Sara was growing up in Santa Fe, she lived a life which many girls would envy. She and her father moved from the apartment on Washington Avenue and became caretakers for a large house at the corner of Canyon Road and the Acequia Madre, which had been bought by fellow painter Gerald Cassidy. She had inherited a small income from her grandfather, which enabled them to live more comfortably, and with the return of his strength Parsons was painting steadily. There was no public school and, although Sara kept house for them both, she had time to wander over the whole town. She had begun even then to follow in her mother's footsteps, and made photographs which sold well enough to enable her to buy a riding horse. She was already trying her hand at painting as well, and in 1916 the fifteen-year-old girl had a painting exhibited in the Palace of the Governors.

Parsons, who had been a prominent portrait painter in the East (he had made portraits of many of the leading figures of the time, including President McKinley, Vice President Hobart, and Senator Mark Hanna), turned to producing the romantic high-key landscapes which have made him famous as a southwestern painter. Although never drawn to Cubism or other experimental styles himself, he was deeply interested in innovative work by others. In his painting, Parsons was a direct descendant of the

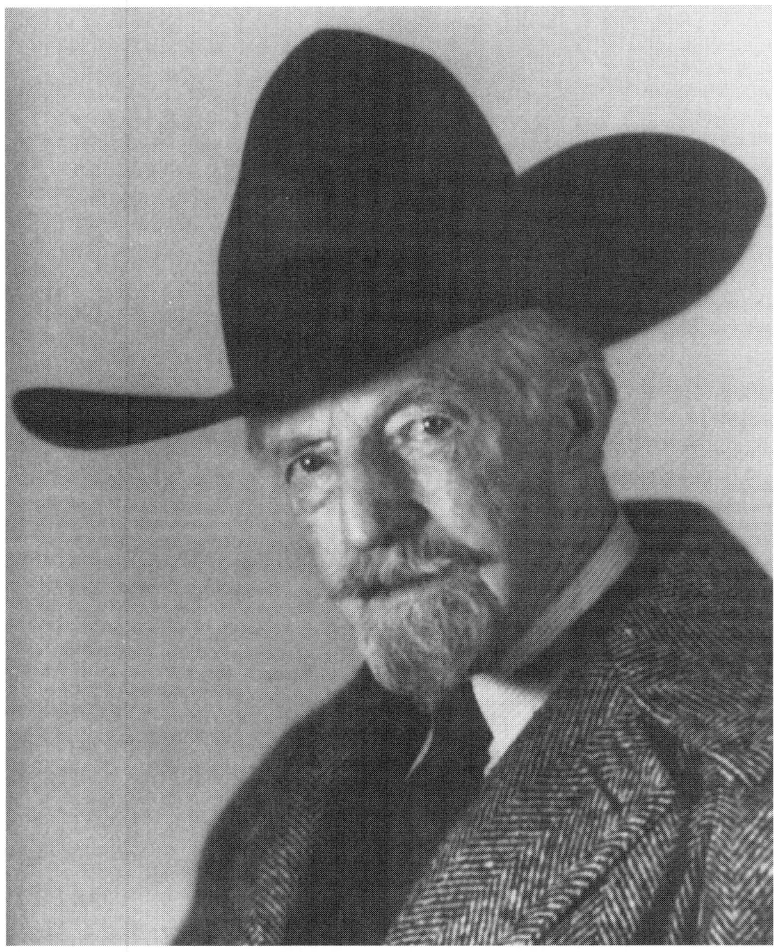

Sheldon Parsons. Parsons and his daughter Sara both showed paintings in the first exhibition for Santa Fe artists only, which was hung in the Palace of the Governors in 1916. Another father-daughter pair in the exhibit were William P. and Alice Henderson.

Barbizon and Impressionist painters, but he maintained a friendly and open attitude toward the younger painters with whom he came in contact, and firmly believed that each artist must seek his own form of expression. As the first director of Fine Arts at the museum, he showed the work of such painters as Paul Burlin, Marsden Hartley, and George Bellows when they visited Santa Fe. His sophisticated views eventually cost him his job at the museum—it was felt that he hung the work of too many modernist artists.

For many tourists and other visitors, Sheldon Parsons exemplified their idea of a perfect western artist and aristocrat. He was a quiet, gentle man, always impeccably dressed, with a neatly trimmed beard, and usually wearing his beloved Stetson hat. After his death in 1943, Hester Jones, then curator of the Art Museum, wrote: "Mr. Parsons's presence in the museum is greatly missed. He was almost a daily visitor. He took a live interest in every exhibitor, old and new. He made many kindly gestures to help the newcomer." Perhaps he was remembering the help and concern extended to Sara and him when they came to Santa Fe many years before.

Sara left Taos with her young daughter following her divorce from Higgins when she was twenty, and returned to New York. She established herself there as a top-ranking photographer, working under contract for *Vogue* magazine before her marriage to Robert Mack. Since her retirement, she and her husband have been living in Santa Fe, where she continues to paint.

Parsons's friend Gerald Cassidy and his wife Ina Sizer Cassidy had visited Santa Fe before Parsons, although they did not settle permanently until some years after their first visit in 1912. That was the year of New Mexico's admission to statehood, and the Cassidys, just arrived from Denver, attended the inauguration ceremonies of the new governor, William C. McDonald. Mrs. Cassidy later wrote that at that time Santa Fe had "no paved streets, no automobiles, one sewer line. . . . A passenger could ride all over town in a horse-drawn taxi for a quarter."

The year 1913 found the husband and wife in California. In a letter to Dr. Hewett dated March 29, 1913, John P. Harrington wrote:

Mr. Cassidy has been making his headquarters at Los Angeles, but has been living at Ventura. This is a surprise which he has planned for you, and he is now ready to show you his pictures. I urged him to come to Ventura last August so that he could make a painting of Fernando before Fernando died. He made a splendid one, a masterpiece. It is the old Indian of Santa Cruz with his white hair and his withered face. Mr. Cassidy has also made a fine lot of sketches of other Chumashan Indians and many landscapes of places about Ventura and on the island of Anacapa. These are ready to show you.

There were two expositions being planned in California at that time—the one at San Francisco for which Parsons had been promised a commission to do murals when his illness stopped him in Denver, and another in San Diego to be called the *Panama–California Exposition*. Harrington refers to the San Diego "fair" in the next paragraph of his letter to Hewett:

I hope that you will like them [Cassidy's paintings], and that you can arrange for him to continue such work this summer, but at a salary and for the Fair. He has had to sell some of his best Ventura pieces. Mr. Cassidy will do anything, he says, in order to get put on a salary by the Fair. He wants me to tell you that he will work for a small Salary if need be and would especially like the mural decoration work. He is a genius in his line, and a very hard worker. He gets up at 5:00 a.m. every morning and works right through the day until 4 or 5 o'clock p.m. . . . Mr. Cassidy never drinks, chews, or smokes; is a free thinker; and of a very poetic temperament. I took him to be rather commercial when I first knew him, but find on better acquaintance that he is not at all so. He is very generous and spends his money very freely for the things in which he is interested. He buckles right down to work and turns it out. He says that he wants you to examine his Southern California work and if it pleases you he wants you to give him a job. He wants you to give him a job and wants it in the worst way.

Born in Covington, Kentucky, in 1869, Gerald Cassidy moved shortly afterward with his family to Cincinnati, which was also the home of Joseph Sharp and a leading art center at the time. He and his two brothers attended the Institute of Mechanical Arts (later called the Cincinnati Art Institute). Gerald studied with the famous teacher and painter Frank Duveneck, and under his influence became interested in lithography. Later, he joined his brother in New York, where he became known as one of the best commercial lithographers in the profession.

Following a year and a half of study in Europe, Cassidy was stricken with a severe attack of pneumonia, and in 1890 was sent to a sanitorium in Albuquerque with a life expectancy of six months. There, while he regained his health, he came to know and paint his first Indians. He was living and working in Denver on commercial assignments when he met Ina. She was the daughter of pioneer parents who had homesteaded in Colorado on the Rio de los Animas near the northern branch of the Old Santa Fe Trail. She had shown an unusual gift for writing from early girlhood, and as a young woman was a correspondent for several Colorado weeklies. She met and married John B. Davis, and moved to Detroit; but shortly thereafter her husband died, so she returned to Denver.

When Gerald and she were married, they decided that he must devote his talents to serious painting. They were looking for a place to settle when they made the 1912 trip to Santa Fe, and decided that they would make it their permanent base. Several reasons influenced this decision. Cassidy needed to be near a railroad in order to ship his work east; near a telegraph office—in those days the fastest means of communicating with his eastern office; and in a community with subjects for him to sketch. Santa Fe had all of these to offer. In 1915, they bought a

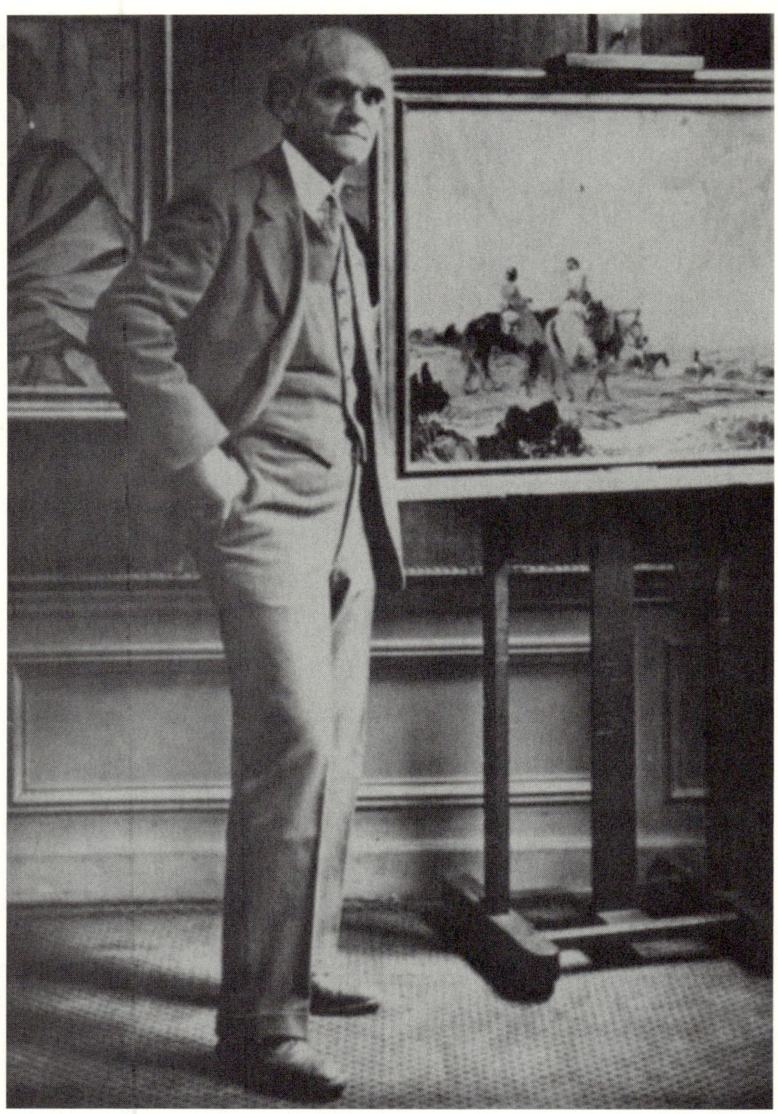

Gerald Cassidy in his Canyon Road studio with his painting Navajo Romance.

house at the corner of Canyon Road and Acequia Madre (the house Sheldon Parsons and Sara later lived in while the Cassidys were on their travels), on property which had formerly belonged to Juan de Archevecque. Archevecque, said to have been one of the murderers of the French explorer LaSalle, had fled to Mexico

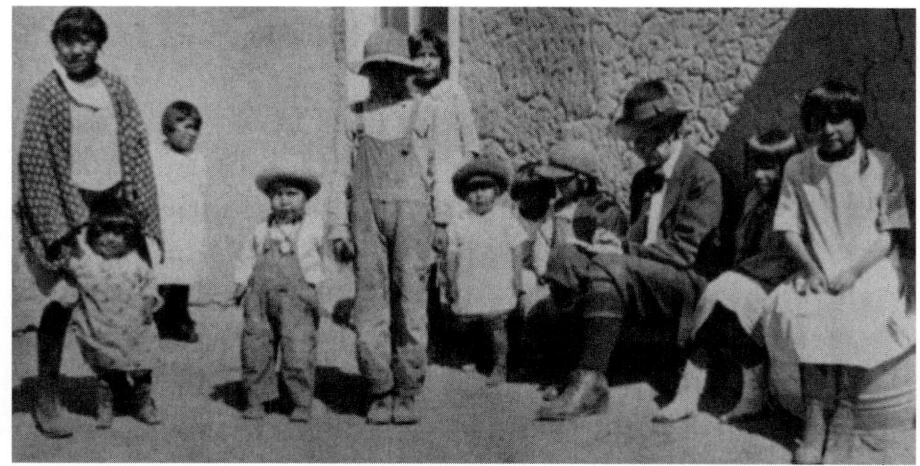

Gerald Cassidy sketching at an Indian pueblo.

following the murder and joined De Vargas's army for the reconquest of New Mexico in 1692. The Cassidys remodelled and enlarged the old house, incorporating corbels, carved vigas, and altar paintings from the ancient, ruined Nambé mission church, which they preserved and used with a loving sympathy.

Ina Sizer Cassidy, who wrote a column on the artists of New Mexico for the *New Mexico Magazine* for many years, wrote of her husband after his death in 1934:

> *Cassidy was primarily interested in light, color, atmosphere. . . . [He] was a prodigious worker, but left comparatively few canvases, preferring to experiment in his studio, destroying his work or keeping it for future reference or study, giving the public only such sort as met his own standard. He spent hours, as well as days and weeks, in the hills he loved and among the Indians, studying them, the light and color effects and relations, making color sketches and notes for later elaboration in the studio. During these studies he came to know the Indian as a human being, trying to understand their point of view and life. That he succeeded in the latter to an unusual degree was shown, I think, in his sympathetic*

rendering of their ceremonials and in their portraits, and also at the time of his death when Indian friends came from pueblos far away and near to add a bit of their ritual to his burial and to mourn with us.

Cassidy's tragic death resulted from turpentine and carbon monoxide fumes from a newly installed gas heater in his studio, the year that natural gas was first brought in to Santa Fe.

Undoubtedly, one of Cassidy's most loved works is a large portrait of a Taos Indian, owned by the Museum of New Mexico, *Cui Bono? (Who Benefits?)*, which was first exhibited in the San Diego Panama–California Exposition in 1915. A fine example of his mural painting may be seen in the U.S. Post Office in Santa Fe. Two large panels face each other, one showing the arrival of the Spanish conquistadores and the other the Indians watching the strangers.

Donald Beauregard was drawn to Santa Fe by the exciting work being done by the archaeologists, and like other artists, he was helped extensively by Springer. Born on an isolated farm near Fillmore, Utah, Beauregard worked his way through school and at twenty-six was head of the art department at the University of Utah. In the summer of 1910, a momentous one for him, he joined an archaeological team working under Prof. Byron Cummings at Frijoles Canyon near Santa Fe. Springer's interest was roused, and he became the patron of the young Mormon artist. California was planning its Panama–California Exposition in San Diego, and Springer commissioned Beauregard to paint the murals to be installed in the New Mexico building. He sent Beauregard to France, Germany, and Italy to study art and the life of St. Francis of Assisi. Beauregard's early letters from Paris express great joy, but later on there are ominous remarks about his health. For a time he was threatened with tuberculosis and spent some months in Switzerland, then he made references in his letters to stomach disorders. In 1913, he returned to the United States and to Santa Fe and was assigned a studio in a building at the rear of the Palace of the Governors, where he commenced work on the murals. But the day came when he

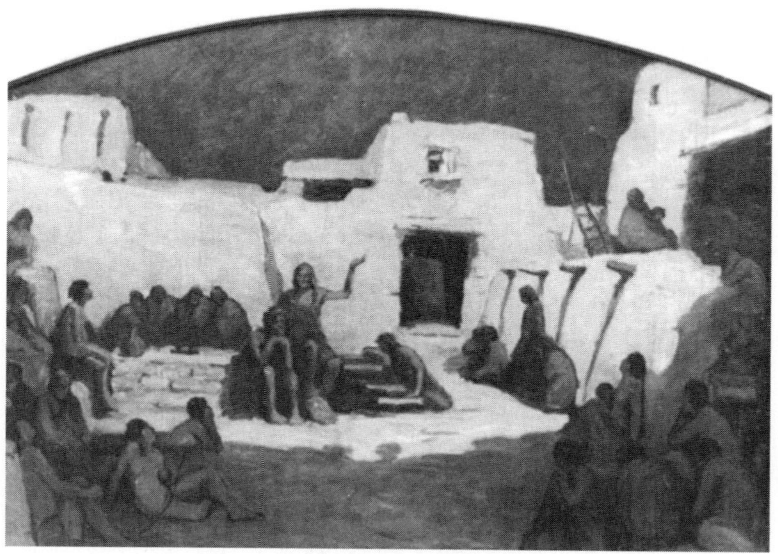

Donald Beauregard, Evening in the Pueblo, *n.d. Oil, 28 1/2 x 39 in. Museum of New Mexico.*

could work no longer; he literally laid down his brushes, left a note to a friend asking him to pack his things, and went to the hospital in Denver, where he was told that he had cancer and had just a short time to live. He returned to his parents' farm near Fillmore, Utah, where he died two weeks later.

In 1916, the art group in Santa Fe was enriched by the arrival of an important couple—a painter and a poet. Like so many of the early artists, the poet Alice Corbin Henderson came to Sunmount Sanitorium in Santa Fe with advanced tuberculosis. Her husband, William Penhallow Henderson, had a successful painting career in Chicago before she was stricken with illness, and many of their friends in the East were anxious when he gave up his work there to bring her and their little daughter Alice to New Mexico's life-saving climate. Henderson, however, was delighted to be in the West again. He had first visited Santa Fe as a two-year-old. In the late 1870s his mother, a friend, and the little boy rode from their ranch in Texas to Santa Fe in an Army ambulance at the invitation of the wife of the commandant of the nearby Army Post. It was an unconventional conveyance, but fairly comfortable, as it had beds along the sides!

Henderson was born in Medford, Massachusetts, in 1877, but his family moved to a ranch near Turkey Creek, Texas, when he was two years old. In 1885, the family returned to the East, and sometime later he attended the Massachusetts Normal Art School in Boston and the Boston Museum of Fine Arts, where his teacher was Edmund C. Tarbell. In 1901, he won the Paige Travelling Scholarship to Europe. Once back in America, he taught at the Chicago Academy of Fine Arts. He also made a trip to Mexico, the Grand Canyon, and the Hopi country in 1904 on the Santa Fe Railroad. In 1905, he married Alice Corbin.

When the Henderson family arrived in Santa Fe in 1916, they all lived at the sanitorium for several months. Then Henderson and Alice moved into a house near the bottom of the Camino del Monte Sol. Mrs. Henderson was later able to leave the sanitorium and live with her family. The house was small and quite primitive when Henderson moved in and started working on it. Nine-year-old Alice helped strip vigas and whatever else she could manage—all of her jobs paid her fifteen cents an hour, and she was firm about her rate.

During World War I, Henderson worked for the Navy in San Francisco doing camouflage, as did many other painters. When the war ended, he came home to Santa Fe in time for Christmas, bringing with him the painter and printmaker B.J.O. Nordfeldt, whom he had known in Chicago. Nordfeldt was born in 1878 in Tullstrop, Sweden. In 1890, he came to the U.S., settled in Chicago, and enrolled at the Chicago Art Institute, where Albert Herter, the mural painter, saw Nordfeldt's work and made him his assistant. Herter took him to New York; shortly afterward, he was chosen by the International Harvester Company to do a mural for their booth at the Paris Exposition. Nordfeldt remained in Paris, painting on his own. Before this, he had been strongly influenced by Manet, Gauguin, and Cézanne; now, he became interested in the woodblock techniques developed by Toulouse-Lautrec and went to England to study the process. After more time in Europe, he returned to Chicago. From 1910 to 1913, he exhibited at the Thurber and Roullier Galleries, where Henderson also exhibited. On his first visit to Santa Fe with Henderson,

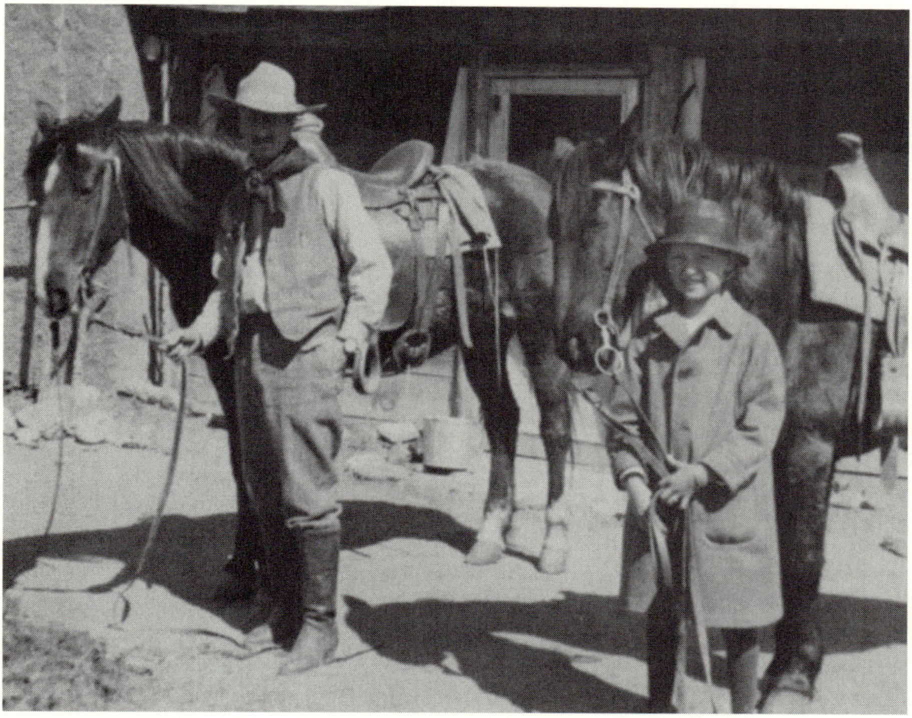

William P. Henderson and little Alice with their horses on the Camino del Monte Sol.

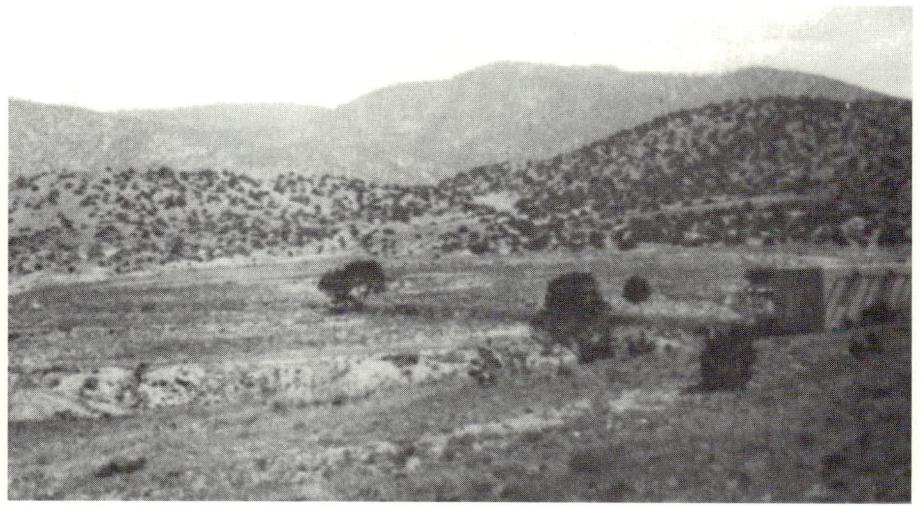

Henderson's first studio on the Camino.

Nordfeldt found that he felt happy and energetic, and so he spent the next twenty years primarily in New Mexico.

When Henderson and Nordfeldt came to Santa Fe together, Sara Parsons and her father Sheldon were living in the Cassidy house, and the Henderson and Parsons families were very close friends. They shared visitors, such as Nordfeldt; artist Gustave Baumann (another Chicagoan); painter Maurice Sterne; writers Carl Sandburg, Robert Frost, and Vachel Lindsey; the composer John Alden Carpenter; and Chicago's great mayor, Carter Harrison. Many of the visitors gave lectures while they were in town.

Mrs. Edgar L. Rossin (Henderson's daughter Alice), in talking about the early Santa Fe years, has pointed out that while they all were quite poor, they were a remarkable group of sophisticated and cultivated people, and were able to live in a very interesting manner when thrown back on their own resources. It was this group which in 1917 decided to revive the yearly fiesta. Mrs. Rossin recounts that many of them dressed in cowboy, Indian, or Spanish costumes, and she remembers fringing a khaki riding skirt, which ruined her hands for days. She, herself, is credited with the first designs for the popular denim and bandana clothes seen all over the Southwest today.

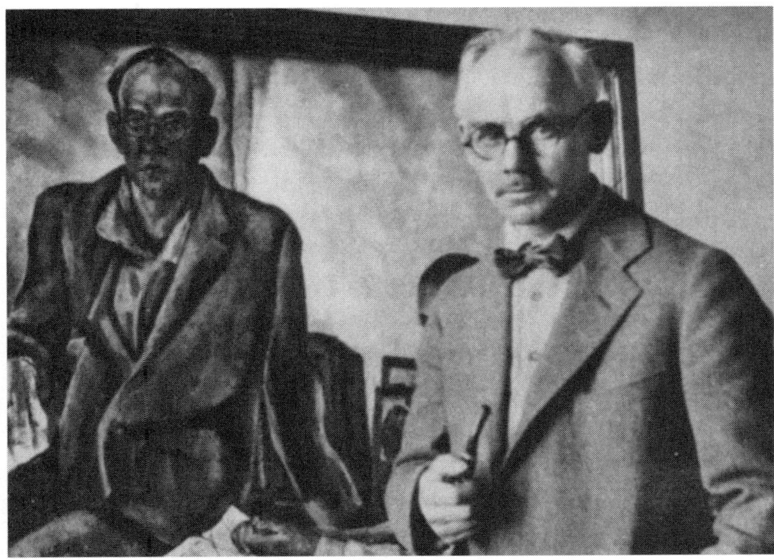

B.J.O. Nordfeldt.

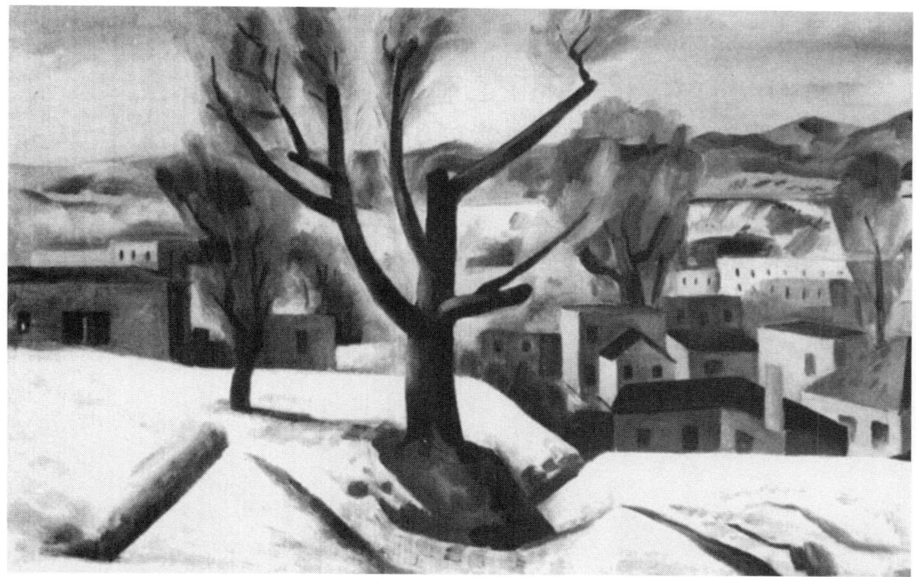

B.J.O. Nordfeldt, Santa Fe, *ca. 1926. Oil, 34 x 36 in. Museum of New Mexico.*

By 1925, Henderson had formed the Pueblo Spanish Building Company. Remarkable in the diversity of his talents, he was a master at making furniture and designing buildings—he restored the old Sena Plaza on Palace Avenue and designed and built the Museum of Navajo Ceremonial Art, the Fremont Ellis house on Canyon Road, and the Santa Fe Railroad ticket office on the plaza. During the 1920s, he helped produce plays. As a benefit for the Indian victims of a terrible drought of those years, one play, written by Henderson and E. Dana Johnson, editor of the *Santa Fe New Mexican*, featured Henderson in the part of a character called the "Desert Whip-poor-will"—and thus he acquired the nickname "Whippy."

Of Henderson's painting, Carl Sandburg said, in a foreword to the catalog for the Henderson Exhibition of 1921:

> *It is my guess that most anybody would enjoy the [pictures] . . . by William Penhallow Henderson. . . .*

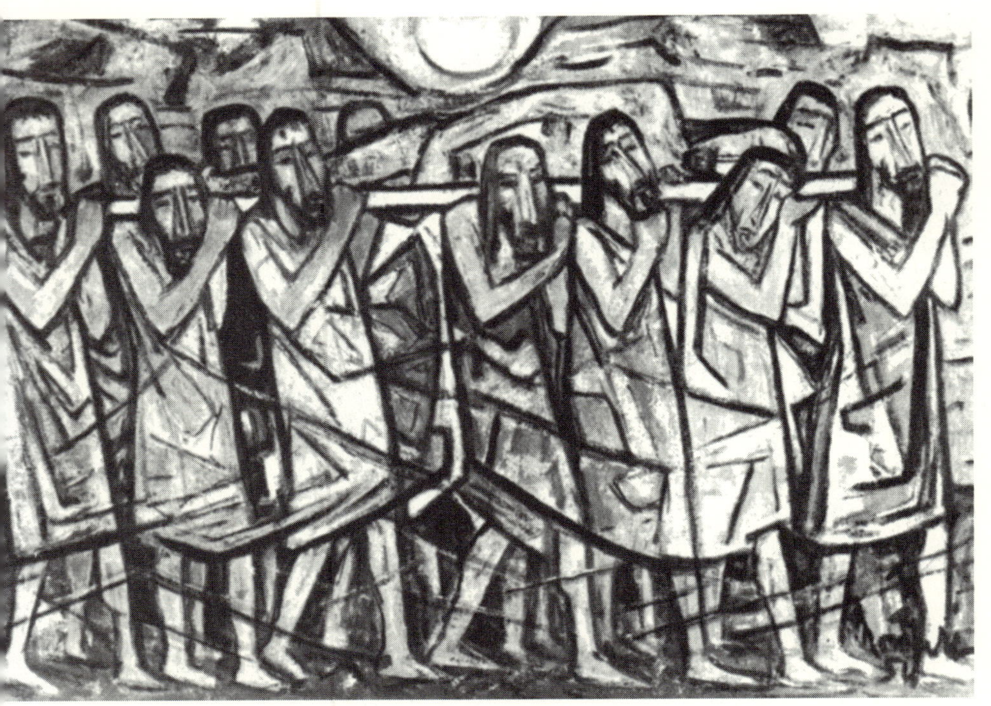

B.J.O. Nordfeldt, Carrying the Dead Christ, *n.d. Oil, 32 x 40 in. Museum of New Mexico.*

It is another guess of mine that Henderson did these . . . because the spirit of the inevitable sat upon him. That is, he had to do 'em.

He spent his best years mixing with the material here dealt with and was spiritually mortgaged to the still and living objects, the forms and gestures, colors and shadows, flickering their suggestions back of these projections. He pays them for what they gave him by a setting forth of fine human and cosmic implications that rise behind and out of the portrayed Indians, mountains, houses, sparse trees—and sometimes thin momentous blossoms—brief desert breaths of whispered blossoms. . . . Yes, the inevitable is over this work.

Look 'em over. Take a second and third look. The more looks, the farther these sink in and multiply their

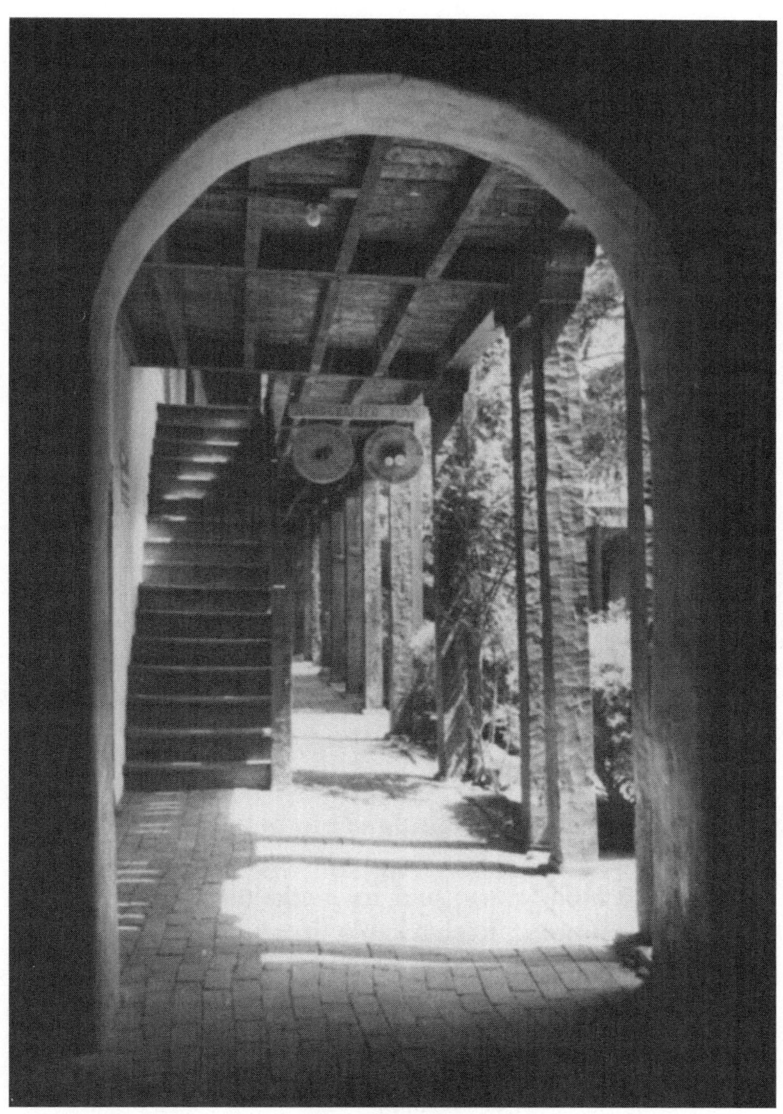

Sena Plaza as restored by William P. Henderson.

> *human pull. . . . They will last a long time. Barring fire and quake and the unforeseen, they will . . . be telling their haunting tale of vanished lovers of marvelous dances when our tallest bank buildings and our longest railroads are shrunken possessions of rust and dust.*

Mrs. Henderson, associate editor of *Poetry Magazine*, became a catalyst for poets and writers, publishing her poetry anthologies and the classic book on the Penitentes, *Brothers of Light*, which was illustrated by her husband. She started the Poets' Roundups held in Santa Fe in the 1930s, and also studied Indian and Spanish poetry.

The Hendersons' life in Santa Fe was another world from the one they had left. Little Alice rode to school on her pony; a trip to Taos took three days; and when Indian friends—of whom they had many, with very close ties—came to town to visit, they stayed at the Hendersons' house where the little girl made great pots of "Alice's potato soup." But the Hendersons also kept in touch with the outside world by means of their frequent guests.

There were many other artists who discovered Santa Fe in the years before World War I, but only a small group was permanently located there until that tremendous convulsion closed

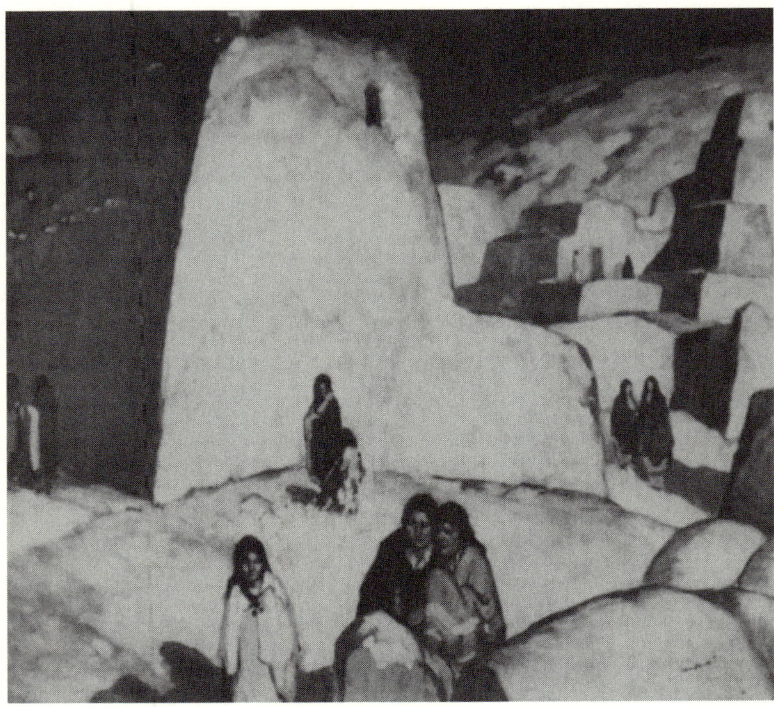

William Penhallow Henderson, The Taos Pueblo, *n.d. Oil, 32 x 40 in. Museum of New Mexico.*

Europe to travellers and students. During World War I and immediately afterward, however, more and more people came to the remote and romantic town at the foot of the Sangre de Cristos.

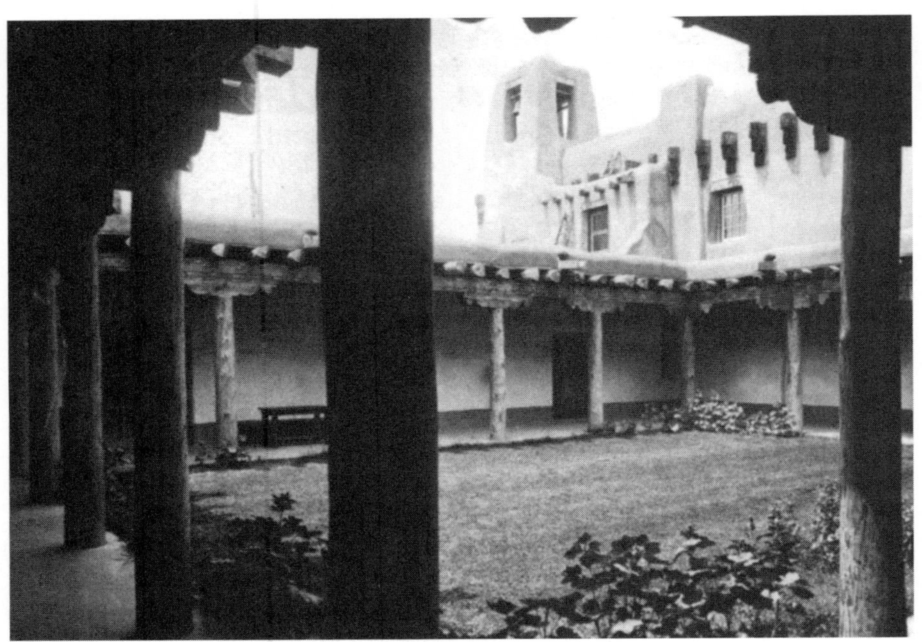

The Art Museum patio.

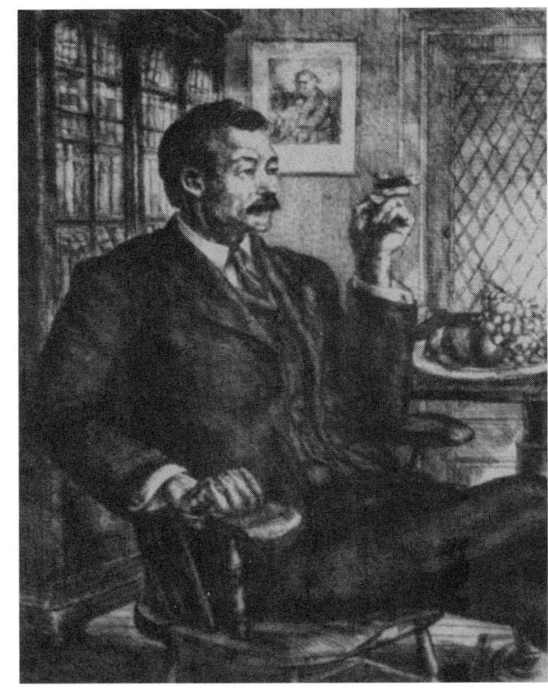

John Sloan, Robert Henri, Painter, *ca. 1931. Etching, 13 1/4 x 10 3/4 in. Museum of New Mexico.*

3
"The New Museum Is a Wonder . . ."

Since its formation in 1909, the Museum of New Mexico had made attempts to draw artists to Santa Fe, helping them financially and making studios available to them, finding them places to live during their visits, and purchasing their pictures. Combined with the Taos group, a formidable colony was developing, and interested citizens began to dream of a building devoted to the fine arts.

Tangible shape was given to the dream by a building designed by Rapp Bros. Architects for the Panama–California Exposition at the 1915 San Diego Fair. The building housing New Mexico's exhibits was romantically called "The Cathedral of the Desert," According to the description in the San Diego Exposition official guide, it had "the irregular wall and rough beam construction of the Pueblo Indians. Two belfry towers flank the portal. A second story loggia or tribune is over the entrances. Within is a galleried patio. The carving of the woodwork and fireplaces reproduces the ancient work at Isleta and Acoma"—all of which gives Santa Feans a peculiar feeling of déjà vu, as it not only could be but is a description of the Fine Arts Museum as it was finally built again in their own city, following the Rapp Bros. plans. Dr. Hewett, director of the Museum of New Mexico and the School of American Research and also connected with the San Diego Museum at that time, had much to do with planning New Mexico's building, as well as arranging for the exhibits.

In San Diego he met Robert Henri, who, along with John Sloan, was one of the leaders of the New York Independents group that was trying to achieve freedom from the academies and jury systems of the day. In 1908, Henri and his friends had presented their revolutionary exhibit of "The Eight," which caused a storm of criticism but opened the way for their later nonjuried shows. After the two met in San Diego, Hewett persuaded Henri to travel to Santa Fe. In a letter dated July 13, 1916, he wrote:

> *I sincerely hope that you have not changed your plans. . . .*
>
> *For something more than personal reasons I have hoped that you might come to Santa Fe this summer. We are just building our new Art Museum and have some plans with reference to future work in art here in which we need advice. You may have noticed that the artists of both East and West are turning more and more toward this region. It is our privilege to have something in the way of exhibits nearly all the time. The building of the new Art Museum, together with the facilities which we can offer in the way of studio and exhibition galleries will be a great additional stimulus.*
>
> *Now, before things get much farther along I am tremendously anxious to have the ideals in art that you stand for brought into the ken of our people. . . .*
>
> *However, it is not altogether for selfish reasons that we hope to see you in Santa Fe. I really think you might find it a place of exceptional advantages along your particular lines.*

Henri wrote back about the same time, saying:

> *I hope this will prove to be only a* first *season for us at Santa Fe, for I should like very much to so like a place that I would not have to worry every season over the question "Where shall we go?" Santa Fe may be the place for I fare well in high, dry, and sunlit climates, and*

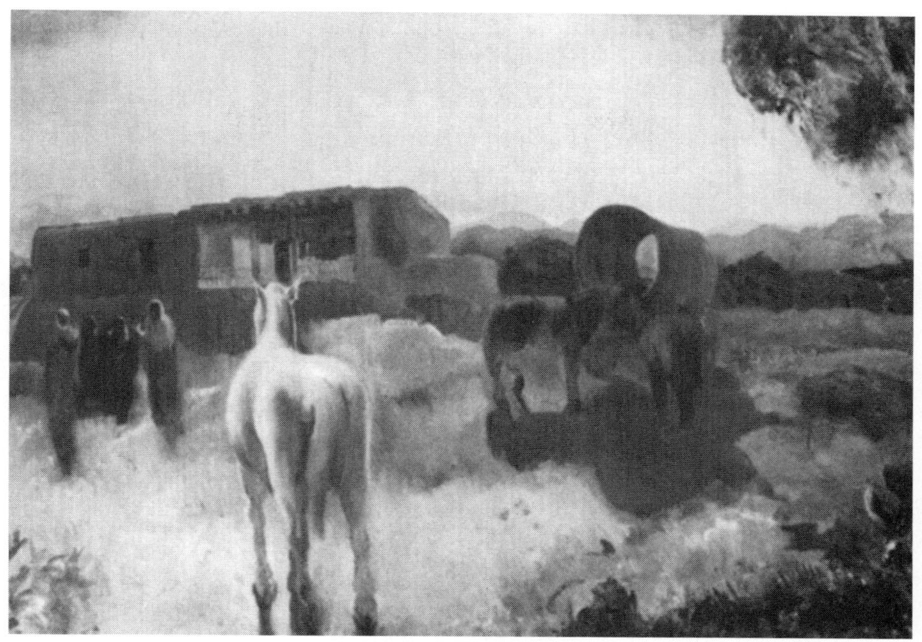

George Bellows, Chimayo, *1917. Oil, 30 x 40 in. Museum of New Mexico.*

> *I am sure there are children, Indians, and others I shall want to paint and who will be willing to be painted.*

This first Santa Fe summer delighted Henri, and 1917 found him back. A note in the Museum's publication, *El Palacio*, of July 1917 mentions under "Art and Literary Colony" that "Robert Henri has built himself a studio in Santa Fe which he expects to occupy not only all summer but also the greater part of the winter, before returning to New York City with Mrs. Henri and her sister, Miss Violet Organ."

The word that Santa Fe was a very exciting art colony was now spreading rapidly. Taos had been a gathering place for artists for a number of years, and people working in both towns had long intermingled; but with the plans for the great new art museum building, Santa Fe was coming into its own as an art center for the whole area. In 1917, several of Henri's New York friends had come after listening to his praises of the town and its vicinity. Among them were Paul Burlin, George

Bellows, and Leon Kroll—important names in twentieth-century American art.

George Bellows's visit in 1917 was the result of an operation. Bellows had been under contract to teach at the Art Students League in New York that year, but when he became ill in San Francisco, he persuaded John Sloan to take his place. This delayed the Sloans' discovery of Santa Fe, but did permit Bellows to join the Henris there. On September 22, 1917, the *Santa Fe New Mexican* announced that "George Bellows, the noted N.Y. artist, and his family will arrive tomorrow noon from Calif. to stay for a month or longer. They will accompany Mr. and Mrs. Robert Henri to the San Geronimo Fiesta at Taos next week."

In his book *George Bellows, American Painter*, Charles Morgan tells the story of Bellows's illness and visit to New Mexico:

> *After a week in the hospital, he drove to Carmel [that other center of creative life with its own artists' and writers' colony]. They closed the house and drove to L.A. in 3 days, picked up old Mrs. Bellows, put the Buick on a flat car, and spent an agreeable month in Santa Fe with the Henris. Kroll was there, and a strange and stimulating countryside, the communal pueblos fascinated B. as much for their picturesque qualities, and he painted them many times.*

After Bellows's death in 1925, *El Palacio* wrote:

> *The summer that the late George Bellows occupied a studio facing the patio of the Palace of the Governors he offered the Museum the choice of 2 of his lithographs ["A Stag at Sharkey's" and "Artists judging Works of Art"]. . . . It may also be recalled that the Bellows exhibit of paintings created a mild sensation locally in Santa Fe because of what was then considered its extreme modernism . . . and one local critic had considerable fun in referring to one of the paintings as "Bellows's Green*

Cow." The late Robert Henri, even more eminent than B. in American Art, occupied the same studio for several seasons. . . . Bellows never returned to Santa Fe.

Leon Kroll, another important Eastern artist to discover Santa Fe in 1917, was in Colorado Springs during the summer, and decided to pay a visit to his friends Henri and Bellows while he was so near. During the brief visit, he painted a picture called *Santa Fe Hills*. Much later, when *Santa Fe Hills* was acquired for the museum's collection in 1968, Kroll wrote: "The painting is unique in a way. At least as far as I am concerned. It is the only major work done in Santa Fe (what a beautiful city). I spent some weeks in 1917 with Henri, Bellows, Randall Davey, and others there. A grand period," (Kroll's memory was in error in regard to Davey, as he did not come to Santa Fe until 1919.) Kroll's painting, one of Bellows's called *Chimayo*, and Robert Henri's portrait of *Dieguito Roybal, the Drummer of the Eagle Dance, San Ildefonso* were all created in that splendid summer, and were included in the opening exhibition of the new Art Museum in November of that same year.

While the Great War caused many artists to concentrate on the American land and people, it also required that some of those who had been living in Santa Fe should travel away from New Mexico. The Cassidys, for instance, had been in San Diego, where he had painted murals for the exposition of 1915. "When he finished, they equipped an automobile and began to drive east. They did not stay in Santa Fe but continued all the way to New York, and, with automobile travel and roads what they were at that time, it is no wonder that the trip took a whole summer. "It had been the intention of Cassidy to visit Paris this year," Cassidy's wife Ina later wrote in a letter, "but the war has prevented that, and he is industriously working at his New York studio with occasional visits to the West, which he loves."

Henderson was working in camouflage, Mrs. Henderson was director of publicity for the Women's War Effort, and Parsons and some of the others were making something called range-finder paintings for the army. Ina Sizer Cassidy wrote from

New York to Paul Walters, the secretary of the museum, on November 14, 1917:

> *We are feeling the pinch of war here. No sugar and none to be had for at least two weeks, if then! We are using honey for sweeting tea and coffee. Milk 14 cents a quart, and can't always get it at that! . . . Mr. Cassidy has just made a stunning poster for the new Liberty Loan. It is being submitted to Washington this week, but of course, do not know if it will be accepted or not, but we are hoping, of course, that it will be.*
>
> *I was very busy for the three weeks before election, speaking for suffrage, and we won! Of course, I am delighted. Now we mean to work for the federal amendment just as hard as we have worked for the state, and hope to be as successful.*

Ina was also writing a book on "American Natural Foods, Edible Weeds, etc.," and she wrote to Walters:

> *It is rather a jump to come down (or up?) to art! Is it not so? And I am rushing this food book out, so it may save the nation! . . . It has been a very great disappointment to us that we were not able to come back to Santa Fe for this summer, but the war has changed our plans entirely, and now we have stopped making any more, until we know a little more of what is going to be. I suppose you do not hear very much of it in quiet Santa Fe!*

Santa Fe, the state capital, was very much aware of the war, even though Europe must have seemed much farther away than it did in New York. But in spite of the war, plans went ahead to open the Fine Arts Museum in November 1917—a gesture of great confidence in the future. There was a sort of cheerful vitality about it, with the country at war and the first American soldiers shortly to go overseas to help the allies.

The faith and pleasure the artists felt about Santa Fe as a place to live and work, and about the Fine Arts Museum then nearing completion, is beautifully expressed in a letter written at the time by Robert Henri to a friend, Henry Lovins:

> *Things are very interesting here. The new museum is a wonder. With the influence of Dr. Hewett and the excellent men about him, Santa Fe can become a rare spot in all the world. Nearly all—one might say, all cities and towns strive to be like each other and not to be like themselves. Under this surprising present influence, Santa Fe is striving to be its own beautiful self. Of course, there are negative influences which combat but the beautiful thing has taken root and the museum has grown in its beauty and it is likely that it will spread its healthy kind. Most museums are glum and morose temples looking homesick for the skies and associations of their native lands—Greek, most likely. The museum here looks as though it were a precious child of the Santa Fe sky and the Santa Fe mountains. It has its parents' complexion. It seems warmly at home as if it has always been here. Without any need of the treasures of art which are to go into it, it is a treasure of art in itself, art of this time and this place, of people and related to all the past. My hope is that it will shame away the bungalow with which a few mistaken tastes have tried to make Los Angeles of Santa Fe, and the false fronts with which other mistaken tastes have tried to make New York of Santa Fe. Santa Fe may do the rare thing and become itself. The painters are all happy. The climate seems to suit well both temperaments—to work or not to work—and here painters are treated with that welcome and appreciation that is supposed to exist only in certain places in Europe. Being of the "to work" temperament myself, I am having a fine time.*

When the opening date for the museum approached, an exhibition was hung, and a tremendous celebration planned. The *Santa Fe New Mexican* announced on November 17, 1917:

> *The preparations for the dedication of the new museum have occupied the time of many Santa Fe men and women during the past week, and the work will be even more intensive during the days that are coming, preceding next Saturday, when the program of exercises will begin. . . . The latter event will be open to the public and will also include the opening of the exhibit of Southwestern art. This exhibit is being hung at present and is by far the most ambitious and impressive that has thus far been given by Southwestern artists. Almost 300 canvases are being hung in the well-lighted galleries. At the exercises on Saturday evening, Dr. Edgar L. Hewett will preside and addresses will be made by United States Senator A. A. Jones, Governor W. E. Lindsey, Secretary of State Antonio Lucero, and Col. D. C. Collier, all of them to be brief and snappy. The meetings held this week disclose how much more beautiful even than planned is the noble structure that commemorates the martyrdom of the Franciscans in New Mexico. It is more than a monument already; it has become a community center. The Red Cross and Woman's Naval service are meeting within its walls, forenoons, afternoons, and evenings of almost every day, and the hum of their industry is heard from one end to the other.*
>
> *When illuminated in the evening, the building becomes a veritable fairy palace and everyone who has seen it is sincerely enthusiastic in its praise and in saying that in many ways it is the finest building in the Southwest. Most impressive and beautiful are the native timbers hewn and carved by native craftsmen. The color-blending is harmonious and striking. Every*

portion of the building is expressive of the skillful touch of human hands and of careful planning by human mind. It is not a mere replica or copy as most public buildings in this country are, but expresses American originality, and yet is based upon primitive precedents and reproduces some of the greatest and most ancient Franciscan missions.

The exhibition for the opening included an important list of Santa Fe and Taos painters, many of them still regarded as among the most important artists of that time in American art. The list included Henry Balink, George Bellows, Oscar E. Berninghaus, Ernest L. Blumenschein, Paul Burlin, Kenneth Chapman, Edgar S. Cameron, Gerald Cassidy, E. Irving Couse, Katherine Dudley, W. Herbert Dunton, William Penhallow Henderson, E. Martin Hennings, Robert Henri, Victor Higgins, Alice Klauber, Leon Kroll, Ralph Myers, Arthur F. Musgrave, Sheldon Parsons, Bert G. Phillips, Grace Ravelin, Julius Rolshoven, Doris Rosenthal, Joseph H. Sharp, Eva Springer (Frank Springer's daughter), G. C. Stanson, Walter Ufer, Carlos Vierra, and Theodore Van Soelen. Included too, although he had died in 1914, was Donald Beauregard. Many of the artists listed donated their paintings to the museum, where they still form the heart of the collection of early New Mexican work.

On November 21, as *El Palacio* describes it:

The tolling of the old Algodones Bell in the Acoma Tower announced the dedication hour for the new Fine Arts building. No services were held in any church, the congregations joining in the exercises. Long before the hour of opening, the building was thronged. At one time more than 2,000 people had gathered within its walls, although almost half of them could not get into the auditorium and many hundreds left without even attempting to get into the building. It was a solemn moment when

Dr. David R. Boyd, president of the University of New Mexico, invoked the divine blessing upon the house that had been builded, upon the builders and the donors, upon the commonwealth and its people, upon the young men fighting the nation's battles and the leader in the White House standing watch in the tower. The audience remained standing and joined in the singing of "America" with a fervor that came from the heart. . . . Mr. Springer spoke for almost an hour and it was nearly 10 o'clock when the art galleries and reception rooms were again thrown open, for the thousands to enjoy the magnificent exhibit. It was almost midnight when the doors were closed upon another day that had broken all attendance records as far as any institution in the Southwest is concerned.

The article goes on to describe the art exhibit itself:

From the auditorium, the throngs poured into the art galleries and lingered to admire the art exhibit, the significance of which Dr. Hewett had pointed out. The Woman's Museum Board, assisted by the artists and their families, received. It was a much appreciated opportunity that the visitors, especially the educators, whose names stand at or near the head of American art and whose pictures made the exhibit the greatest of Southwestern art that had ever been attempted anywhere. Artists like 0. E. Berninghaus, came direct from St. Louis to attend this opening of the exhibit, and among the other artists present were Mr. and Mrs. Robert Henri, Mr. and Mrs. Julius Rolshoven, Mr. and Mrs. W. P. Henderson, Mr. and Mrs. H. Paul Burlin, Arthur F. Musgrave, Sheldon Parsons, Miss Sara Parsons, Mr. and Mrs. Carlos Vierra, Ralph Myers, Mr. and Mrs. K. M. Chapman, and others almost as well known, and whose paintings

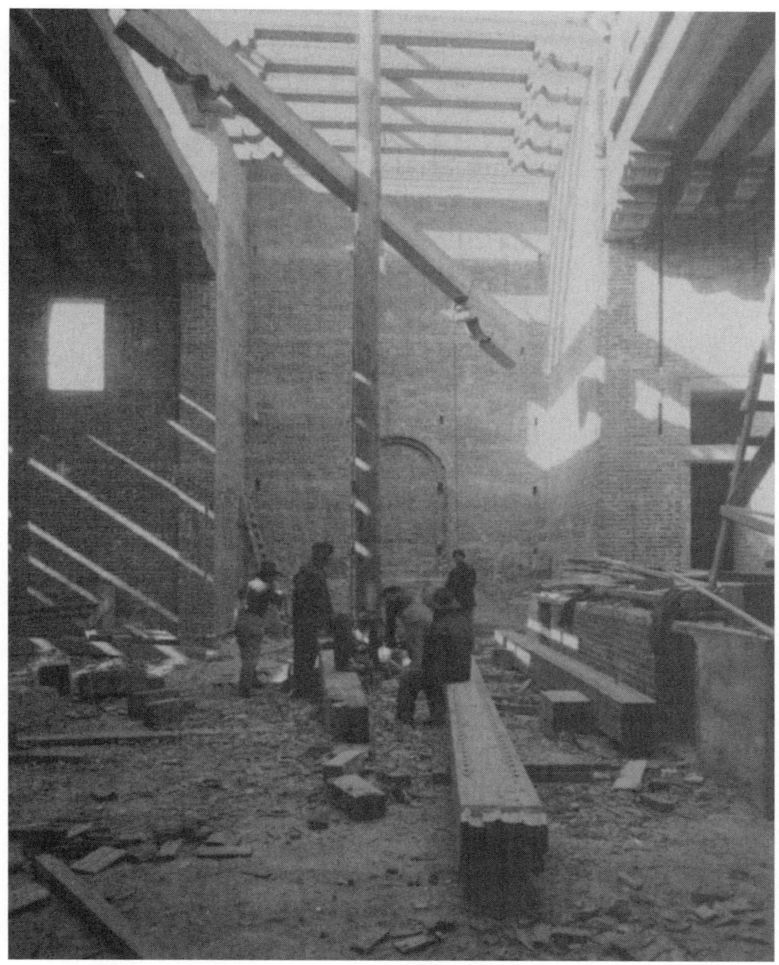

St. Francis Auditorium under construction.

> *are among the finest on exhibit, some forty artists being represented in this the first complete exhibit of Southwestern art.*

Frank Springer's address had been a broad statement about the ideals of science and art. Dr. Edgar L. Hewett, the director of the museum, was more specific. He thanked the workmen who, under Jesse Nusbaum, had done the actual construction. He spoke of the strokes of their axes, gouges, brushes. Then he quoted the words of the donors of funds: "This fund is contributed by a small group of men and women residents of or interested in the state, who desire in this manner to attest their loyalty to New Mexico, their solicitude for its progress and their appreciation of the benefits which its opportunities have afforded them."

His speech on the opening of the galleries reflects the tremendous pride the community felt at opening a museum during the horrifying cataclysm of the First World War, and its depth of idealistic feeling and thoughtfulness justify quoting it at some length.

> *On throwing open to you this exhibition of Southwestern art, I would, if I were capable, express the deep sense of obligation that we of the Southwest feel toward the painters who are producing here the most characteristic art of the new world. It is not our debt alone; it is the debt of this nation. These artists are revealing to the world the beauty of the Southwest. Beauty is indescribable, and a world full of it is, for the most part, unseen. The beauty of the Southwest is subtle, mysterious, elemental. We of the Southwest have rather silently felt it—the eternal character of these vast spaces, silent but vibrant with life and color—earth masses on which man through the ages has wrought no change nor ever can; and in it all, of it all, our people, simple, gentle, lovable. We are particularly grateful that these artists appreciate our people. We know of nothing finer than humanity—nothing greater than the spirit of man striving to be in harmony with the forces about him. That striving unifies life, and makes it strong and beautiful.*
>
> *We feel that our people here in the Southwest do have a life in keeping with the soil, the skies, winds, clouds, spaces—that they have ordered their lives in honest, simple harmonious ways. We are glad that the artists understand them.*

I trust that no one will attempt to dissect, to classify in the language of criticism, this noble art of the painters of the Southwest; nor should we wish to see it circumscribed by any local name. Pride might lead us to hope that it might come to be known in its big universal character. It is, in my estimation, the most democratic group of painters in America that is now painting in the Southwest. Here are the canvases of thirty artists working under the same potent influences, and remaining absolutely independent in method of expression, each sincerely concerned with the unfolding of his own spirit. Yet with all this diversity, we discern the golden thread of sympathetic comprehension, of elemental meanings, which makes this exhibition of Southwestern art a splendid unified thing.

There is a glorious future for art in the Southwest—for art in America. Fortunate are we in having some part in it. This building that we have erected expresses something of our gratitude for, and appreciation of, their works, to bring them to the attention of the world, to the end that multitudes may share our pleasure. It is the least that we can do. We shall not be satisfied with this. It will be the policy of this institution to provide all possible facilities to the artists who come to the Southwest—studios that can be freely at their disposal, and other conveniences to save their time and make the most of their powers.

We feel that in encouraging the production of art and in bringing it into the lives of the people, we are doing our proper service in the world. Art is for everyone. It should be universal. Think what it is! The truest, finest, most enduring record of the activities of the human spirit. It is our immutable heritage from the people of the past. It tells their story truly, faithfully, long after they have descended from the pinnacles of power;

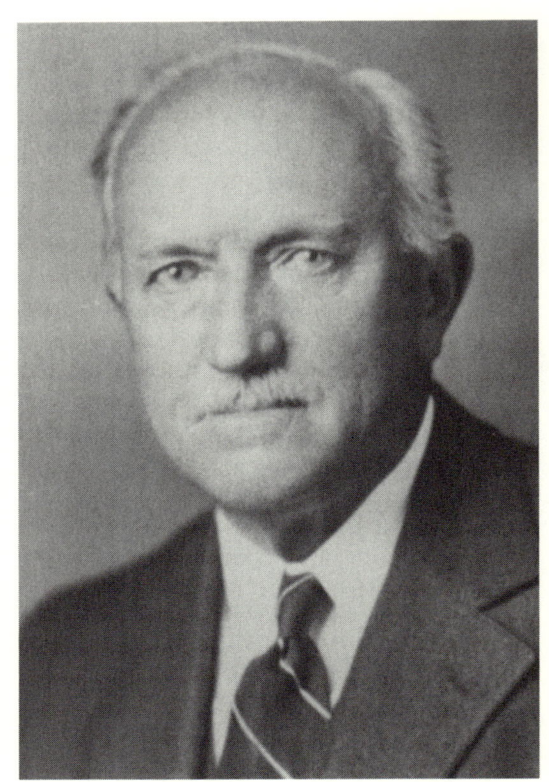

Dr. Edgar L. Hewett.

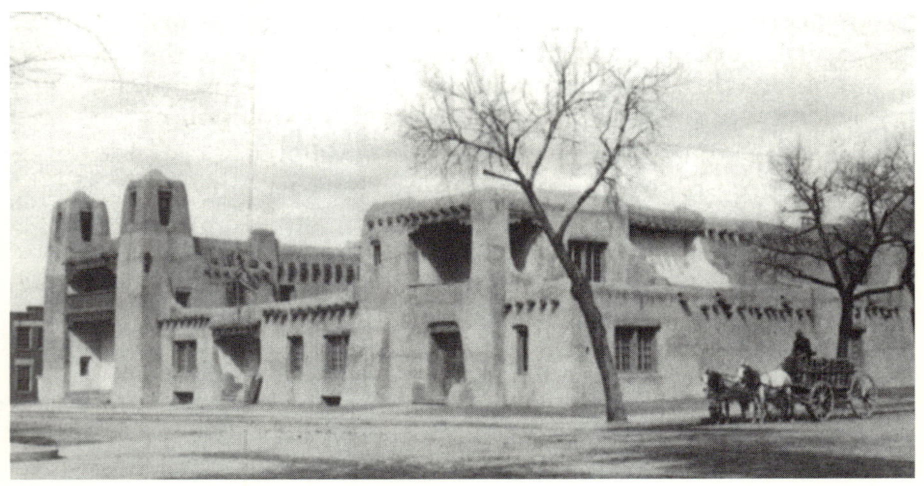

The new Art Museum.

their dynasties gone, their boasted evidences of greatness crumbled, their arts alone remaining to disclose, in spite of everything they ever said or did, the real life and spirit of the people. Art is the great, lasting, self-revealing activity of life. Through it, we transmit our spiritual power through the ages.

We are looking forward to the time when the vast energies that we are now organizing and dedicating to the defeat of despotic power, may be released and rededicated to the activities of peace. When that time comes, let us hope that art will be one of the chief concerns of this great nation. Perhaps the part we play here may not be important. It may fall to us to help carry through times of great darkness the torch from which new fires may be kindled to illuminate greater days than humanity has hitherto known. At any rate, we have taken our part, whatever it is to be, and we offer to you, tonight, the first fruits of our efforts in the opening of these galleries with the exhibition of Southwestern art. We are proud that it has been permitted to us here in Santa Fe, to do this. We dare to hope that this may become an annual event—that we may look forward every year to an exhibition of the new art of the Southwest. I believe I speak for the entire state, when I thank the artists who are represented in this exhibition that we are now about to view and say to them that they have added an inexpressible charm to our environment here, that this is their gallery as well as ours, that we want it to become not only a place of beauty, but of deep, abiding personal friendship.

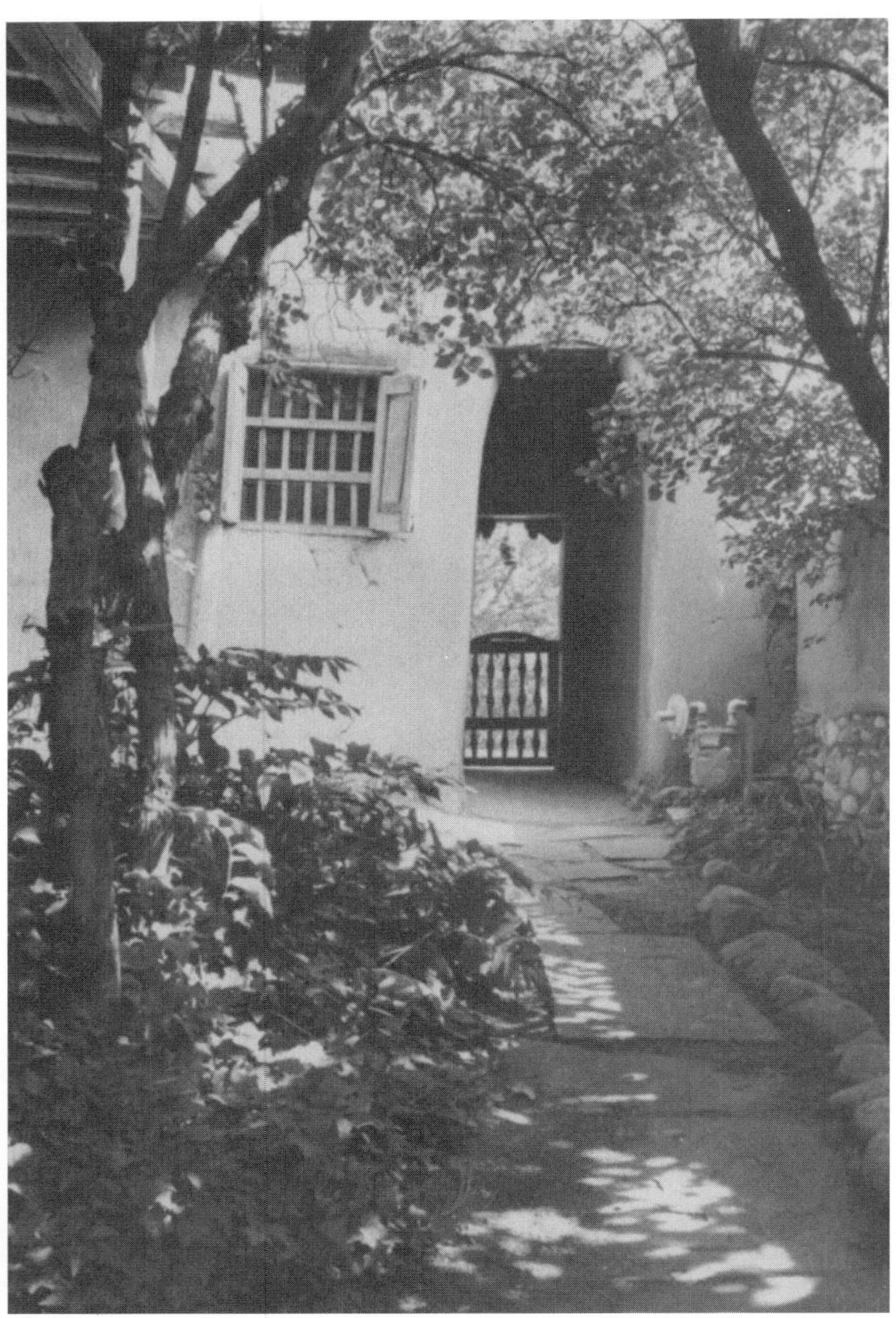

The Olive Rush house on Canyon Road, now the Quaker meeting house.

4
Artists' Haunts

Because many galleries and studios have been established along Canyon Road and the Camino del Monte Sol through the years, there has grown up a mistaken conviction that the early Santa Fe art colonists all lived on those streets. The Hendersons were the first to live on "Telephone Road" that led to Sunmount Sanitorium. (Its original name had been Camino Del Monte Sol. That name was reestablished through Alice Corbin's appearance before the city council with a new sign, which was put up by the big and little Alices on horseback.) The Cassidys had purchased their place at the corner of Canyon and the Acequia Madre, where Sheldon Parsons was living. In 1920, Olive Rush bought and restored one of the beautiful old adobes on Canyon Road. But in the early years painters, writers, and photographers settled in all areas of the little town.

Around 1920, a large concentration of their homes and studios was in the area of College Street (later renamed the Old Santa Fe Trail) and Buena Vista. Although it's now well within the city, at that time the area was on the outskirts of town. Ben Muñiz owned the corner property (which ultimately was purchased by Witter Bynner), and several little houses on it which he rented out, often to artists. The next plot to the east on Buena Vista belonged to the family of Mrs. Gladys Gilmour. In an interview, Mrs. Gilmour, who still lives in the house bought in 1875 by her grandfather, discussed the painters and writers who lived in the vicinity when she was a little girl, shortly after the end of

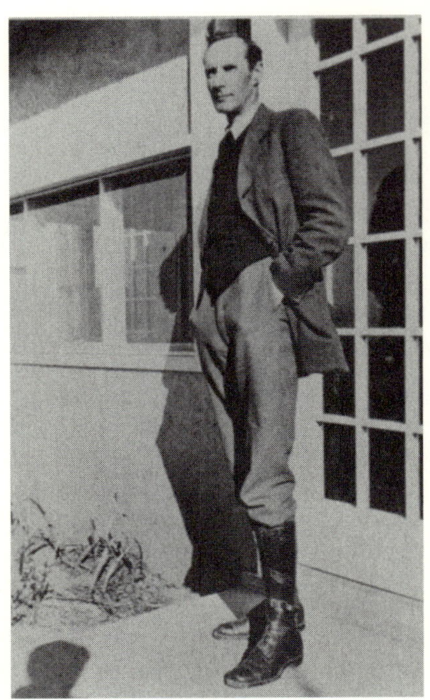

Arthur F. Musgrave at Sunmount Sanitorium.

the First World War. One she remembers was Arthur Musgrave, a handsome young lieutenant invalided out of the British army who was sent to the Southwest to recover his health. On September 14, 1916, Musgrave wrote to the director of the museum, asking:

> *Do you know of any lodging I can obtain in or near Santa Fe that would suit my purpose as an artist and where the charges would be very reasonable?*
>
> *Could I obtain a few acres, say five up the Cañon of Espiritu [Holy Ghost Canyon] at the price advertised by the Chamber of Commerce—10 dollars per acre. Is this near Santa Fe?—and what means would I have of easily getting there and back? Are houses easily and cheaply obtained? I believe there is a small artists colony nearby. I should very much like to join them. . . . Any particulars that you think will help me I should be most grateful to you for and trust it is not putting you to any great inconvenience.*

Would they indeed be able to help! With the people at the museum just completing the construction of the Art Museum, and with their readiness to find homes, lend studios, and in fact do anything in their power to promote the "small artists colony" in Santa Fe! Paul Walter, the secretary of the museum, immediately wrote back:

> *It isn't difficult to obtain lodging at reasonable prices in Santa Fe. The Forest Service grants five acres to the person, under terms mentioned for summer homes, on the Santa Fe Forest Reserve which covers two million*

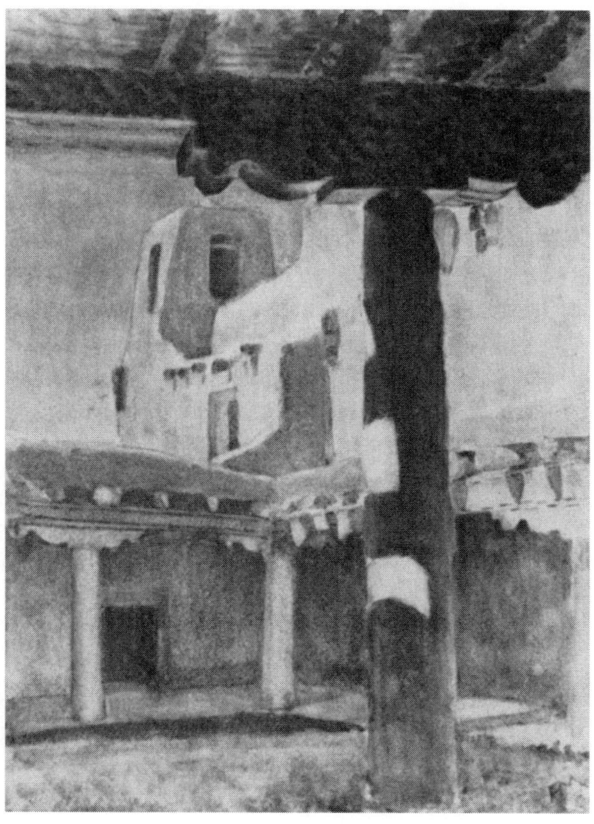

Arthur F. Musgrave, Untitled, *1917. Watercolor, 15 x 11 in. Museum of New Mexico. This watercolor was hung in the Art Museum's opening exhibit.*

acres in the vicinity of Santa Fe. The Canyon Espiritu is twenty-five miles east of Santa Fe by horse trail but forty-five miles by wagon or automobile road. Horses are easily and cheaply obtained.

The artist colony of which you will find an account in El Palacio, *which I am sending you under different cover, I am sure would be delighted to have you with them.*

The description of the road to the Canyon Espiritu must have sounded a little daunting, although it certainly fit the popular dream of coming to the Wild West and living a rugged, manly life. In the end, Musgrave rented two rooms from Muñiz.

Musgrave was only one of many artists who called Muñiz "landlord." Muñiz was an influential Santa Fean, editor of the *Santa Fe New Mexican* Spanish edition, and the man in charge of the weekly band concerts on the plaza. It might be mentioned that these weekly concerts were an important part of the social life of the town, and an opportunity for carefully supervised flirtations. Young ladies and their *dueñas* were accustomed to promenade around the plaza in one direction, and young men in the other, as was recorded in John Sloan's painting *Music in the Plaza*.

Another of Muñiz's early tenants was Paul Burlin, a noted New York painter who spent several years in Santa Fe. He was married to Natalie Curtis, the musician and author, in Santa Fe in 1917. As artists, no two could have been more different than Musgrave and Burlin. While Musgrave's paintings are sunny, impressionistic landscapes, Burlin's work is full of harsh angles and heavy, murky color. He had been an exhibitor in the International Exhibition of Modern Art (commonly called the Armory Show) in 1913, and his New Mexico work reflects the eagerness with which he responded to what was then the radically modern work he had encountered in the exhibition. He spent part of each year from 1913 through 1920 in Santa Fe, and was powerfully influenced by Indian art.

These two widely different painters were part of a long procession of artists who lived near Muñiz's corner property. The house where Gladys Gilmour lived was just west of the corner on

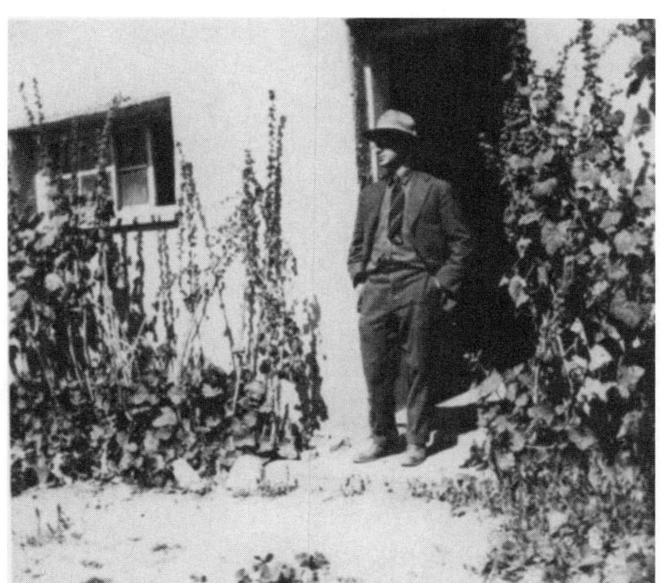

Paul Burlin.

Buena Vista, and across the street was the Dorman house, where two neighboring children lived. All three children were avid artist-watchers, and were adept at getting a foot into a door with gifts of wildflowers, or even, on one occasion when they were curious about a new lady artist, with a toad in a lard bucket! They also hid in the bushes to check on all comings and goings. There were a large number of lilac bushes then, started from cuttings which Archbishop Lamy had given the Gilmours' gardener. Even now the entire area around that corner is filled with the scent of lilacs each spring.

Among the subjects of the children's curiosity were Carlos Vierra and his wife Ada, who lived across the street on College before Vierra built a house further up the hill. And behind the Dorman house one year were the Daveys, Randall and Florence, and their young son Billy. The Dorman house still stands on the corner of College and the Camino de las Animas, where it presently houses the Unitarian Fellowship.

A couple of blocks to the west of the Gilmours, at Buena Vista and Galisteo, was the tiny adobe house of another convalescent from the war, Will Shuster. Later he was to become famous

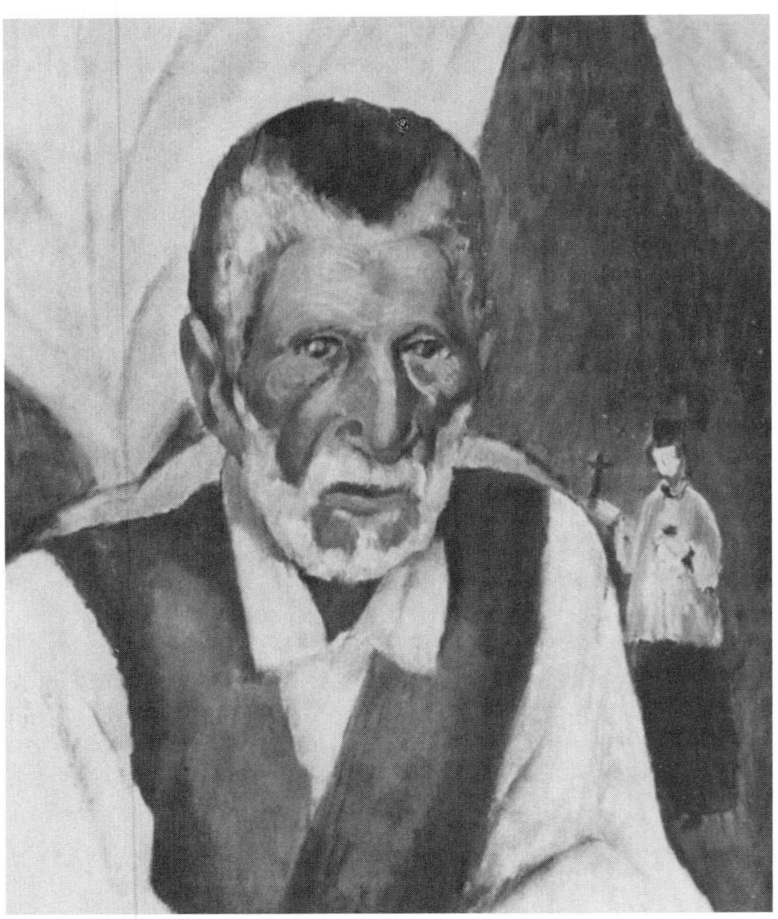

Paul Burlin, The Sacristan of Trampas, *n.d. Oil, 24 x 20 in. Museum of New Mexico.*

as one of the group of painters known as the Cinco Pintores and to be a close friend and student of John Sloan. In these early Santa Fe days, the Shusters had a hard time existing on Will's small pension. He had been badly gassed in France and was trying to recover his health. When his son, Don, was born in 1921, Mrs. Gilmour's grandfather commissioned Shuster to paint her portrait so that he could pay the hospital bill and retrieve his wife and baby.

Painter Louise Crow and her mother lived in one of Muñiz's little houses before they went to Paris, and directly across the street on Camino de las Animas lived two other painters,

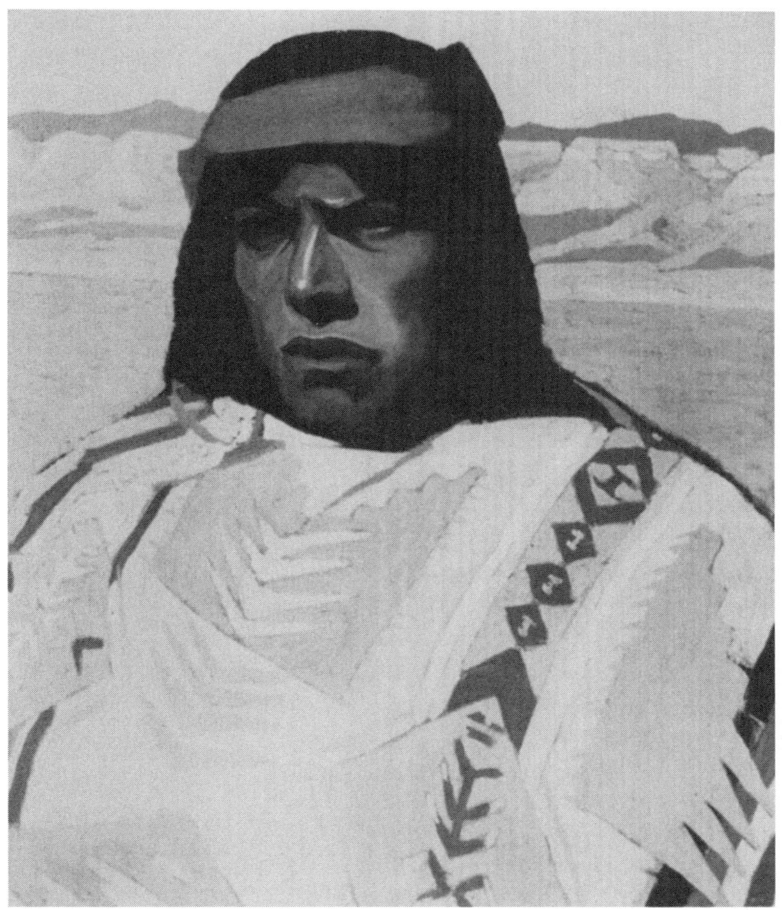

Louise Crow, Yen-See-do, *n.d. Oil, 26 x 20 in. Museum of New Mexico.*

Raymond Jonson and B.J.O. Nordfeldt. In 1923, Gustave Baumann built his house on the same street after having rented a place on Canyon Road for a while, and his friend, the Dutch painter Henry C. Balink, built his studio/home around the corner on the Old Santa Fe Trail. After the arrival of Witter Bynner in 1920, the College/Buena Vista neighborhood continued for many years to be a center and meeting place for the artists and writers.

Henry Balink arrived in New Mexico just in time to show several paintings in the Art Museum's opening show in 1917. Balink was born in Amsterdam in 1882. His parents were violently opposed to his becoming an artist, so in order to pay his way through the Art Institute at Rotterdam, he worked as a bicycle racer and ice skater from the age of fourteen on. In 1909, at the age of twenty-seven, he entered the Royal Academy. After studying there for five years, three of which were as a protégé of Queen Wilhelmina, he graduated from the master class. When World War I broke out, young Henry came to New York, and then travelled to Chicago. He explained his migration to the West by saying, "I saw a tourist picture of the state in the window of a railroad office in New York. I liked it so much I bought a ticket and came out." On this first visit he stayed in Taos, but immediately made contact with the museum people in Santa Fe, writing:

> *I made a large Mural Decoration [in Chicago] 10 x 16 foot, but after that painting was finished they wanted to cut the price for the others because US went into the war. [A painter's lot is not an easy one!] I was not satisfied with it so I wanted to go more West and I landed in Taos. Where I am now 6 weeks, and all ready I sold 5 pieces of work. I like the country very much. And hope to move from Chicago soon as possible.*

In 1918 he again stayed briefly in Taos, and in 1924 he finally settled in Santa Fe, first living on the Camino del Monte Sol, then building his house and studio on the Old Santa Fe Trail.

Balink's painting and etching techniques always reflected his early Dutch training, although as time went on, his palette became much brighter, no doubt influenced by the brilliant color he found in New Mexico. An article in *El Palacio*, June 1927, reports:

> *A striking exhibit of Indian portraits by Henry Balink was hung in the Art Museum the past week. The portraits are vivid in color and strong in characterization. . . . Since coming to New Mexico from Amsterdam, Holland, some years ago, Balink has become one of the foremost limners of Indians physiognomy, and he was recently given the Marland commission to paint a series of portraits of*

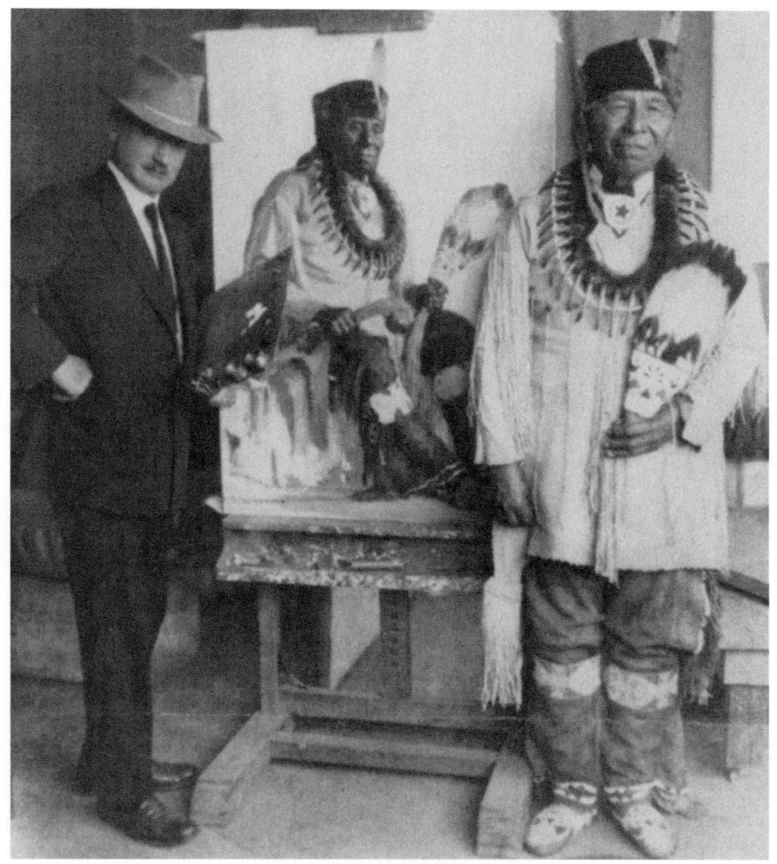

Henry C. Balink with the son of Sitting Bull.

> *chiefs of Oklahoma Indians for an Oklahoma art museum [at Ponca City]. He built himself a pueblo-style studio home at Santa Fe, which has become one of the showplaces of Santa Fe's art colony.*

Balink lived in his house on the Old Santa Fe Trail, just across the fields from his friend Gustave Baumann, until his death in 1963, and painted almost until his death. He never entered into the life of the art colony's younger artists, and probably disapproved of their experimental way of working, but he has left a fine and solid body of work in his paintings of his many Indian friends.

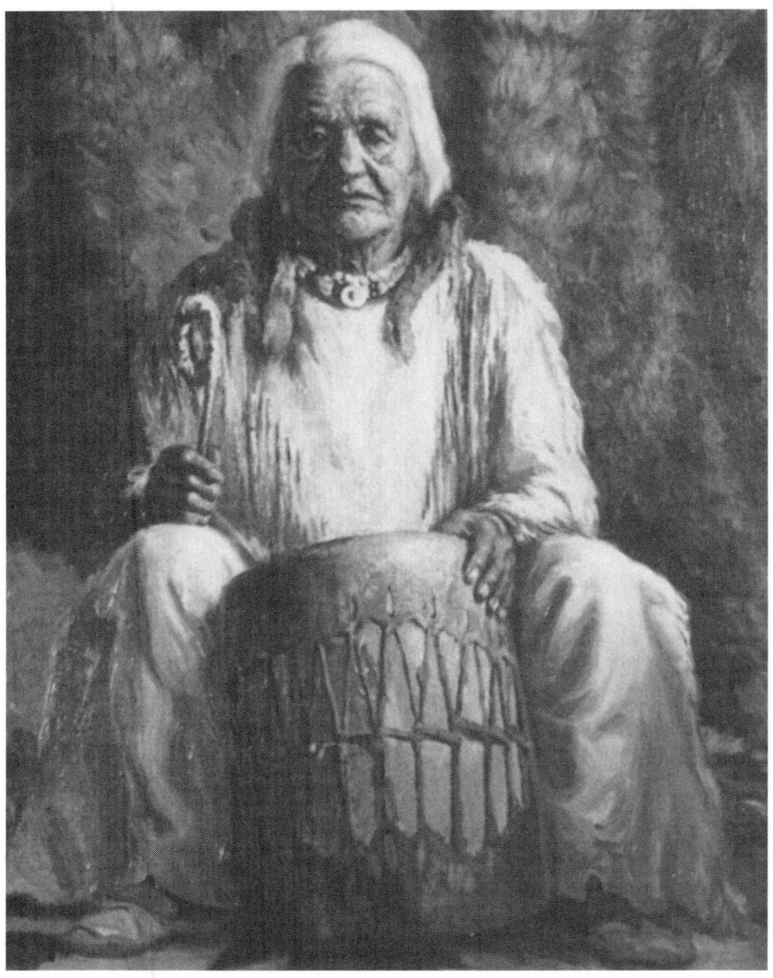

Henry C. Balink, Santiago Naranjo, *n.d. Oil, 29 3/4 x 24 3/4 in. Museum of New Mexico.*

Theodore Van Soelen was another important artist to settle in the area in the early years. Like so many others, it was pneumonia followed by tuberculosis which brought the young Minnesota-born artist west. He had been studying at the Pennsylvania Academy of Fine Arts, and had also toured Europe on a Cresson scholarship from the Pennsylvania Academy. A trip west held no mystery for Van Soelen, however, as in 1910 he had spent time in Nevada driving mules for the construction gang of the Western Pacific Railroad. In those days the Wells Fargo stage carried passengers and express, and also gold from the mines. The company had offered Van Soelen a job as driver on their coaches—a job which he turned down in order to return east to study art. But he always looked back on those romantic adventurous days with great fondness and said that they made up one of the most interesting periods of his life.

He did not come directly to Santa Fe, but went to Albuquerque, then later, during his convalescence, he worked as a ranch hand. From the first, Van Soelen loved New Mexico and the life on the ranches—his paintings and lithographs portray the reality of the cowboy's life with genuine fidelity. His son Don wrote later of one of his father's lithographs:

> After Supper *is a group of Fernandez cowboys with "Uncle Lou" rolling his own. It was the experiences on this ranch which gave Father the feeling and knowledge of ranch life that he drew on years later, for he didn't print his first lithograph until 1950. . . . He rode the range, was at home in the camp, slept on the ground in all sorts of weather, ate at the chuck-wagon, roped, branded, gathered cattle, and for many years followed the roundup. Knowing the ways of cattlemen, he was one of them. Nothing pleased my dad more than when some crusty, old cowhand would say, "Mr. Van, that's what a horse looks like."*

Van Soelen married Virginia Carr, the daughter of a cattle baron from Albuquerque, in 1921, and in 1926 they built a beautiful house in Tesuque, a little town directly north of Santa Fe, where they spent the rest of their lives. Van Soelen's art was not only known in the Southwest, however; he continued to exhibit in the East with great success, eventually becoming a National Academician. The Van Soelens were active in a variety of community affairs, but in his painting he held to his own style, and he never tried the bohemian life although he had many artist friends. He lived rather more like a country gentleman, hunting, fishing, and raising Labrador retrievers.

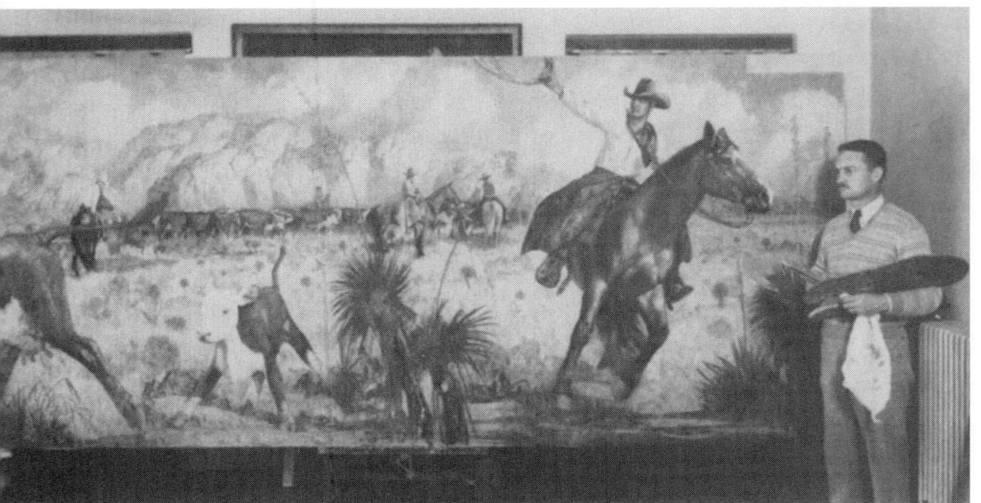

Theodore Van Soelen painting a mural for the Treasury Section, one of the Federal Art Projects.

In his work Van Soelen was, as Oliver La Farge has said:

> *Not merely an artist who moved to New Mexico, but deeply a New Mexico artist.*
>
> *He has never been limited to the New Mexico scene, as witness his portraits, but he has done a mighty work of recording that scene, including drab, wooden shacks and adobe houses with pitched, tin roofs. To this layman, it seems that he takes scenes that it is a cliché with us to deplore and, with effective underemphasis, reveals the beauty in them.*

One of the most important events to happen to the growing art colony occurred in 1919, when John Sloan, one of the great painters and etchers of the twentieth century in America, decided, with his friend Randall Davey, who was Henri's teaching assistant and friend, to investigate the situation in Santa Fe. They had talked of making the trip before, but that summer the two men and their wives set out from New York in a 1912 90-horsepower Simplex chain-drive touring car.

Henri had written a letter of introduction for his friends to Paul Walter at the museum, telling him that "John Sloan, his wife, and Randall Davey, his wife, are all coming to Santa Fe. They are coming overland by means of automobile all the way. " Later Sloan wrote that the trip took them some weeks, as every time they stopped in a tourist cabin they were only able to get their wives on the road again with the greatest difficulty. With the conditions of cars and roads in those days, one can feel a certain sympathy for them.

Henri continued:

> *I think you must know them both very well by reputation and perhaps you know that they are very close friends of ours. Sloan is one of my lifelong friends and is a man of very great character, a strong and very original artist—painter, etcher, draftsman. Davey is of a younger generation. You will all like them, find them artists of the first order, and they will be new and other interpreters of Santa Fe. I am very much interested in their going there and in seeing what will come of it in the way of work.*
>
> *As for ourselves we don't know yet. I am in much doubt. The case is like this. For both of us there is no place we would like to be in so much as Santa Fe—but for painting I want a change of subject—or rather a change of skin—light skin instead of red.—At Santa Fe we can hardly hope to extend our model supply much beyond what we already developed and our supply was confined to our Indian and Mexican friends. Last summer, I did not paint people at all—only landscape (woods); now, I have a craving to do some fair-skinned people and will probably go somewhere where I can get them. Have thought of Canada—but nothing is decided. Don't think that we have cut allegence to Santa Fe—we will come back, for we love the place and our friends and*

all the atmosphere you put about us when we are there. What I would like would be to find a half dozen kids I might use to satisfaction and import them to Santa Fe—have our old place back again and paint the imported ones alternately with new paintings of our old group of Santa Fe subjects.—However I can't just arrange that.

After all, I don't know yet what we will do—so there is nothing fixed. I'm really hungry for the sun, the feel and the look of Santa Fe.

Henri was not completely finished with Santa Fe, as he came for the summer again in 1922 and rented the Lansing Bloom house near the Capitol. *El Palacio* noted that it had been several years since his last visit, so it is apparent that he was serious in wanting a new type to paint. The 1922 visit was the last, however; from 1923 until his death in 1929, he spent each summer in Ireland.

It was a very different story with the two friends about whom Henri wrote to Paul Walter in 1919—Sloan and Davey. From their first dramatic arrival into town they both made lifetime commitments to Santa Fe. Sloan spent over thirty summers in New Mexico, returning each winter to New York, where he continued to teach privately and at the Art Students League. Davey established his permanent residence in Santa Fe, although he was for many years a noted teacher at the Chicago Art Institute, the Broadmoor Art Academy in Colorado Springs, and the University of New Mexico. Both men had exhibited in the Armory Show of 1913, were active in the movement for freedom from the academic art world, and were much impressed with the attitude developing at the Art Museum at Santa Fe, with its open door policy for exhibition and the free and welcoming attitude of the community.

It was a hot summer's day when their dust-covered car rattled to a stop at the plaza and Davey, who was driving, asked a man sitting on one of the park benches the way to the museum. Following the direction of his pointing finger, they went on to the northwest corner of the plaza and pulled up at the two-year-old building. Later Davey recalled, "They really treated us nicely over there at the museum. Fixed us up with studios so we could get right to work." This evidently suited him very well, as the next May *El Palacio* was noting:

> *Randall Davey, the young New York artist, who spent last summer in Santa Fe, has returned to Santa Fe, after a successful season in New York City, where he filled several commissions for portraits, and at Chicago, where he had large classes at the Chicago Art Institute which petitioned for his return and several members of which expect to follow him to Santa Fe during the summer and to New York next winter. . . . Mrs. Davey and young son arrived a few days after Mr. Davey who has purchased the picturesque Candelario Martinez home and orchard at the entrance to the Santa Fe Forest and Santa Fe Cañon above the big reservoir.*

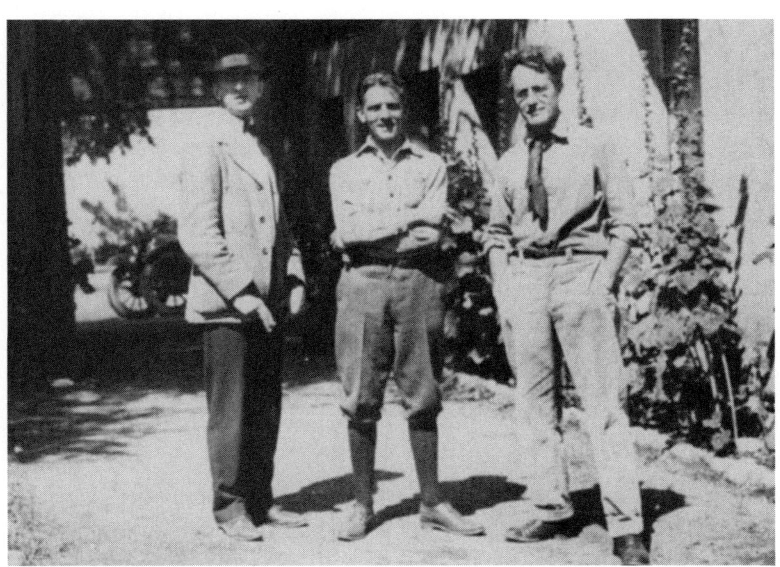

Marsden Hartley, Randall Davey, and John Sloan on the patio of the Palace of the Governors, near the studios provided for them by the museum, 1919.

This house had been built in 1847 by the United States Quartermaster as Santa Fe's first sawmill, to provide lumber for the woodwork at the army post, Fort Marcy. Later it was owned by Ceran St. Vrain, the famed frontiersman, before becoming the property of Martinez. After Davey (who had trained in architecture at Cornell) had restored and enlarged it, the house became famous as a meeting place for musicians and artists.

In 1938, long after Randall Davey had settled in New Mexico, Henry McBride, art critic for the *New York Sun*, wrote:

> *Randall Davey has been around a considerable while and enjoys a fairly good reputation as an artist, but the idea persists that he might enjoy considerable more reputation if he lived in this neighborhood rather than in New Mexico. Why does he lose himself in the ambience of Mabel Dodge? She owns that state. Why does he insist upon living down there?*

Perhaps the best answer to that question was given by Davey himself when he said on one occasion: "I wouldn't trade my life here where I can hunt, shoot, ride, for all that committee going and bootlicking you've got to do in a city for anything. An artist might starve for food here, but he'll starve spiritually in a place like New York." The life the Daveys lived in Santa Fe was a gracious one. Their house was full of music and books as well as paintings, and outside there were chickens, dogs, horses (Davey was an avid polo player), an orchard, and beautiful gardens.

In his painting, Davey was strongly influenced by the French Impressionists and by Velasquez and Franz Hals. His pictures radiate light and motion and a flickering vitality of line. He was a highly regarded portrait painter, but perhaps was best known for his racetrack scenes with their crowds of people and jockeys in colorful silks, an air of tension and an eagerness showing in every line of both people and horses.

Recognition had come early to Davey. He was born in 1887, and by 1916 was a member of the board of directors of the Independent Artists, the group of which John Sloan was president

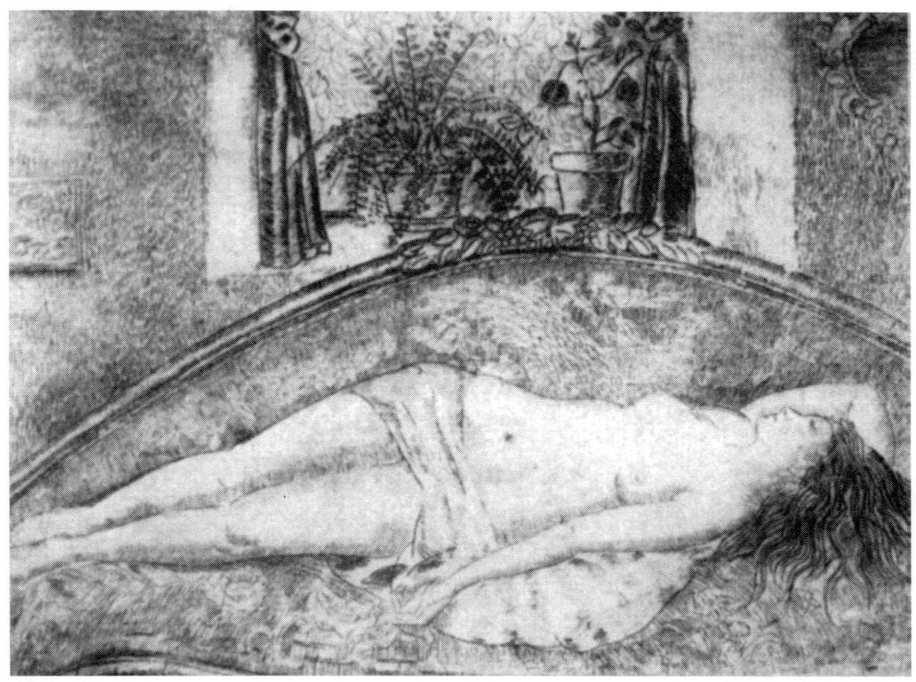

Randall Davey, Nude, *n.d. Etching, 4 x 5 ½ in. Museum of New Mexico. Davey was noted for his racetrack scenes and his gracious and romantic portrayals of women. Note the echo of the curve of hip in the curved back of the couch.*

for many years. In 1915, Davey had won the second Julius Hallgarten Prize of the National Academy of Design, as well as an honorable mention for his painting in the Panama Pacific Exposition. While still in the East he had painted portraits of a number of nationally known figures; many of the portraits can be found today in the collections of leading museums.

Davey never went back to the big city to stay, but lived the life he loved in the West until in 1964 he was killed at age seventy-seven in an automobile accident while driving from Santa Fe to California. Santa Fe had lost a beloved citizen with tremendous flair and sophistication. His personality was enchanting. He loved to talk about horse racing, and looked like a gentleman jockey himself: small, full of tension, and beautifully dressed in boots and tweeds. Someone said that even when Randall was very poor he lived as though he were rich; certainly he was a man full of richness and joy.

In the June 1957 *El Palacio*, Dr. Reginald Fisher, then director of the Art Museum, wrote:

> *At the time of Davey's emergence into art from the study of architecture at Cornell University, near the turn of the century, a groundswell against the spell of Europe was developing in America. In the wake of French Impressionism, which had swept the hemisphere during the latter nineteenth century, a new realism adapting the luminous colors of Impressionism to the American subject surged among painters here.*

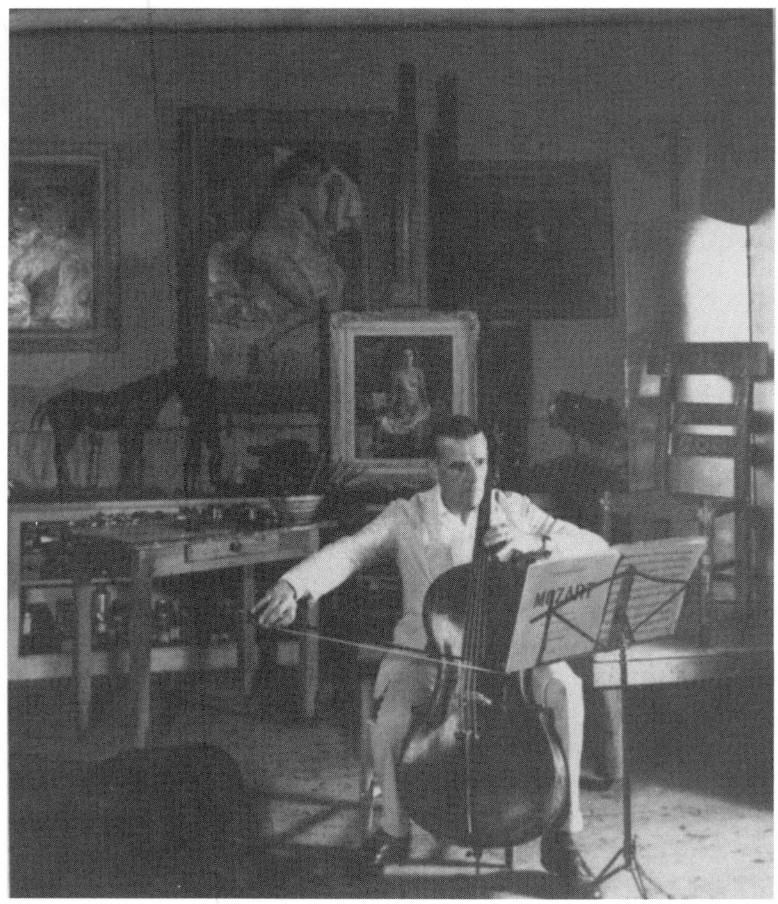

Randall Davey in his studio.

From this interest in American life and landscape, a new institution was born—the artists' colony. Woodstock, New York, and Taos, New Mexico—these came before 1900. Provincetown on Cape Cod, New Hope on the Delaware, and Carmel in California were in existence by 1905; and before World War 1, Henri had discovered Santa Fe and had inspired several of his followers with its attractions for artists. Randall Davey was one of these.

The early twenties was indeed the first great period for Santa Fe as an art colony, and some of the best known and most influential artists in the country were coming to New Mexico. Robert Henri, who brought so many here, and who so strongly influenced the policies of the new Art Museum, was one of the foremost teachers and painters in the country; John Sloan was one of the leading influences toward a new American realism; William P. Henderson, too, was highly regarded in eastern artistic circles, as was his wife, Alice Corbin Henderson. Cassidy and Parsons had both been highly successful artists in New York before bad health sent them west. Andrew Dasburg had lived and studied in Paris with many of the leading Cubist painters. The coming together of such men and women as this in the setting provided by the lovely, romantic, and ancient town of Santa Fe made it inevitable that other young artists and writers would flock to join them.

Fremont F. Ellis, who settled in Santa Fe in 1919, has stated that this was the main reason for his coming: "I came because of the interesting and important artists who were there. I wanted to know and work with them." Unlike many of the newcomers to Santa Fe, Fremont Ellis was born in the West and received very little art training in the East. He was born in 1897 in Virginia City, Montana, where his parents had gone in the Gold Rush days. Their house was one in which a former sheriff and his gang of stagecoach robbers were captured and hanged by the enraged citizens of the town. Ellis's family did not stay there long, however, and his father, who had been a dentist, went into theatrical work.

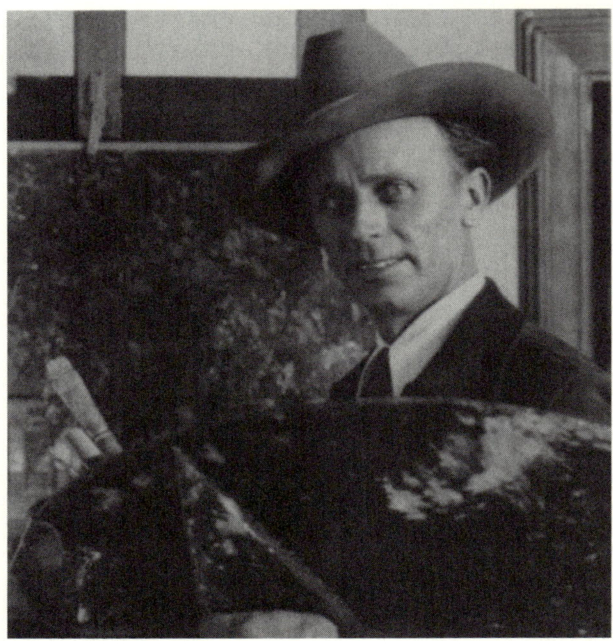

Fremont F. Ellis.

At one point, young Fremont played the drums in his father's movie theatre.

Their travels took them all over the country, including New York City. There the boy spent hours at the Metropolitan Museum where he used to stand in front of a particular painting and then rush home and work at copying it. He has said that he was too shy to do copying in the gallery, as many art students did at that time, and that the practice he got in this visual memorizing has helped him throughout his artistic life. He attended the Art Students League for a short time, but soon decided to return west to study and paint directly from the landscape which he loved. He went first to El Paso, Texas, where he was doing very well painting and teaching art, when he left to join the artists in Santa Fe and, with four of his new friends—Willard Nash, Jozef Bakos, Will Shuster, and Walter Mruk—to form the noted group Los Cinco Pintores.

Of the five young men, only two had known each other before joining forces in Santa Fe. Walter Mruk and Jozef Bakos were both from Buffalo, New York, and both were of Polish parentage. Both had studied at the Albright Art Institute and with John Thompson in Denver. In 1920, Mruk was in the Santa Fe area working as a forest ranger and doing political cartoons for the *Santa Fe New Mexican*, while Bakos was teaching art at the University of Colorado in Boulder. When an influenza epidemic closed the school, he decided to visit Mruk. While he was in Santa Fe, the two men shared an exhibit at the museum; the next year Bakos returned to Santa Fe to stay. Following Mruk's example, he took the old Denver and Rio Grande Railroad to Buckman and went to work for the Forest Service at Frijoles Canyon. Bakos was, and is, a sociable, ebullient person, an emotional and dramatic painter, while it appears that Mruk was a more introspective man. An article in *El Palacio* states that Mruk's work is "starkly, if not grossly, realistic."

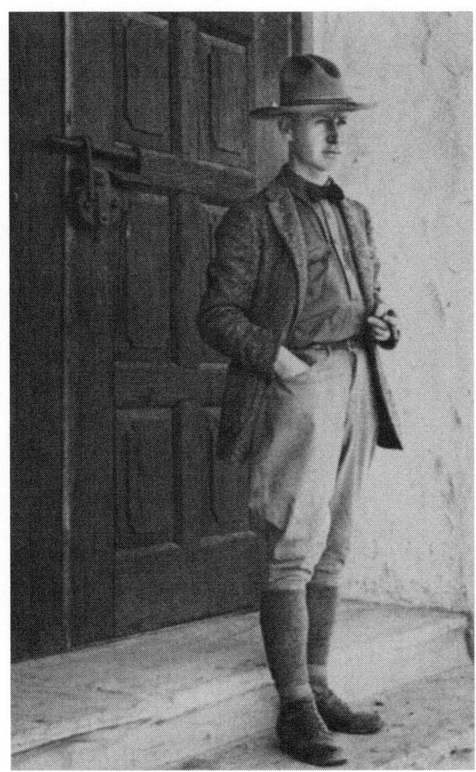

Walter E. Mruk.

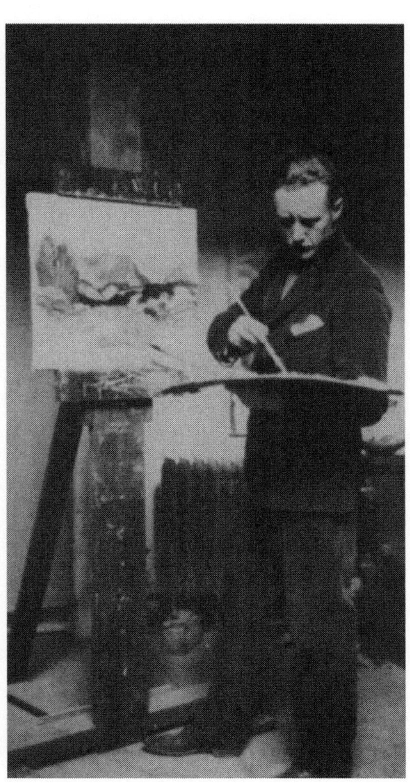

Willard Nash.

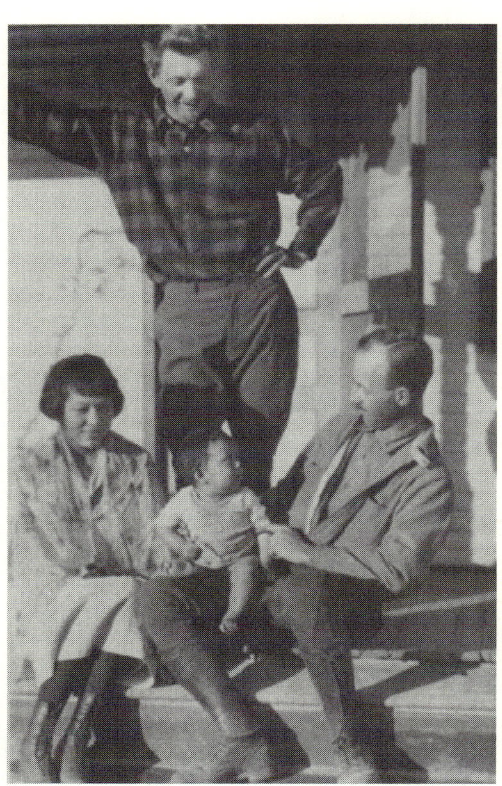

Jozef Bakos (standing) with friends.

Willard Nash first came to Santa Fe in 1920 to gather data for a mural which he had been commissioned to paint. He returned to stay the following year. He had been born in 1898 in Philadelphia and had studied art there and in Detroit under John P. Wicker. In a September 1921 *El Palacio*, it was reported:

> *Willard Nash, the Detroit artist, has completed several attractive Santa Fe landscapes which will be exhibited shortly and which prove that as a colorist he has made great advancement since his visit last summer. At least, he found a palette that is of greater brilliance than the subdued tones which characterized his fine canvases last year. He has brought more light into his landscapes and there is a greater feeling for the luminous colors of the Southwest. While Nash can hardly be classed as a modernist, yet he is not bound by academic*

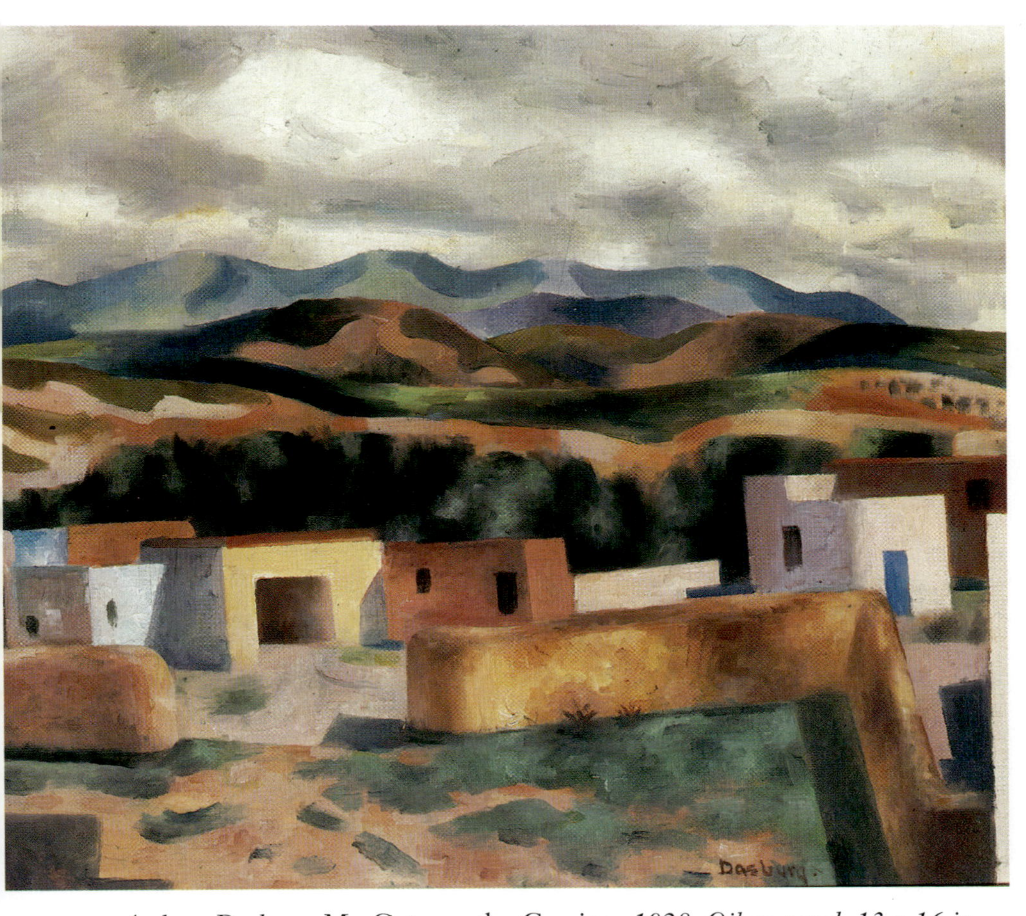

Andrew Dasburg, My Gate on the Camino, *1928. Oil on panel, 13 x 16 in. Museum of New Mexico.*

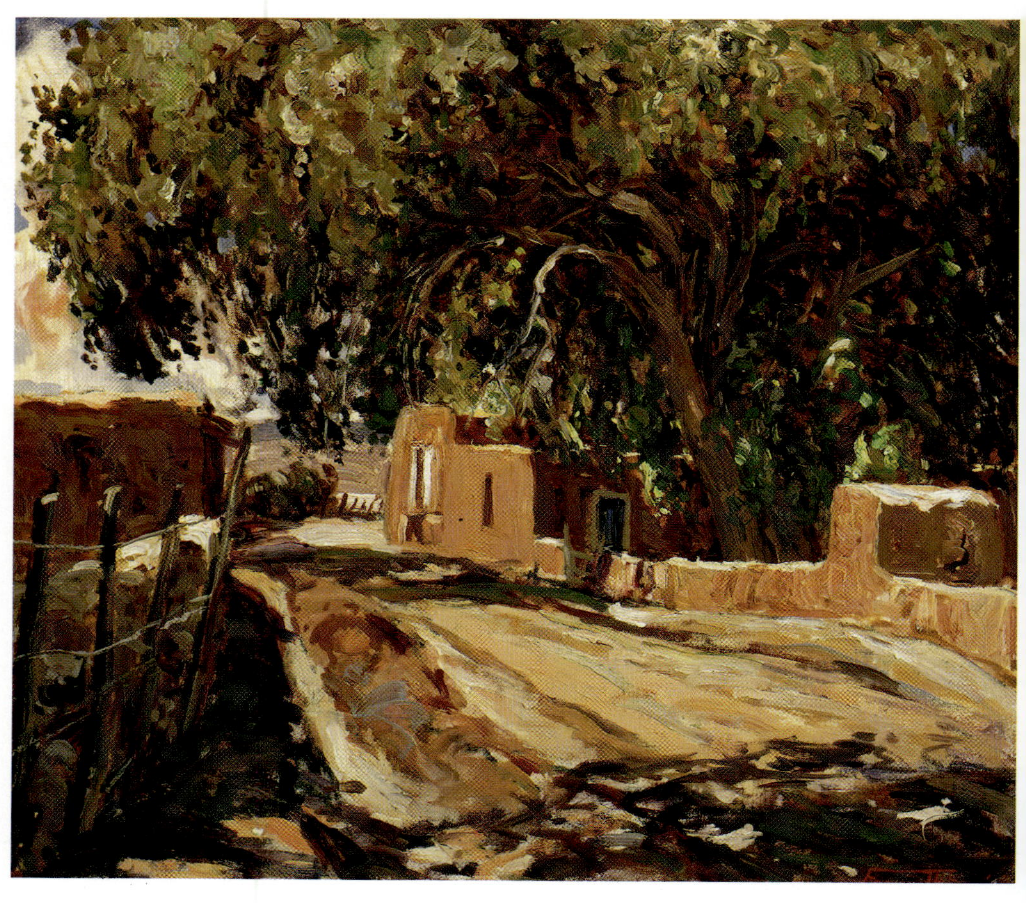

Fremont F. Ellis, Street Scene, Galisteo. *Oil on canvas board, ca. 1934, 20 x 24 in. Museum of New Mexico.*

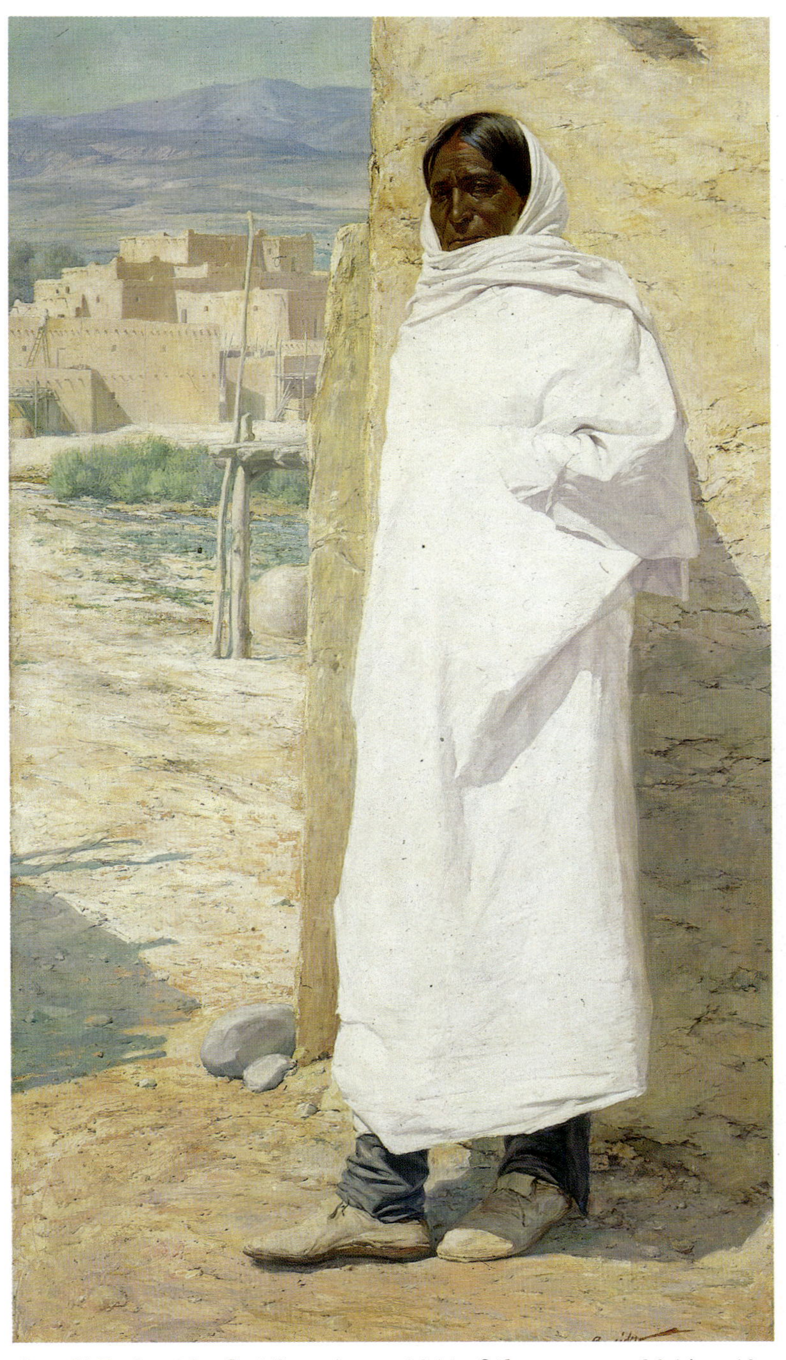

Gerald P. Cassidy, Cui Bono?, *ca. 1911. Oil on canvas, 93 1/2 x 48 in. Museum of New Mexico.*

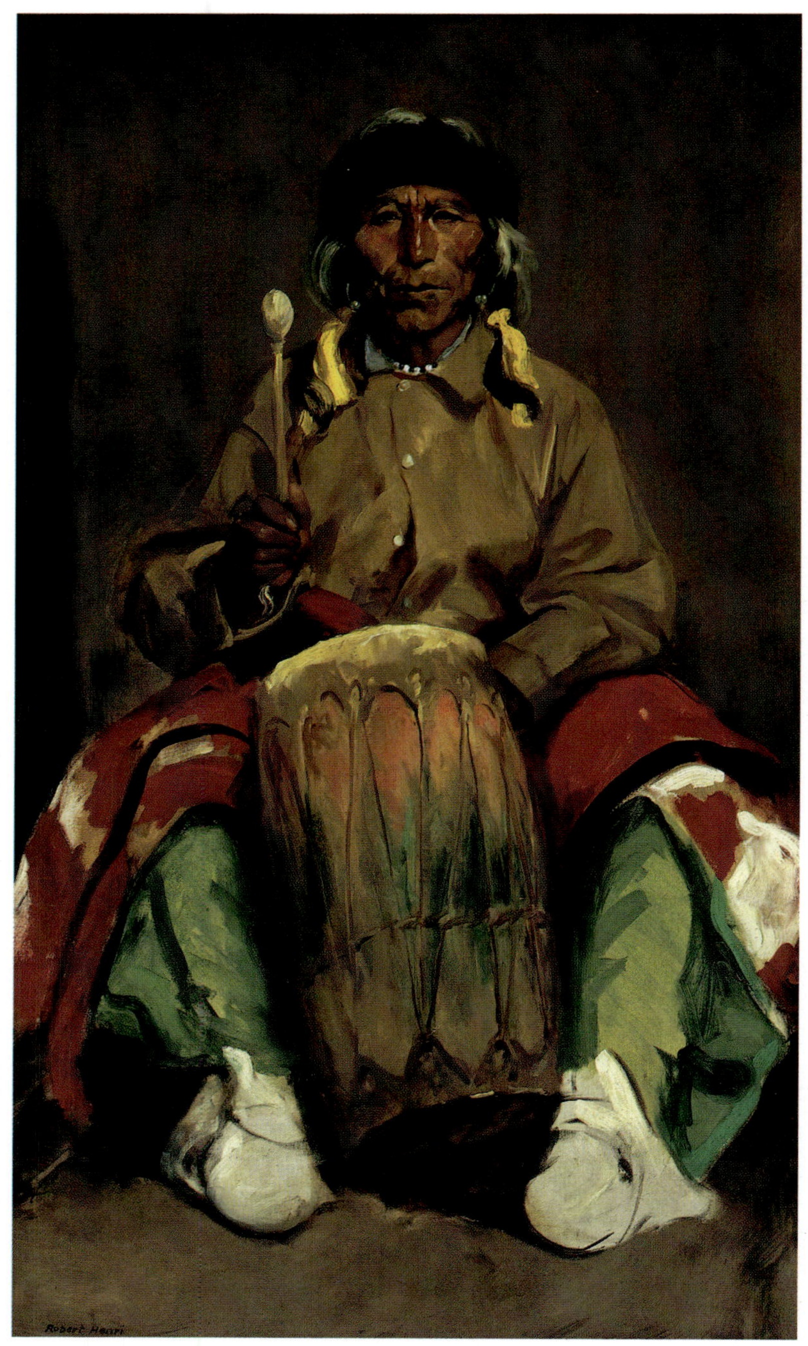

Robert Henri, Portrait of Dieguito, *1916. Oil on canvas, 65 3/8 x 40 7/8 in. Museum of New Mexico.*

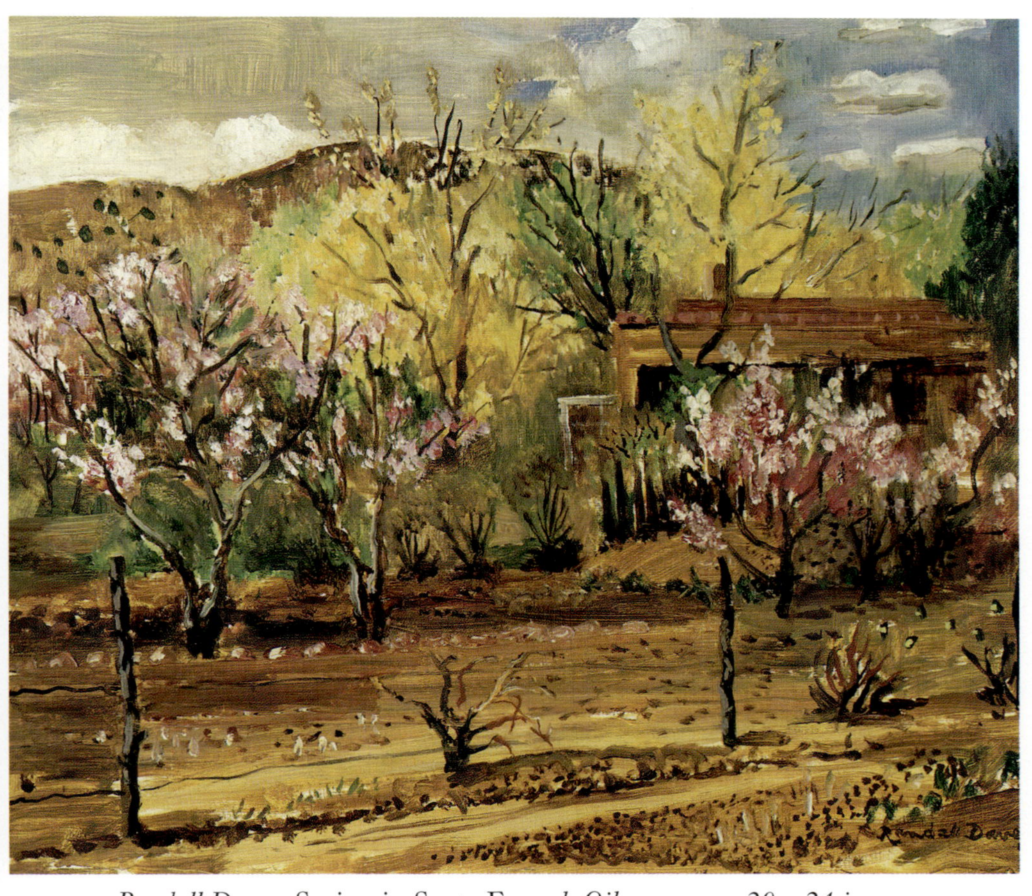

Randall Davey, Spring in Santa Fe, *n.d. Oil on canvas, 20 x 24 in. Museum of New Mexico.*

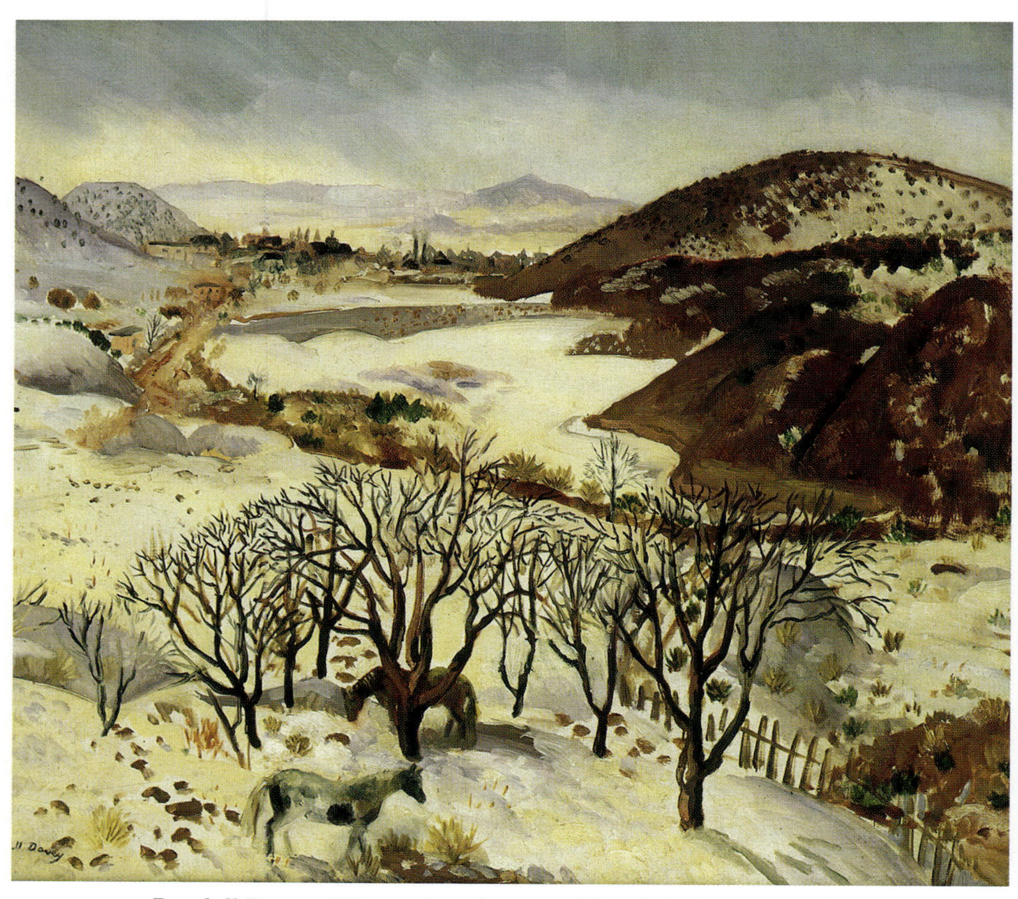

Randall Davey, Winter Landscape—New Mexico, *1923. Oil on canvas, 26 x 32 in. Museum of New Mexico.*

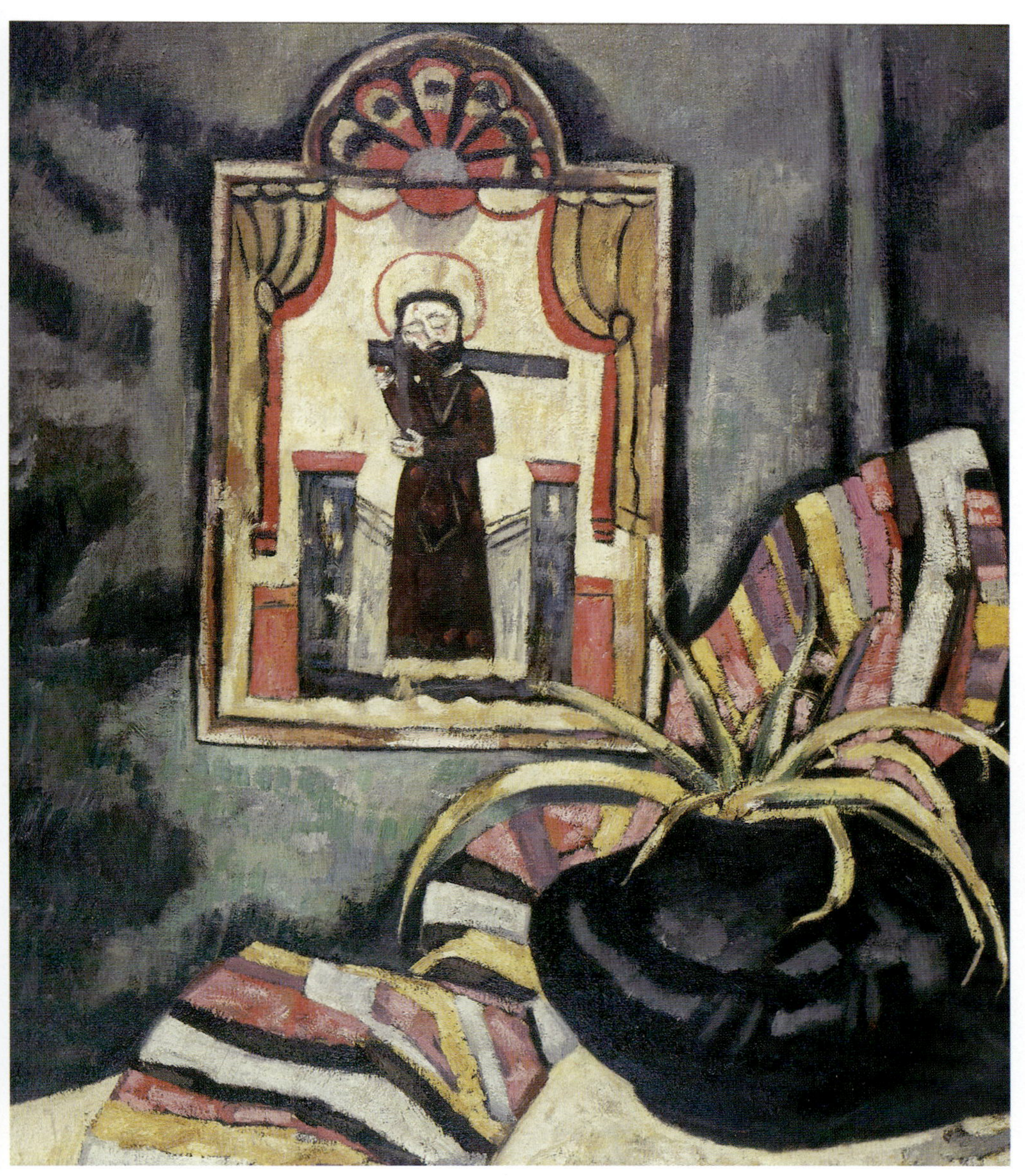

Marsden Hartley, El Santo, *1919. Oil on canvas, 36 x 32 in. Museum of New Mexico.*

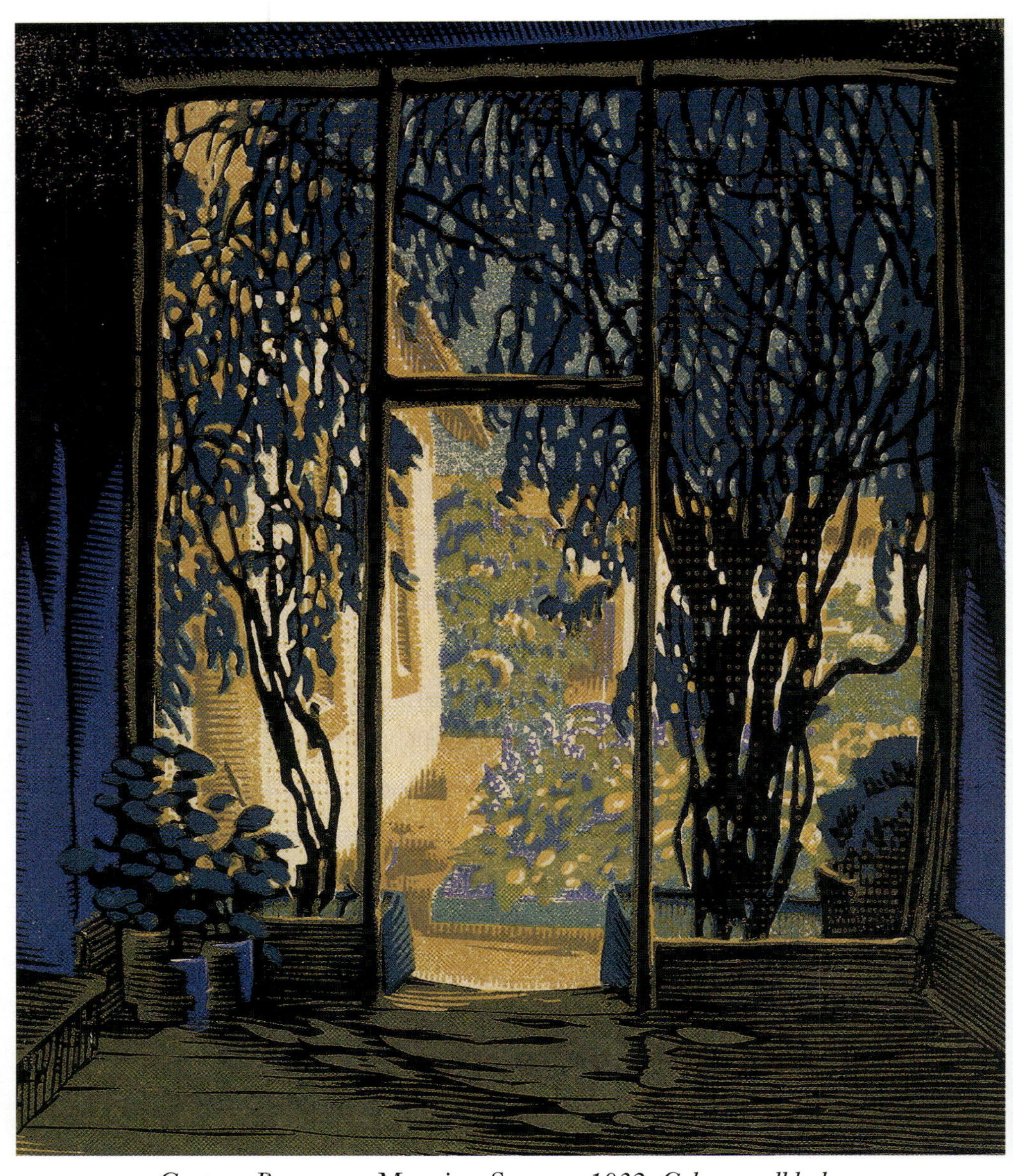

Gustave Baumann, Morning Sun, *ca. 1932, Color woodblock,
10 1/2 x 9 1/2 in. Museum of New Mexico.*

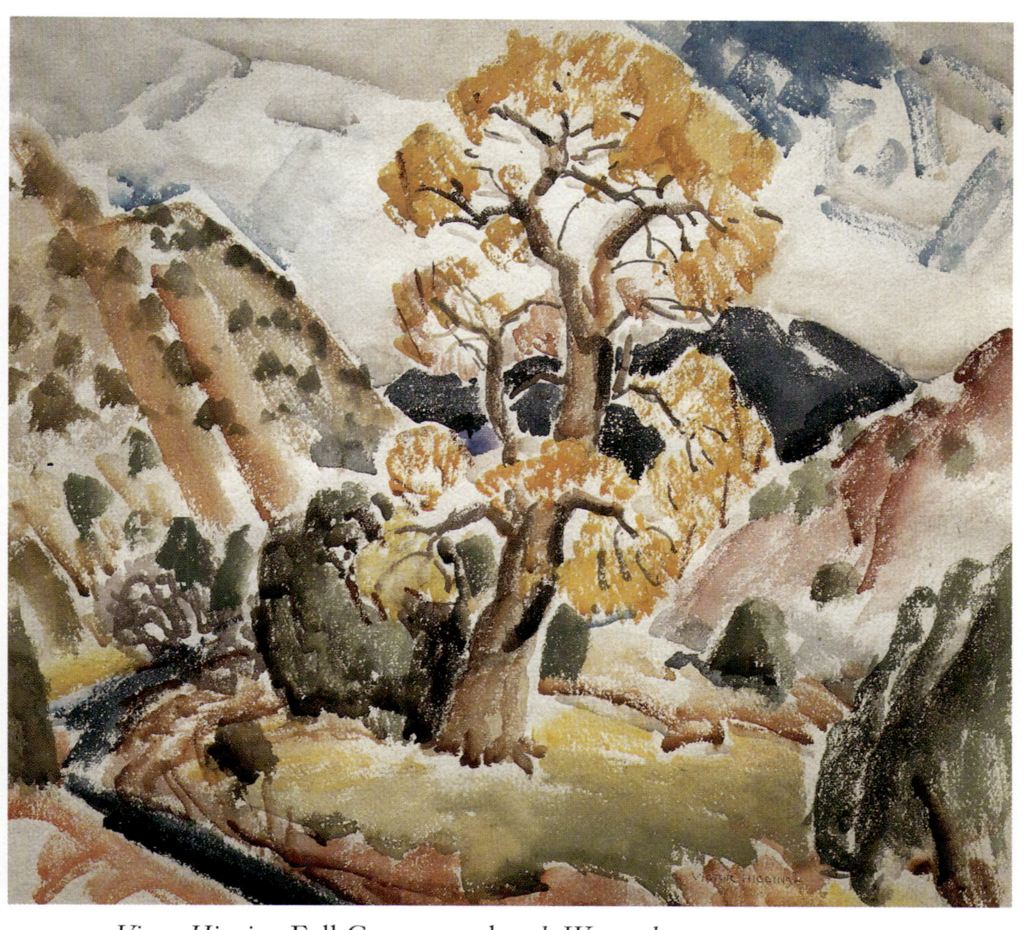

Victor Higgins, Full Cottonwood, *n.d. Watercolor on canvas, 22 x 18 in. Museum of New Mexico.*

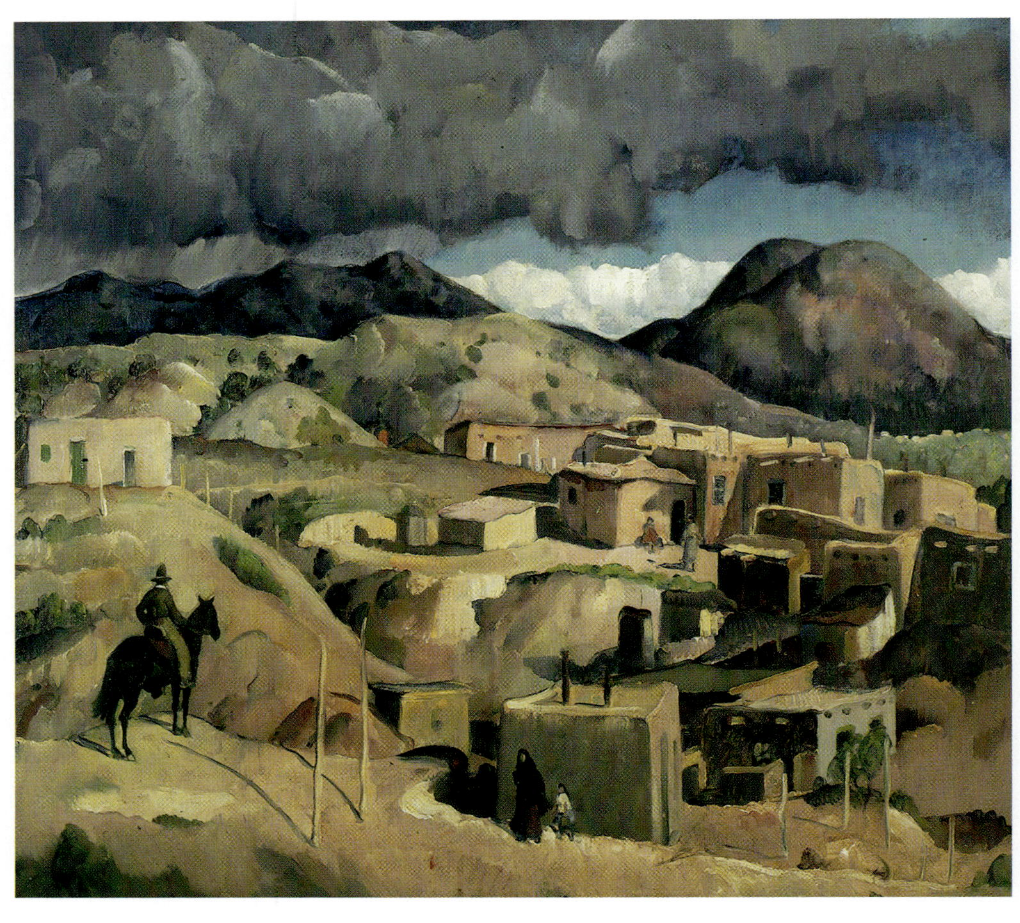

Leon Kroll, Santa Fe Hills, *1917. Oil on canvas, 34 x 40 1/4 in. Museum of New Mexico.*

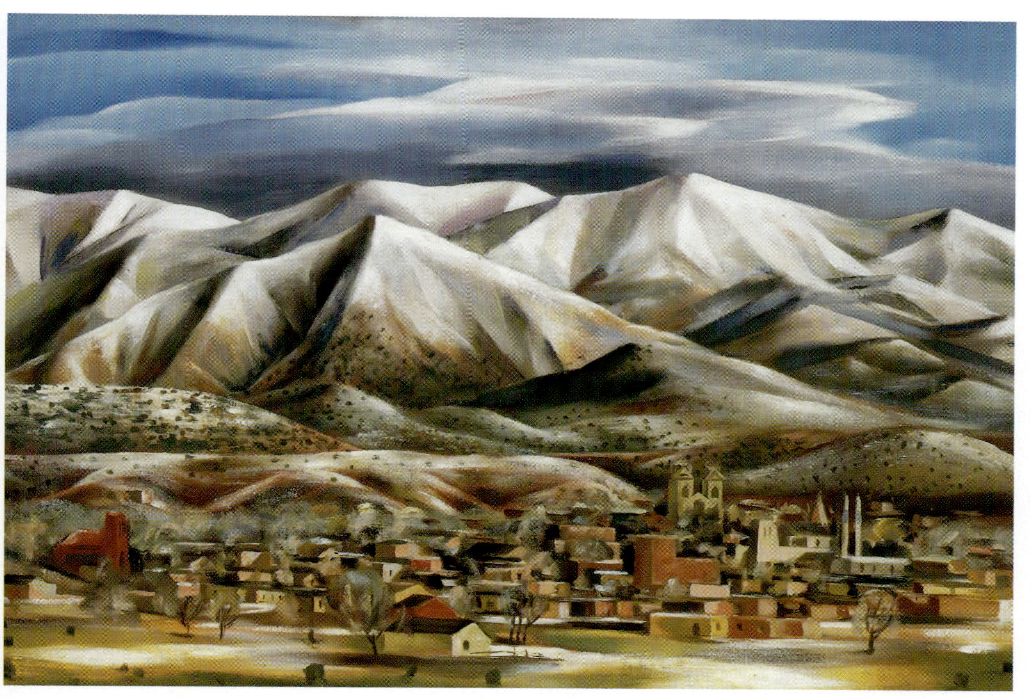

Paul Lantz, Snow in Santa Fe, *ca. 1935. Oil on canvas, 30 x 40 in. Museum of New Mexico.*

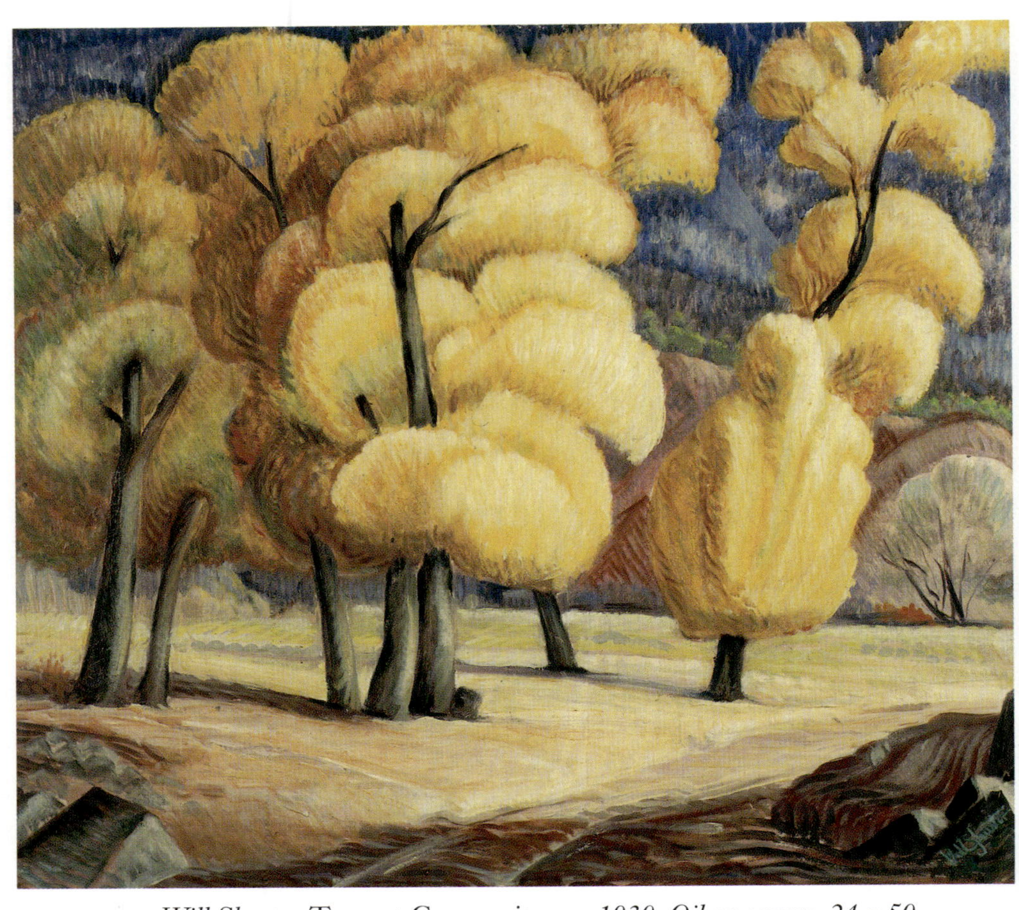

Will Shuster, Trees at Canyoncito, *ca. 1930. Oil on canvas, 24 x 50 in. Museum of New Mexico.*

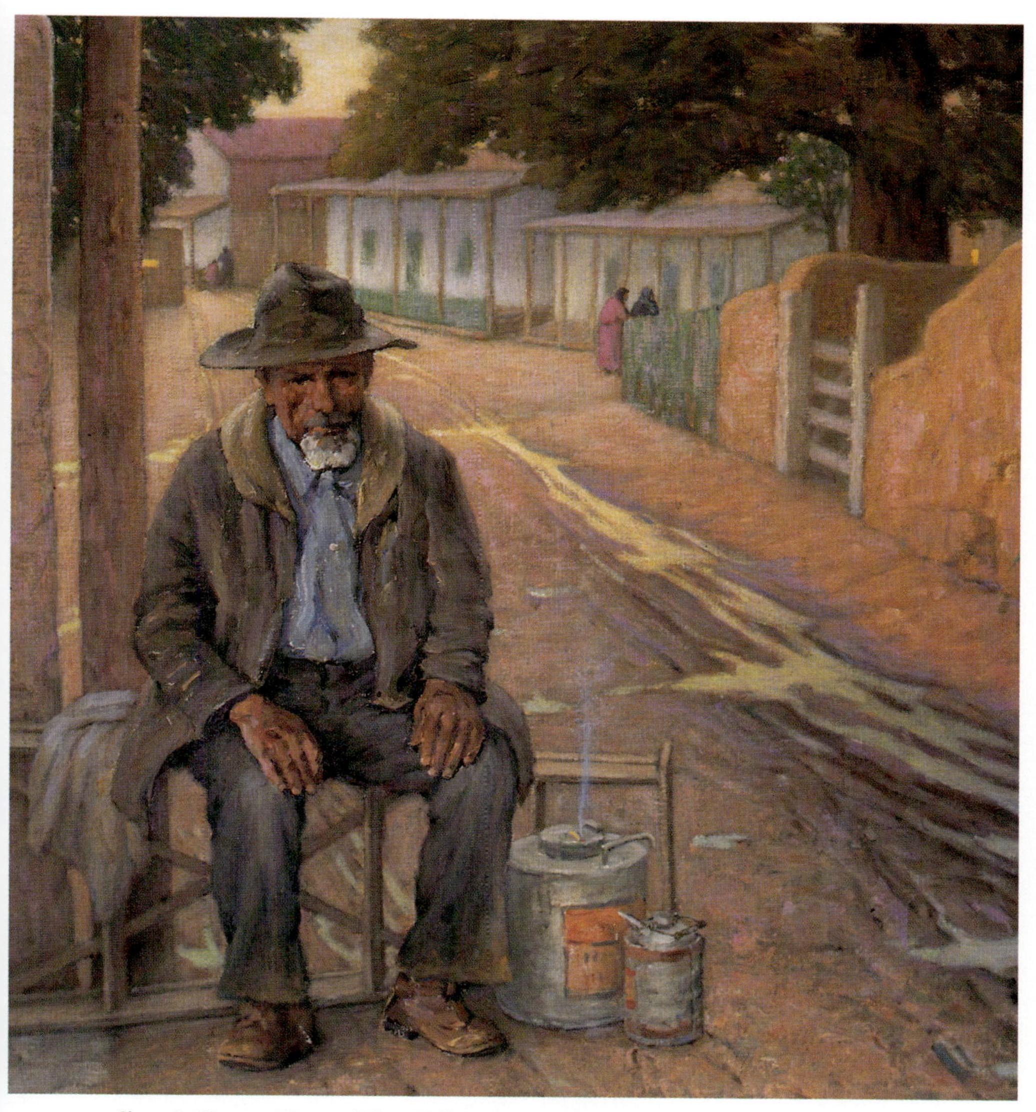

Joseph Henry Sharp, The Village Lamplighter, *n.d. Oil on canvas, 25 x 30 in., Museum of New Mexico.*

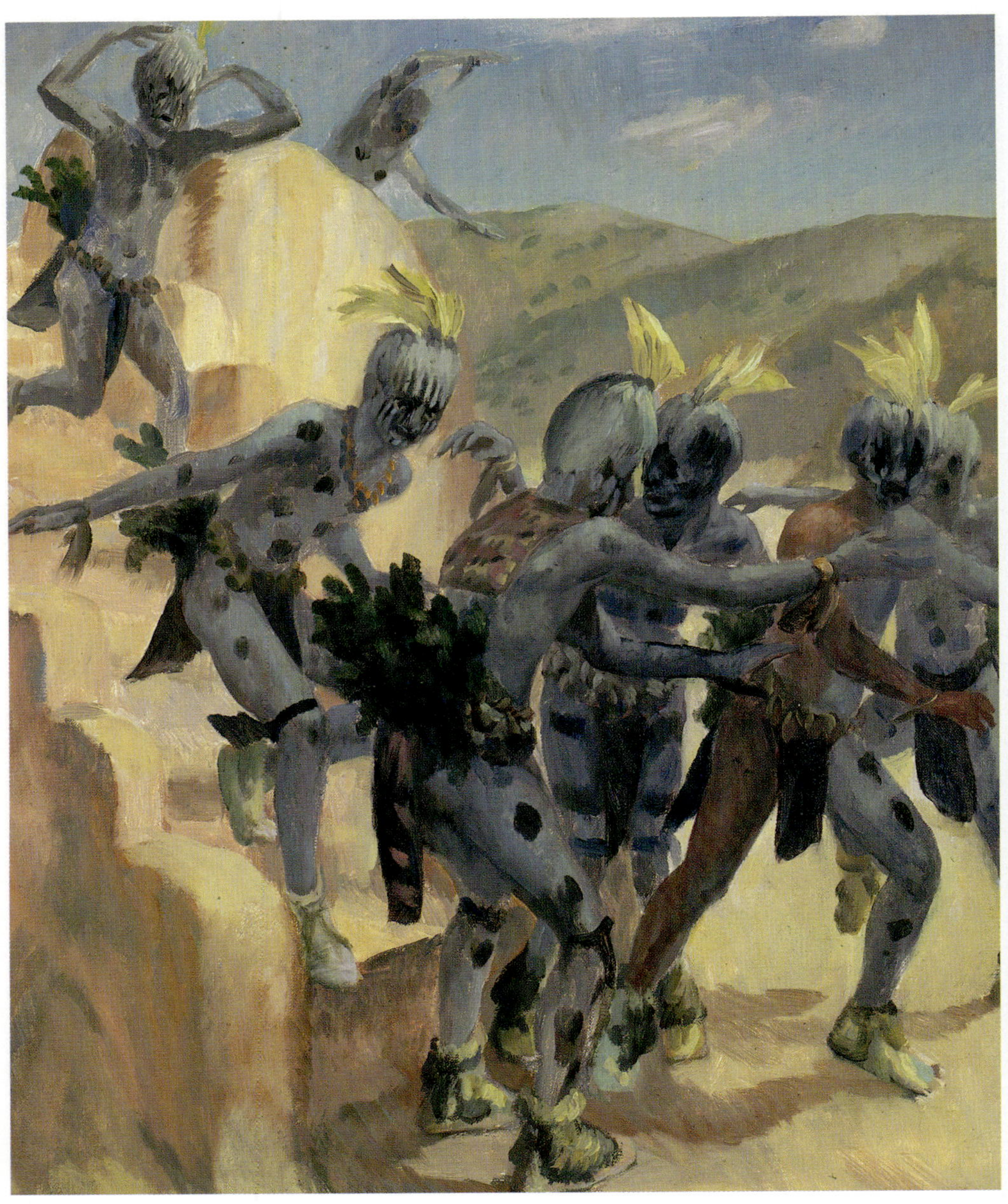

John Sloan, Ancestral Spirits, *1919. Oil on canvas, 24 x 20 in. Museum of New Mexico.*

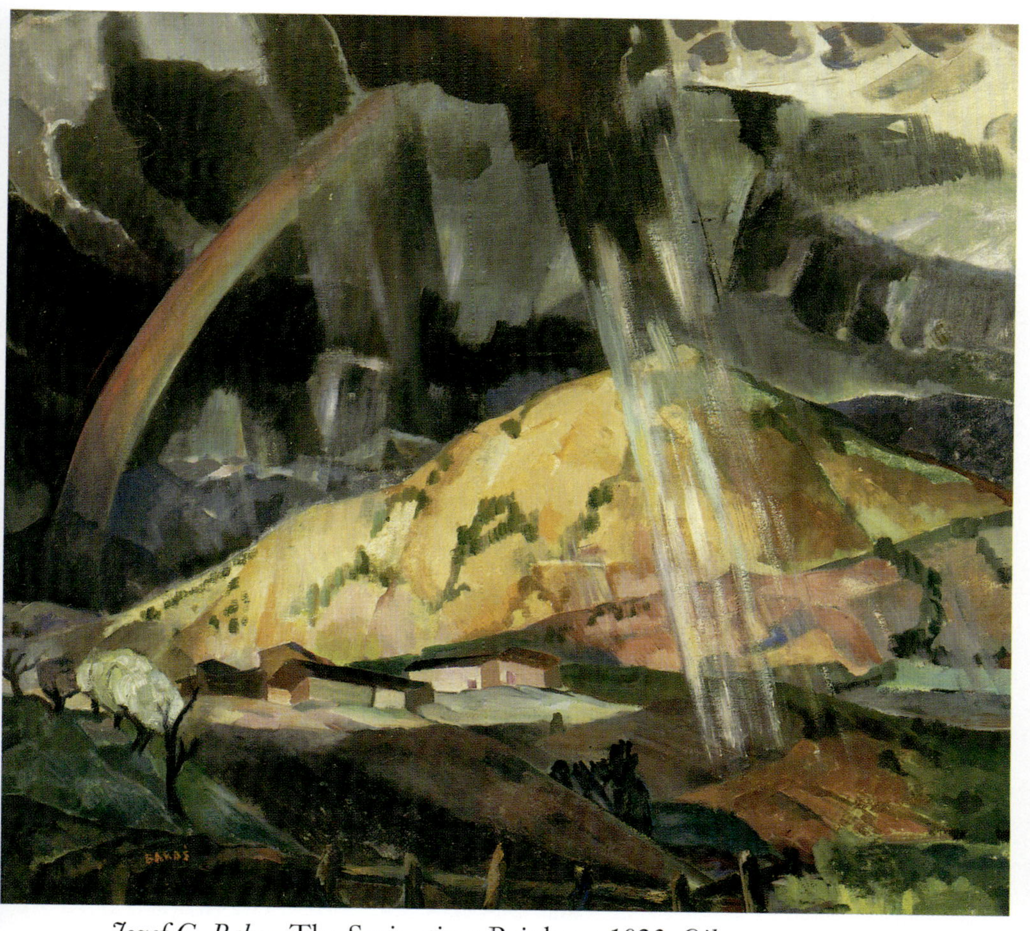

Jozef G. Bakos, The Springtime Rainbow, *1923. Oil on canvas, 29 1/2 x 35 1/2 in. Museum of New Mexico.*

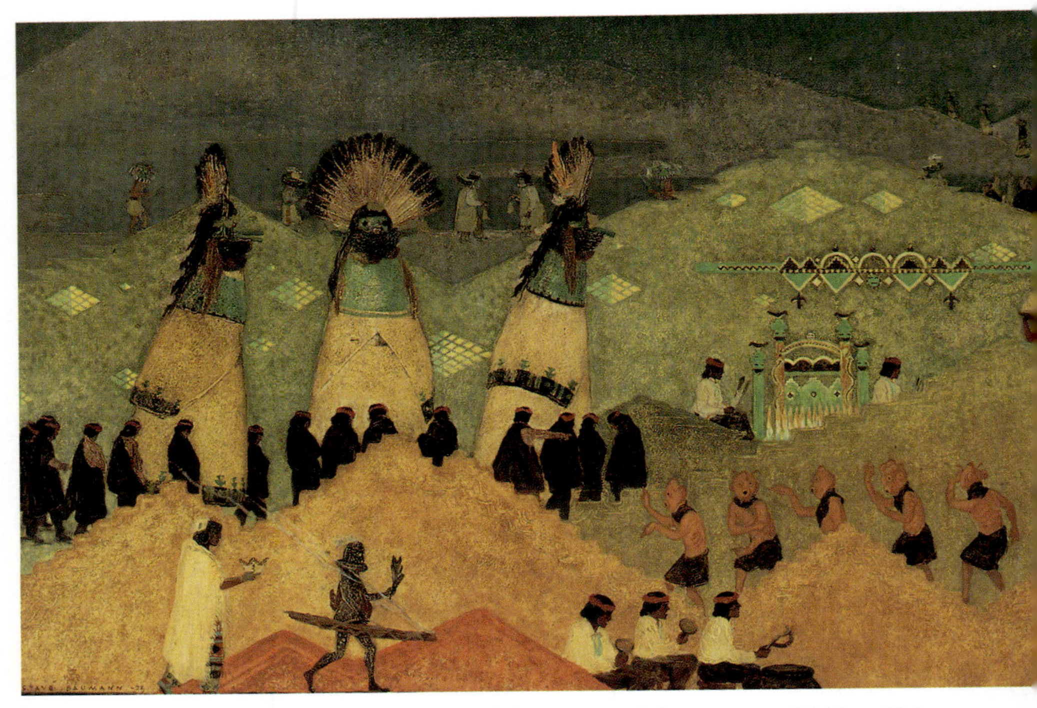

Gustave Baumann, The Shalako, *1923. Oil on canvas, 35 1/2 x 60 in. Museum of New Mexico.*

or classical traditions, and there is a freshness about his work that is very pleasing.

As he was just twenty-two years old at the time, this was high praise.

The fifth member of this dynamic group of young artists was Will Shuster, who has already been mentioned. Shuster was born in Philadelphia in 1893, and there studied electrical engineering at Drexel Institute. When his health brought him west after the war, he planned to go to Taos, but he was so delighted with the number and quality of the artists he found in Santa Fe that he settled there instead.

When the Cinco Pintores held their first of several annual exhibitions at the Art Museum in December 1921, Santa Fe was a town of 7,000. It had, according to Shuster, about fifteen resident artists, but this number was greatly increased by the close connection they had with the rugged souls living and working in Taos. The Taos Society of Artists, made up of Joseph Sharp, Ernest L. Blumenschein, Bert G. Phillips, Oscar E. Berninghaus, E. Irving Couse, Herbert W. Dunton, Victor Higgins, Walter

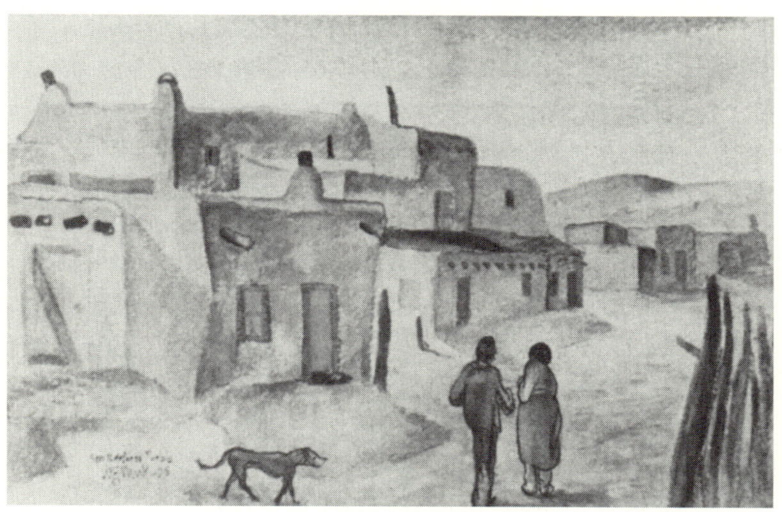

Walter E. Mruk, San Ildefonso Pueblo, *n.d. Watercolor, 11 3/4 x 18 in. Museum of New Mexico. Painted shortly before he returned to Buffalo, this is one of the few Mruk paintings still in New Mexico.*

Ufer, E. Martin Hennings, and later Kenneth Adams, had been established there some years before, and its members were exhibiting widely in the East. Santa Fe was benefited by the anthropologists working at the School of American Research who were interested in art as an expression of a people's culture. Also, the city had the lively excitement of being the state capital. The Santa Fe Railroad and the Harvey Company, which was running its famous Indian Detours (with touring cars and young lady couriers to act as guides), were sending artists west and using their works to promote tourist travel. The increased use of automobiles after the First World War also contributed to the surge of travel, and a trip west was now becoming a popular American adventure.

The new museum was playing an important part in bringing artists to Santa Fe and keeping them there. Will Shuster, reminiscing in the *Santa Fe New Mexican* in 1940 about the early days at the museum, revealed what it was like for the five young friends and other artists in those early days:

> *We are going to look at the place from the artist's point of view.*
>
> *We have always appreciated its noble open-door policy. That was a precious thought which set it off to a fine start. A progressive museum with a new idea, amidst all the museums in this broad land of ours.*
>
> *Now let us go down in the basement. There's Sam Huddleson presiding over a carpenter shop where Joe Bakos and Fremont Ellis and several other artists are busy making frames and crating their paintings. For those who didn't have the know-how, there was good old Sam ready to lend a helping hand or a bit of advice. . . .*
>
> *Look over here in this other basement cavern. There is an etching press and there are the budding etchers—Willard Nash, Fred Monhoff, Will Shuster, and others—working hours on end, sweating and swearing*

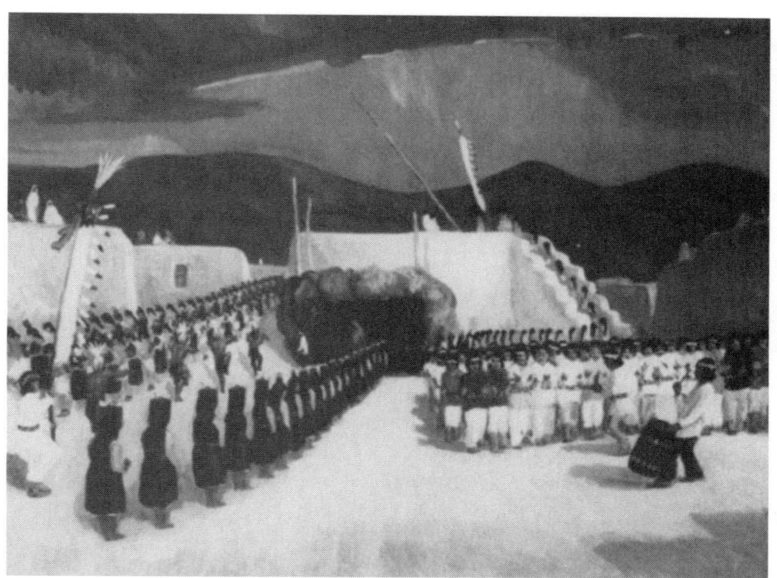

Will Shuster, Santo Domingo Corn Dance, *1929. Oil, 30 x 40 in. Museum of New Mexico.*

over their plates and proofs. And Nordfeldt and Co. chipping in with their own acid criticism and advice. . . .

There's Wes Bradfield, the museum photographer and a thorough archaeologist. Something tall and Lincoln-like about Brad. He did practically all the copying for the artists at a modest fee, and if one was sufficiently skillful the well-equipped darkroom facilities were made available to the artists to do their own work with much good advice thrown in. . . .

Now, out of the basement. Upstairs, Sheldon Parsons is hanging a new show; we take a look-see and then go across Lincoln Avenue to the patio of the Palace. Yes sir, that's right; there are four studios here, available for a time to newcomers until they get settled. George Bellows worked here, Robert Henri, John Sloan, Randall Davey, Willard Nash, Warren Rollins, Julius Rolshoven, Paul Burlin, Andrew Dasburg, on and on goes the list. A great roster of painters. . . .

Upstairs in the women's boardroom about once a month we had gay dinners catered for the artists at a modest price by the Parrot Shop. Lively dinners with the artists, their wives, and friends. A speaker for the evening, usually followed by a hot and lively discussion.

These were the little extra things the museum did to encourage artists to come here and work, that I have shown you.

At that time there were probably about 15 resident artists in Santa Fe and not a great many in the state.

This last remark, of course, helps to explain why the museum could be so hospitable.

At the time of their first exhibition, the Cinco Pintores were all under thirty years of age, and they represented a new generation of painters that was starting to come to New Mexico. They were not European trained, and their work was strongly influenced by Sloan, Davey, Henri, and the others of the Independent Movement which later came to be called, rather slightingly, the Ashcan School. They were sometimes regarded as a "wild bunch," but the world itself was moving into a very different time—the postwar world of the 1920s with jazz, prohibition, a new social unrest, and a surge of travel to what was still regarded in the East as a faraway place of romance and adventure.

It may have seemed a fine romantic place to the five friends, but they were all having a hard time making a living. This, however, did not stop them from deciding to build houses near William P. Henderson's studio home on the Camino, and near their friend Frank Applegate. Shuster had a studio at the time in an adobe building on what is now the parking lot of the First National Bank on the plaza. By a stroke of luck, he sold some paintings to a New York dealer for two hundred dollars, and excitedly went home to tell his wife, "We're going to have an adobe up on the Camino."

The other friends were not in much better condition to become house-owners, but they all decided to start building together. They were short on money and skill (except for Jozef Bakos's knowledge of carpentry), and they started making their

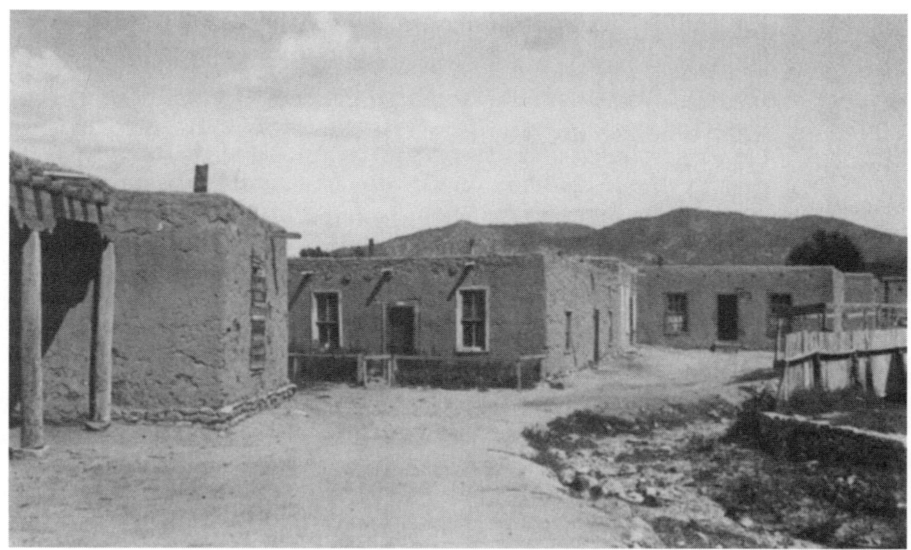

Adobe houses in Santa Fe.

adobes in October, far too late in the year for safety, as the mud and straw bricks must cure in the sun after being shaped. Bakos has said, "This was foolish, but the Lord was with us." With more sublime faith they also installed plumbing and electricity themselves.

Shuster later recalled that Fremont Ellis and he were building their houses side by side. Both were busily working away on adobe walls when "Shus" noticed that Ellis's wall was slowly leaning off center. He hurried to warn Ellis and turned back to his own wall just in time to see it fall over, too. They did not know the primary rule: that one must build a corner with the bricks, not just a wall in a straight line. They learned, however, and in spite of many difficulties the houses were completed and may still be seen on the Camino. The buildings climb up the hill along with the two-story house of Frank Applegate, their close friend and sometimes financial helper.

Applegate had come to Santa Fe with his wife and daughter in 1921, during a tour of the country which he made to study native clays. He was teaching head of the Department of Sculpture and Ceramics at the Trenton, New Jersey School of Industrial Arts, but within a week of their arrival in Santa Fe—a week spent camping in the orchard at the Cassidys' house—he decided to quit his job and move. Less than a year later he bought the piece of land on the Camino and started building. He had majored in architecture in college, and so was well able to plan his own house, and also to give help and advice to the "five little nuts in five adobe huts," as the Cinco Pintores came to be called by some.

The new trend toward "modernism" was certainly encouraged and stimulated by the Cinco Pintores' friend John Sloan. As early as 1908 he had exhibited at McBeth Gallery in New York with the group called "The Eight"—Robert Henri, Maurice B. Prendergast, Arthur B. Davies, George Luks, William Glackens, Ernest Lawson, George Bellows, and Sloan—and an outraged critic wrote that "Vulgarity smites one in the face of the exhibition and I defy anyone who wants to hang Luks's posterior of pigs or Glackens's *At Mongrums* or John Sloan's *Hairdressers Window* in his living room." From this exhibition there developed the Society of Independent Artists, of which Sloan later became president. Each year, the Independents held a large open exhibition, and through the years Sloan encouraged Santa Fe painters, and especially Shuster, who became a close friend and protégé, to enter.

After Sloan's first trip in 1919, he returned to Santa Fe almost every summer for over thirty years, living for most of those summers in a house on Garcia Street. (The studio was later used, from his arrival in Santa Fe in 1948 until his death in 1975, by the Japanese artist Chuzo Tamotzu who had known Sloan in New York.) Sloan's two worlds were wildly different from each other. During the winters in New York, he taught at the Art Students League, went to plays, was delighted by dancer Isadora Duncan, and dined in restaurants (with an occasional illegal celebration in a speakeasy), as his limited money allowed. In Santa Fe, his wife Dolly and he were sparkling participants in everything from painting and picnicking trips to the mountains to marching in the fiesta parades in outrageous costumes. A wonderful record of this time comes through in a long series of letters Sloan wrote from New York to Will Shuster in Santa Fe over the years. Each year as spring approached, he hated to leave the city; and each fall he hated to leave Santa Fe.

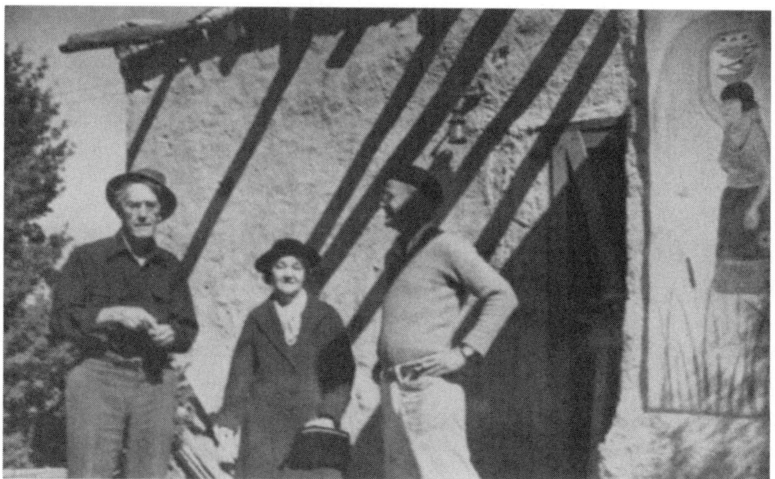

John and Dolly Sloan, Will Shuster.

During the summer of 1919, he produced the first of the many warm and human paintings he created in the West. One of these, *The Old Portal, Santa Fe*, I reproduced in Sloan's book *The Gist of Art*, with the comment that this was "the last survival of the roofed sidewalks which once gave Santa Fe a thoroughly foreign appearance. Coy maids and mashers have not been abolished." Although the new Art Museum, of which Sloan deeply approved, had been built in what was being called the "New-Old Santa Fe style," it was true that at that time many of the old buildings were either being modernized or torn down to make way for progress. Sloan's and the other artists' paintings and prints have preserved for us a view of the gentle old town and the people still holding to their traditions, which they were afraid would soon be lost.

In fact, the artists were among the fiercest fighters for Santa Fe to maintain its character and not become like any other western town. In 1919, Sloan was already nostalgic for the loss of a place which was still there, but which he felt was threatened. He painted the town, the women in black shawls, the Indian dancers—and the tourists who came to stare at them, his neighbor Georgio Valdes digging the Sloans' orchard garden, and the processions. His sardonic humor comes through frequently, as in his painting *Old Jemez Mission*, which shows the looming mass

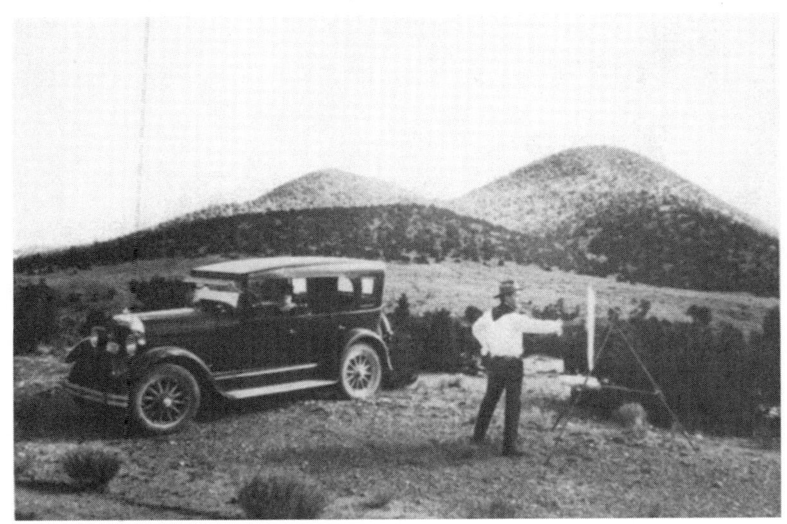

John Sloan painting while Dolly waits patiently in the car.

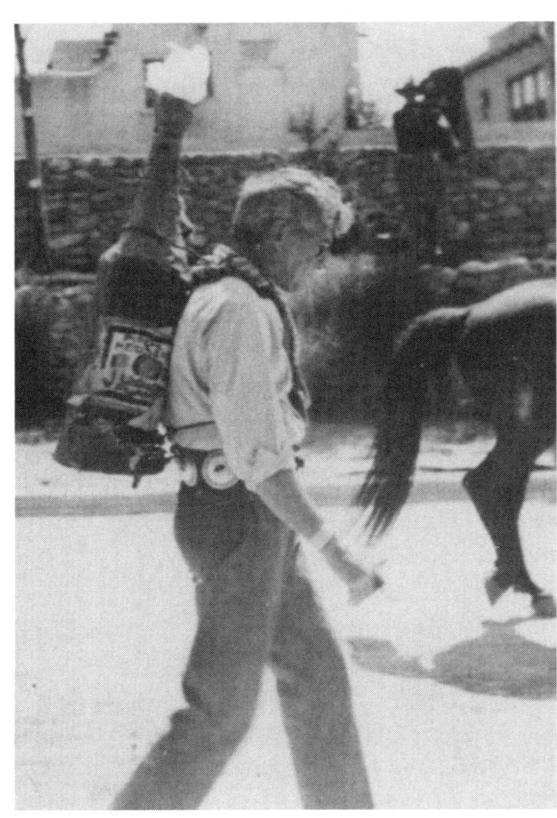

John Sloan in a fiesta parade.

of the ruined church with a Ford car parked in the front of the picture, the "proud owner snap-shooting his family on the almost prehistoric spot."

An interesting friendship developed between Sloan and Shuster. Sloan was the older by twenty-two years, and a highly experienced artist and teacher, while Shuster had not done much serious painting before he came to Santa Fe. The meeting with Sloan, and through the years the letters and personal contact, kept Shuster going in his darkest times of depression and poverty. Sloan was first and last a teacher, and his letters to Shuster scold, praise, and encourage the younger man. A sociable man himself, he was concerned by the banding together of the artists in Santa Fe, and wrote Shuster:

> *Beware of the competitive spirit it is too apt to spring up—and while New Mexico has fewer artists than New York, they get closer to you there than here. Wm. Yeats always said the artist is a hermit—has the hermit's mind. Your little community on the Camino del Monte Sol is too large—not socially, but artistically. Give way to any feeling of aloofness that may find its way into your temper. That's the artist part of you and must be given its share in your conduct.—Here endeth—etc. The habit of teaching (I hope it's not preaching) intrudes—but rereading what's gone before, I say yes to it. Don't try to be good at everything, just be an artist—merge them all to that focus.*

It doesn't seem as though Sloan needed to worry too much about the perils of the Cinco Pintores' living and working so closely together. All five of the friends developed in different directions and, in fact, only exhibited as a group for a few years. Fremont Ellis, the "loner" of the group, soon went his own way. After he married, he spent a period of time living in Española, a small town about twenty-five miles north of Santa Fe. Later, he bought land and moved an old Spanish house—adobe by adobe—

Will Shuster, Untitled mural, *1964. Oil, 48 x 48 in. El Nido Restaurant, Tesuque, New Mexico. Will Shuster painted this mural of Zozobra for Ray Arias, the owner of El Nido Restaurant at the time.*

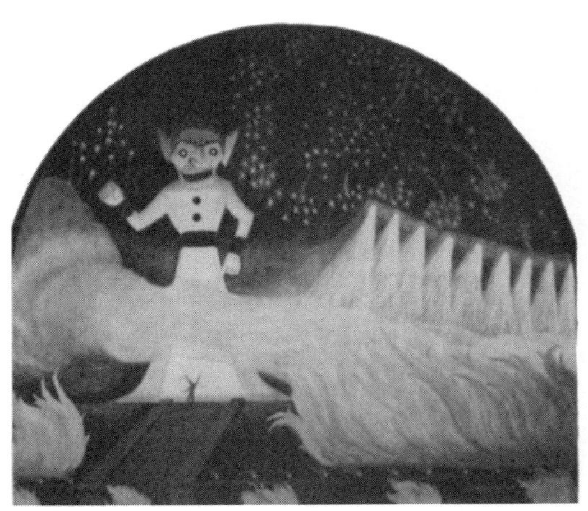

from Galisteo to "Rancho San Sebastian," ten miles east of Santa Fe. It is still considered one of the most beautiful houses in the area—a real hacienda.

Ellis has always loved the Spanish people of New Mexico and respected their ways. His wife was a member of an old and aristocratic New Mexican family which owned a large piece of land at the site now occupied by the Hilton Inn. He feels that a genuine and very beautiful quality of life has vanished now from Santa Fe, and speaks with love of the sound of the church bells which used to fill the city, and of the smell of the piñon smoke from the cooking and heating fires before the advent of gas lines.

He has said that the people, when he first came to Santa Fe, were extremely dignified and courteous—even courtly—in their manners, and that many of the things which we now think of as "native" were really imported from Old Mexico after the artists revived and revised the yearly fiesta. "The songs were different," he recalls. "The mariachi music is all Mexican and so are the caballero type clothes they wear." Sometimes when one watches two of the older men or women meet and exchange greetings, one still can sense the quiet, gentle way of life which he loved so much when he first came to Santa Fe to live.

The emotional and romantic quality which colors Ellis's attitude toward life is very evident in his painting. From the beginning, he responded to the southwestern landscape with an

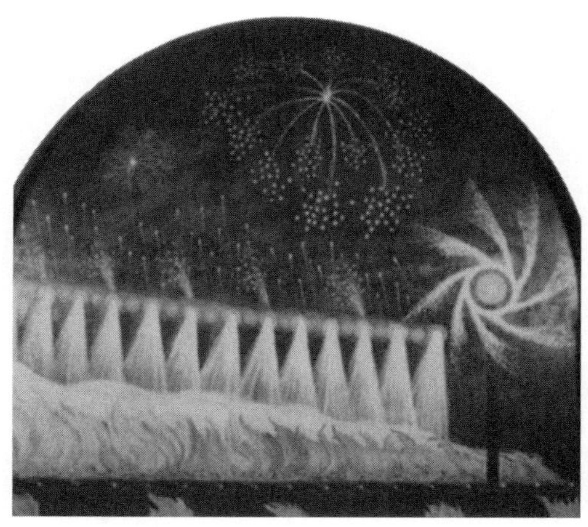

intense love, and his forceful works have always shown a direct response to a particular place and a particular time. Through the years he has become an extremely successful painter, but with characteristic modesty he has said, "I am fortunate. Many people like my work because I happen to have a very common mind—I see and love things the way a great many other people do, so they like the way I paint them." This is indeed too modest. Ellis has tremendous technical ease and such a feeling for the process of painting itself that a young painter recently remarked that when he looked at Ellis's brushstrokes he could feel them in his own painting arm.

A very different approach was taken by both Jozef Bakos and Willard Nash, who moved toward Cubism and abstraction in their work. Nash has said of himself, "I am an individualist, and a self-analytical one. I am an experimenter in art and have worked through many phases, going step by step deeper into the mysteries of esthetics." He has also stated: "Art is not concerned with the outer aspect of things. Art is concerned with the true inner spirit which determines the outer form. That is why people generally could not understand the so-called Cubist movement. They could only see the outward thing and did not understand what the artist was trying to discover inside." While he worked as a member of the Cinco Pintores group, however, Nash's paintings retained a simplified representationalism. Cézanne's

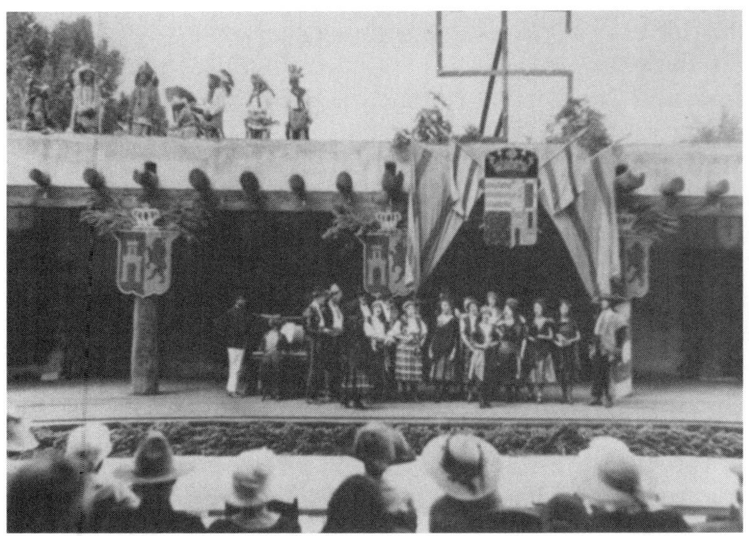

Fiesta program outside the Palace of the Governors, 1921.

influence was predominant in his work of the thirties, while the work he did in the forties became more abstract. But all his paintings have a cool and intellectual quality.

Unlike Nash's paintings, the early work of Jozef Bakos was deeply emotional and affected by Van Gogh, Gauguin, and the painting of the Expressionists. He said once, "I've always been more concerned in painting the weight of a mountain than its atmospheric condition. I feel there are tons and tons of granite, and maybe even gold under there." Bakos's enormous love of people and the land gives power and vitality to his paintings. He has also produced watercolors of lyric charm.

Less is known about the work of his close friend Walter Mruk, as examples of his paintings are rather rare. Van Deren Coke has said in *Taos and Santa Fe: The Artist's Environment, 1882–1942* that "his is a kind of energetic and introspective expressionism which, although conventional in subject, gained strength through the gesture of painting itself."

In their move toward abstraction and Cubism, Bakos and Nash were greatly influenced by Andrew Dasburg, who was called by Lloyd Goodrich and John I. H. Baur, in *American Art of Our Century*, "The most lucid American champion of Cubism, in his writing and teaching as well as his painting." Dasburg was born in Paris in 1887, but came to America in 1892. After studying at the Art Students League and at Woodstock, New York, he returned

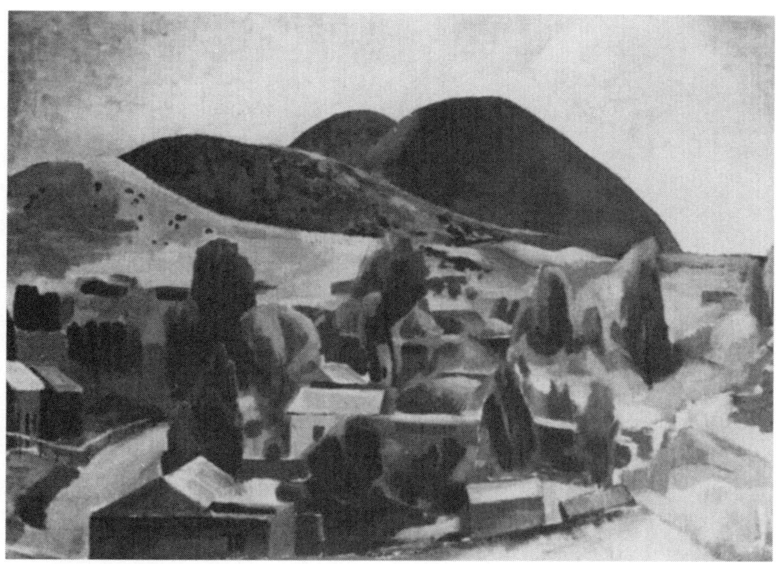

Willard Nash, Landscape. *Oil, n.d., 24 x 30 in. Museum of New Mexico. Josef Bakos, fellow memberof the Cinco Pintores, said they all painted similara views of Sunmount Sanitorium, because they could see it from their houses on the Camino del Monte Sol.*

to Paris in 1909, where he became acquainted with Matisse and the work of Cézanne. Returning to the United States, he was an exhibitor in the world-shaking (or at least U.S.-shaking) Armory Show of 1913. Four years later, in 1917, he visited Taos for the first time. Dasburg said in an interview for the *Santa Fe New Mexican*, "I came as a guest of Mabel Dodge Luhan's. We, Robert Edwin Jones and I, were invited. He was a stage designer. We got a telegram from her, I can still remember it: 'It's a wonderful place. Must come. Am sending you tickets. Bring me a cook.' We brought the cook."

After this first visit, Dasburg went back and forth from Taos to New York City, Santa Fe, and Woodstock. At first, he lived at the corner of Buena Vista and College Streets in Santa Fe. In 1921, however, Dasburg, his second wife Ida (she had been married first to Max Eastman, the radical writer who founded the magazine *The Masses*), her son Dan, and Dasburg's son Alfred, bought a house in Santa Fe on the Camino del Monte Sol, and when the house was finished in 1922 they moved in. Alfred

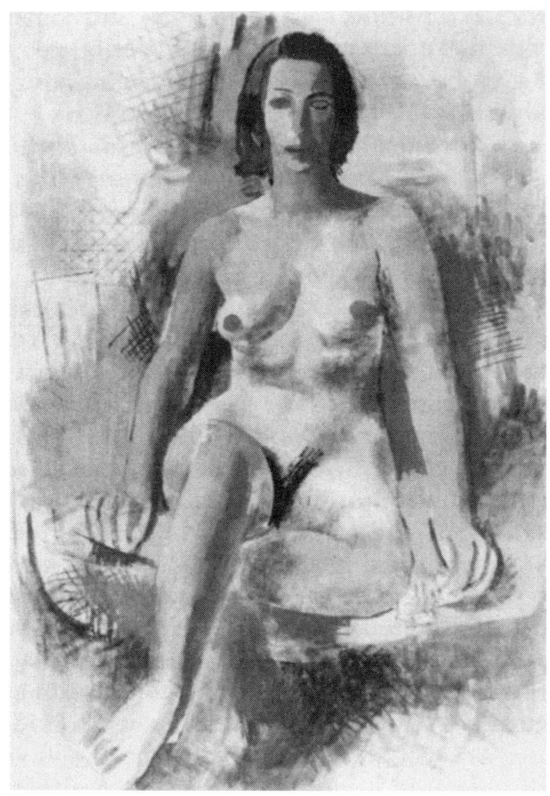

Willard Nash, Nude, *n.d. Watercolor, 22 x 14 3/8 in. Museum of New Mexico.*

Dasburg remembers that the house was very modern for the east end of Santa Fe in those days, and, in fact, had hot-water heat and a brand-new Westinghouse electric stove.

The two boys, Dan and Alfred, loved living in the West. They slept year round on an outdoor porch on wooden shelf-bunks. They had horses and rode each day down the Camino to Canyon Road, then west to Castillo (now the Paseo de Peralta), where the Parish School was located. One of the teachers Alfred particularly remembers was Katherine Van Stone, who sang Spanish songs to the class and played the piano. (Miss Van Stone's mother, Mrs. Mary R. Van Stone, was the curator of the Art Museum and beloved by the entire artistic community for many years.) After school, Alfred retrieved his horse from the pasture next to the school and often rode all the way to the end of Canyon Road and on up the Santa Fe Canyon to fish in the river. The canyon has been closed to the public for many years, but at that time was an open forest area.

There was quite a group of boys and girls living on or near the Camino in the 1920s, who knew each other and whose parents were friends. Alfred Dasburg remembers Betty Applegate, and Raphael and John Dorman, Derek Nusbaum, Fergus Mera (the doctor's son), and Ned Hall (later Dr. Edward T. Hall, noted writer and anthropologist). There is a big arroyo behind the houses on the west side of the Camino where they used to hold track meets. When they were a little older, they played polo in a field behind El Caminito, a little street branching off from the Camino. This game, by the way, was later taken up with enthusiasm and skill by a group of grown-ups there, who held more formal matches for several years.

Andrew Dasburg bought the next piece of land down the hill from their first house, which had a log cabin on it (the logs were vertical instead of the usual horizontal), and during the winter of 1928–1929 Alfred lived alone in the cabin while his parents were in Puerto Rico. The cabin was later incorporated into a house

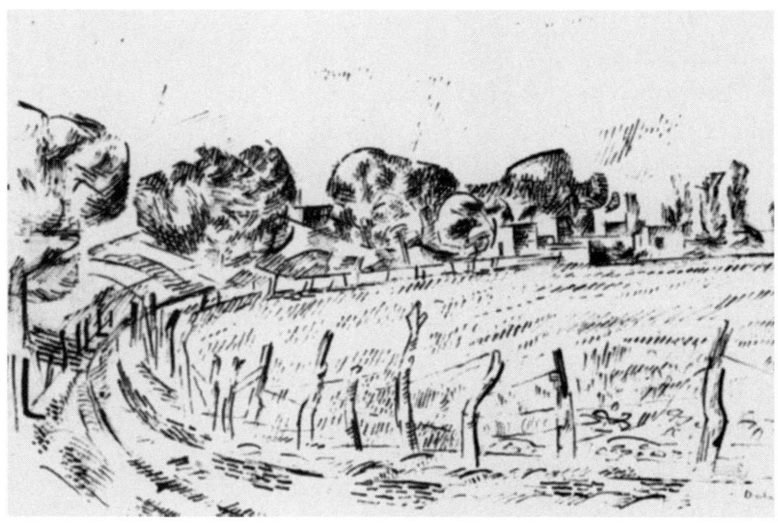

Andrew Dasburg, Landscape, *1932. Ink on paper, 15 1/2 x 22 in. Museum of New Mexico.*

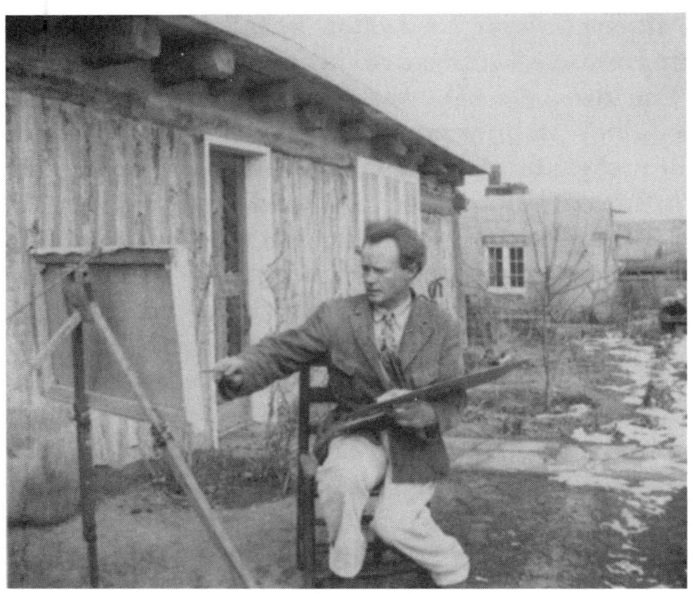

Andrew Dasburg at work outside the cabin on the Camino del Monte Sol, 1929–30.

designed by John Gaw Meem, one of New Mexico's most distinguished architects and a National Academician in his field.

One of Andrew Dasburg's closest friends in Santa Fe was Jozef Bakos, with whom he hunted as well as painted. Another was Lynn Riggs, who was writing *Green Grow the Lilacs*, later to be made into the musical *Oklahoma!* Riggs and Mrs. Dasburg had much in common, as Mrs. Dasburg had organized the Provincetown theater group in the East. In fact, the whole group of friends acted, danced, and sang in their own productions. In some of these efforts, Lynn Riggs played his guitar and Fremont Ellis, the drums. The Dasburgs also saw a lot of the poet Witter Bynner after his arrival in Santa Fe, and Alfred Dasburg remembers that his little brother and he acted in a play written by Bynner called *Let Them Eat Cake*. Other writers living on the Camino included Mary Austin, who began Santa Fe's Community Theatre while she was in town, Calla Hay, who now writes for the *New Mexican*, and the poet Arthur Davison Ficke. Aaron Copland also spent some time in Santa Fe in 1928. This diversity of talents unquestionably lent vigor to Santa Fe's cultural life.

It seems amazing that all of these people managed to make a living in the little adobe town. Some, of course, had private means when they came, but others were extremely poor. Alfred Dasburg recalls, however, that it was hard to tell who was rich and who was poor. Their friendship and activities were not centered on things of monetary value. They shared activities and judged each other by their creativity and wit. The biggest market for their work was not in New Mexico, but usually to collectors or exhibitions in the East. It was a time of major competitions in many leading eastern museums, such as the Corcoran Gallery of Art in Washington, D.C., the Carnegie in Pittsburgh, and the annual show at the Art Institute in Chicago. The competitions continued all through the thirties, and in the lists of accepted works in the big shows one encounters name after name from the Santa Fe area. It should be remembered, however, that while many top-ranking artists came to Santa Fe and found their ideal home, others drawn by its reputation—for example, Edward Hopper, Yasua Kunioshi, and George Bellows—came, looked, and left. The light and space which stimulated some may have dazzled and repelled others.

By the mid-twenties, then, Santa Fe was at its height as one of the leading art colonies of the country. Each train which stopped at Lamy, the closest railroad station, spilled out its load

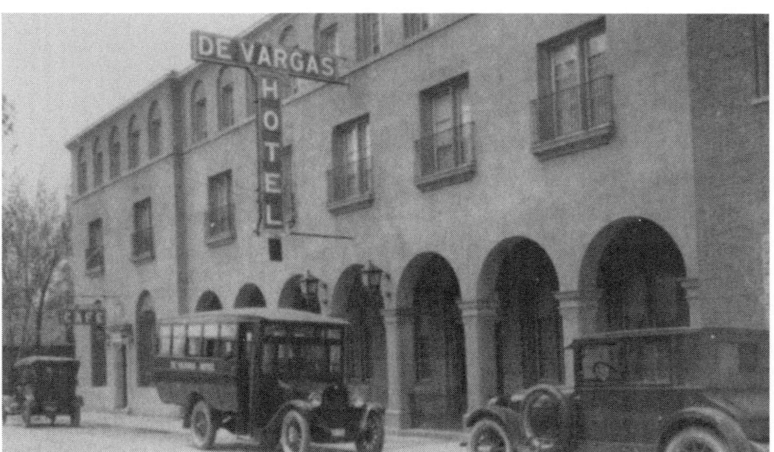

The De Vargas Hotel showing its bus which met arriving trains at Lamy.

of tourists laden with cameras and artists laden with paint boxes and portable easels. The Harvey cars and couriers were there, poised to scoop up *their* customers and offer them the excitement of the Indian Detours. And, in contrast with the relative quiet and isolation of a few years before, many of the artists were now being met by friends who had come ahead and encouraged them to venture out for a summer—and sometimes a lifetime—of exploring the possibilities of expression in the Southwest.

5
The Twenties

All over the United States the Roaring Twenties were at their peak, and in Santa Fe they seem to have roared with particular gusto. The artists threw themselves into the fiesta each year as only artists can, decorating the plaza, inventing fantastic costumes, marching in the Hysterical/Historical Parade, and making batches of homebrew. The Cinco Pintores entered into all of this, and Jozef Bakos has many warm tales to tell about their exploits. They had hilarious times, with a party somewhere almost every night to complement the serious daytime work of painting.

He recalls that they lived in constant fear of the revenue officer. One time when he made a sudden raid on the Camino, they rushed their batch to the next house up the hill via the back door, and when he headed toward that one, on to the next. Before he made his way to the last house, they hurried the kettle back down the hill to the first house.

One evening they all built a bobsled and were pulled by car to Lamy, where they had to decline an invitation to a box-car party as Teresa Bakos (Jozef's wife) was lightly attired in a bathing suit under her fur coat. They formed the Adobe Chamber Music Society, with a violinist and a drummer and several percussionists playing on tin cans and other homemade instruments.

During the twenties, when a bad drought swept through the Southwest, the artists put on plays at the museum to provide a milk fund for children and to buy feed for starving cattle. They also followed political activities, and many of them

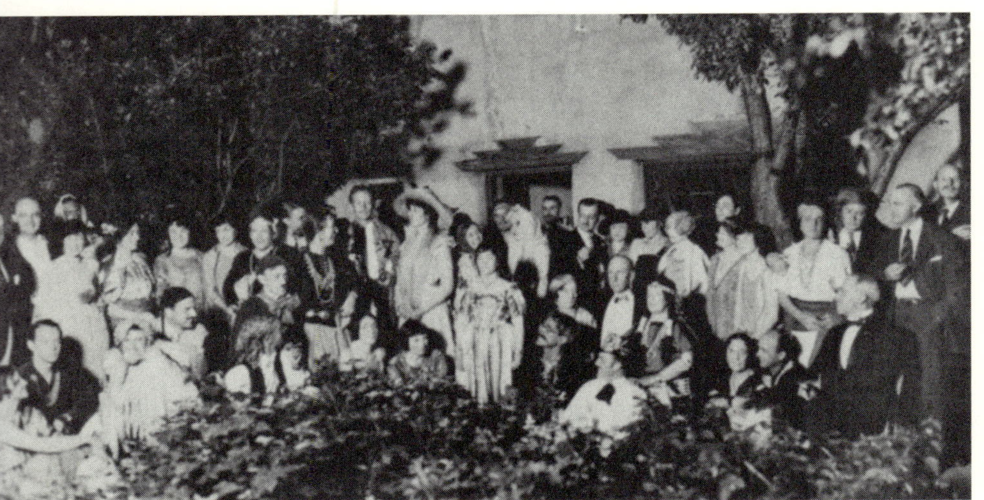

A fiesta party. Some of these parties started with the burning of Zozobra and lasted for all four days—or nights—of the yearly fiesta. Front row 5th from left, Will Shuster; front center, Dolly Sloan; back row to left of Dolly, Willard Nash.

worked for Wisconsin's liberal candidate Robert LaFollette. Unfortunately some of them, like the rest of the country, played the stock market. Alfred Dasburg has said that when the market crashed they lost a good deal, although mostly on paper.

And, although Santa Fe was picturesque, life was often hard for the native-born Spanish Americans. An elderly acquaintance has said that as boys, his brother and he had to carry all of their water from the Santa Fe River up a block-long hill to their mother's house on the Acequia Madre; another has told of not being allowed to go to school to learn to read, as he was needed to tend the goats on his family's little farm. Many of the women worked for the "Anglos" for extremely low pay, and the men worked at odd jobs and sold firewood, for which they walked all the way to the mountains to cut and load it onto their burros. For the artists, all of this added subject matter and lent a romantic quality to the paintings they sent back east.

The Indians, too, while they were never dispossessed of their pueblo lands, were treated at best with a kindly superiority by many. When the Santa Fe Fiesta was first revived in 1919,

Santa Fe painter Gus Baumann later recalled that Colonel Twitchell, a local lawyer and noted historian, "being a stickler for historical exactitude, . . . had talked the Indians into consenting to be shot at—with blank cartridges, of course."

However, many of the artists and writers formed close ties of friendship with both Indian and Spanish neighbors. William P. Henderson and his wife and daughter certainly did so. One of their close friends was Awa Tsireh, or Alfonso Roybal, to use his Spanish name. A native of San Ildefonso Pueblo, he was one of the best of the pueblo painters. Henderson frequently advised and helped Awa Tsireh and other Indian artists, gave them paint and paper, and bought their paintings.

Henderson's daughter, Alice Rossin, has talked about her father's wanting to paint a portrait of Awa Tsireh, who steadily delayed sitting for the painting. He and his whole family would frequently drive up to the Hendersons' house on the Camino and announce that "now we have come to visit." They would stay for several days, and Alice would provide for them. But one day, at last, Awa Tsireh came to the house dressed in a sparkling white shirt and a handsome scarf and said, "Now paint me." And that is the way he looks in Henderson's fine portrait of him which can be found in the museum's collection.

In spite of any surface frivolity on the part of the artists, there was a great deal of serious creative work going on in Santa Fe. The Cinco Pintores regarded themselves as avant-garde and radical artists of the area. They had pledged when they formed their group, to "take art to the people and not to surrender to commercialism." And they did indeed exhibit their work several times in factories and other places where art was not usually found. They were thwarted in their attempt to show their work at the State Penitentiary, however, when the warden told them that knives and forks would be thrown through the pictures if they held an exhibit in the dining hall.

About this time one writer in *El Palacio* stated, with some reservation, that "each of the young men has a viewpoint and a technique of his own. Vigor, originality, and the daring to express themselves are evident. One is convinced of the honesty of endeavor of each artist, and while the trend is modern, it is yet within the bounds of sanity."

Will Shuster and Walter Mruk, by the way, shared an interesting adventure when they went into the Carlsbad Caverns to paint. This was long before the caverns were developed for public admission. They were lowered into the caves in buckets and painted by lantern light. *El Palacio* commented in June 1925:

> *This collection of canvases has created a stir in the art world, not only because the visit of Mr. Mruk and Will H. Shuster was the first that resulted in canvases of the cavern, but Mruk's canvases are said to be imaginative to a high degree. He filled the cavern with mythical grotesques in an effort to interpret his reaction upon entering the dim lit interior. The work is accepted as a distinct achievement, although decidedly unusual, and difficult of treatment. Art critics have differed widely over the paintings, although all have conceded an impressive result.*

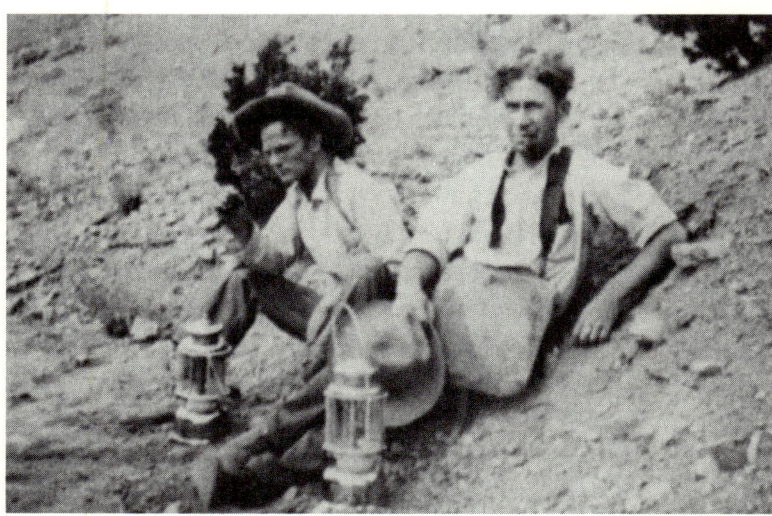

Will Shuster and Walter Mruk at the entrance to Carlsbad Caverns.

While this was the opinion of the local writer, a letter from Sloan to Shuster dated March 4, 1925, shows that neither he nor the eastern experts agreed on the merit of Shuster's cave painting:

> *I suppose you had hoped too much from the Cave stuff and it blued you to have the bottom fall out of your hopes. Just forget it—put 'em away and come to the surface of the Earth again. Perhaps it's time for me to tell you that I never could really understand your interest in the bowels of the Earth—I did like the pictures and I saw how you enjoyed painting them and I'm sure they were great technical exercises and well done and I felt you had to get 'em out of your system—but if my advice is worth anything you can have it: Come back to human life—*

This was a hard blow to Shuster, but he leaned on Sloan's judgment and knowledge, and went back to painting above ground.

All during the twenties, the Sloans came each year to live in their house on Garcia Street, and the first year the Sloans had the house the Shusters lived there too. Sloan was not painting well

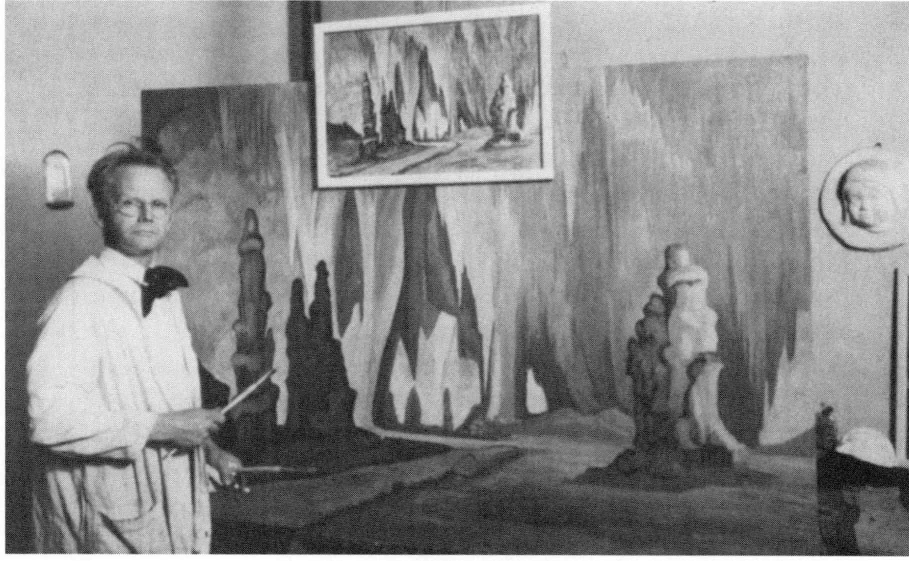

Will Shuster and one of his Carlsbad Cavern paintings.

that year, and he was feeling crotchety and depressed. Dolly Sloan begged Shuster to get him painting again, so Shuster persuaded Sloan to go out sketching. One day when they were lounging in the orchard at the house, Sloan suggested that they paint each other. Shuster agreed. Later he said, "And so it happened. We worked like beavers but with a strange feeling of doing double duty: The consciousness of trying to be kind to the other fellow, and pose a bit and at the same time concentrate on the all-important job of painting."

By the middle of the twenties, the Cinco Pintores group was breaking up. In 1926, Walter Mruk returned to the East; the other four became involved with various groups which were forming and re-forming in the town. In the mid-twenties, art schools sprang up in Santa Fe (the first in 1925), some to have very short lives, others to have considerable influence.

One of the most important teachers to work in Santa Fe was Raymond Jonson. Born in Iowa in 1891, he grew up in Portland, Oregon, where his Baptist clergyman father had been called. Jonson studied art at the Portland Museum School, and when he finished high school, went to Chicago with money saved from delivering newspapers. While attending the Chicago Art Institute he met Nordfeldt, whose enthusiasm and experimentation introduced the young man to the abstract approach to painting which he has continued to follow ever since.

One may suppose that Nordfeldt also talked to Jonson about the little town of Santa Fe. But it was not until after several years working as graphic art director of the Chicago Little Theater, and four years of painting which included a summer in Peterborough, New Hampshire, that Jonson came to Santa Fe to live in 1924. He stayed in Santa Fe from 1924 until 1949, and his influence on the young artists first there, and later in his classes at the University of New Mexico in Albuquerque, was enormous.

Jonson's work developed from Cubism into nonrepresentational painting, following such men as Kandinsky. In an article in *El Palacio* for May–June 1956, Jonson's longtime friend Ed Garman wrote:

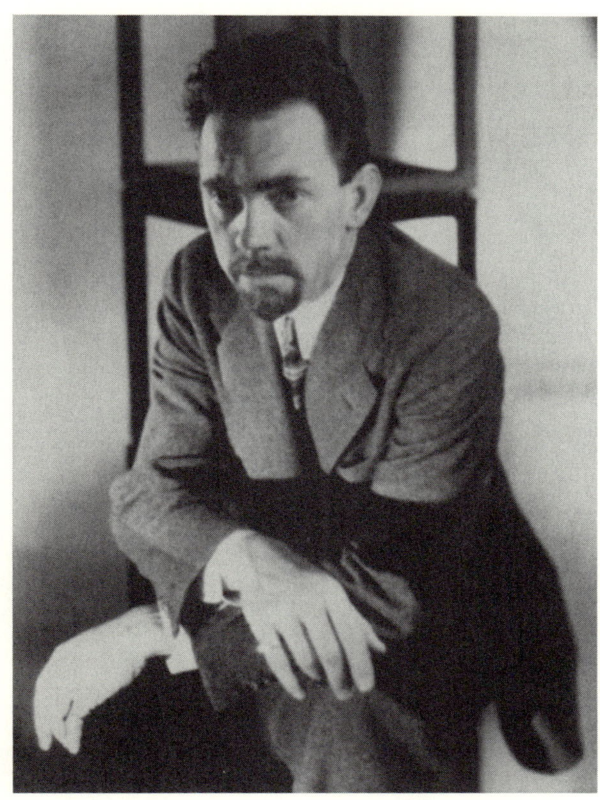

Raymond Jonson, 1932.

> *Jonson stated his aim early in life. It was to work out his salvation. It was to live and work so that his thought might take form. He wanted his work so to become a symbol of order that it would express what he had made of his life in both body and spirit. Working out one's salvation is the big issue which we all have to face. Jonson found his key to this main issue early. He has been devoted to life through the art of painting—not to painting for its own sake, but as a way of life, as a consummation of what intelligent and sensitive living can apprehend and express.*

Jonson himself said in an interview in the *Santa Fe New Mexican* in 1949:

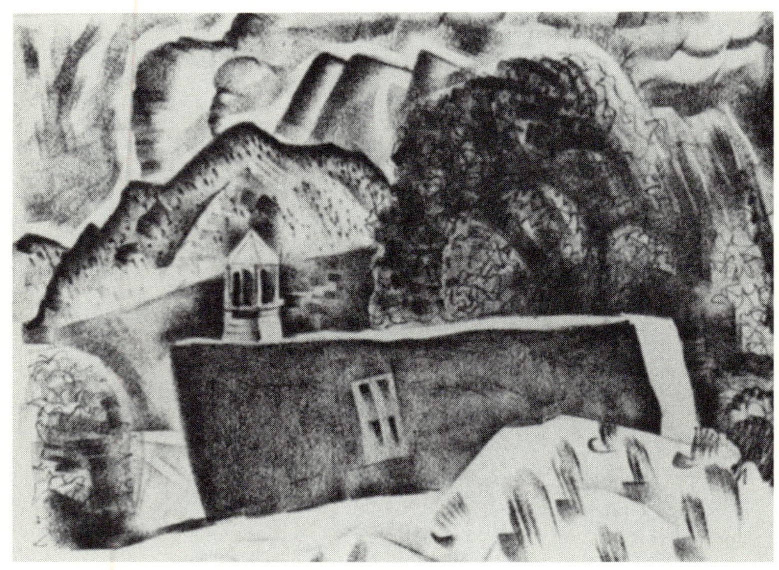

Raymond Jonson, Sanctuario, *n.d. Lithographic crayon, 11 1/2 x 16 1/4 in. Museum of New Mexico.*

> *1 believe that the highest aspect of painting is one that is creative—that quality in every element, especially in pigmentation, functions in a high degree. In order to attain these, the approach is usually abstract or absolute. In these two, painting is very much alive today and I personally think we are living in an age that is producing some of the greatest art of all time. It appears to me that both the abstract and the absolute are consonant with our age. . . . My own definition is: By absolute painting, we mean painting which is entirely creative. All the forms, lines and color relationships, etc., are pure inventions. It is painting which makes no use of the objective world and depends for its comprehension, not on imitation or suggestion, but on structure. Here pure imagination functions.*

During his many years of painting, Raymond Jonson has experimented with new approaches to his art, and he has been an eager exponent of nonobjective painting. He has always, however, been keenly aware of the real world around him, and by no means an ivory tower philosopher in the arts. In a letter to the museum in 1966, he wrote:

> *The M. of N.M. has, from my first visit to New Mexico, and that was forty-four years ago, at which time the museum provided me with a studio, filled an important place in my life as a painter. I look back over the years with a keen appreciation for what the museum has meant, not only to me but to virtually all the artists who have worked in this State. In many ways our museum is a unique one that seems to function in much closer rapport with its environment than is the case with other museums of which I have knowledge.*

Although his own work is a world apart from the romantic bravura of such men as Robert Henri, he too responded to the particular feel of Santa Fe and the museum. Today, Jonson is retired from teaching but he is still painting in eager experimental ways—often with airbrush and acrylics—in his studio at the Jonson Gallery on the campus of the University of New Mexico.

Among all the artists who flocked to Santa Fe in the twenties, two important women stand out—Olive Rush, a painter, and Eugenie Shonnard, a sculptor. Olive Rush's adobe home and studio on Canyon Road was a far cry from her beginnings in Fairmount, Indiana, where she was born in 1873. Her people were Quakers, and she was a devoted member of the Religious Society of Friends for all of her long and significant life.

Miss Rush left home at sixteen to attend the Corcoran Art School in Washington, D.C. Later she went on to the Art Students League and to private lessons with renowned illustrator Howard Pyle in Wilmington, Delaware. Next, working as a magazine illustrator, she financed several trips to Paris. Until this time, all of her thoughts had turned eastward, but in 1914, as a favor to her father, she travelled with him to the Southwest. In

Santa Fe she found her own spiritual climate, and in 1920 she returned to live permanently.

The house she bought, the Rodriguez home, was nearly a century old at that time. During her life, it was a stopping place for young and old Quakers who came to Santa Fe; today, it is the meetinghouse for the Religious Society of Friends. Miss Rush painted frescos in the house and worked devotedly in the huge old garden at the rear. From its windows, she watched Santa Fe grow from what she called a "burro economy" (in 1920, when she came to Santa Fe to live, there were more burros in the town than automobiles) to a modern city. In the early years she rode her horse downtown; later in her nineties, she rode in a taxi. But whatever the means of transport, she always managed to attend exhibitions of art and look at them with a keen critical eye.

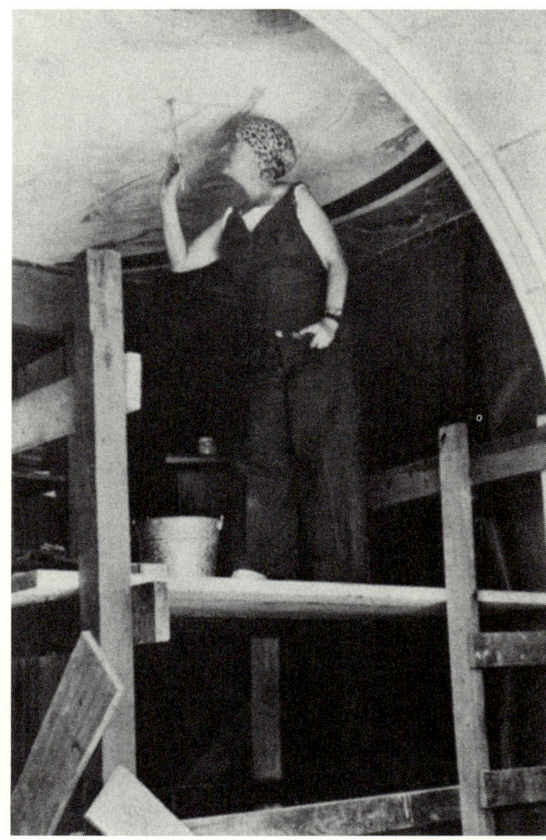

Olive Rush painting the murals at the Santa Fe Public Library.

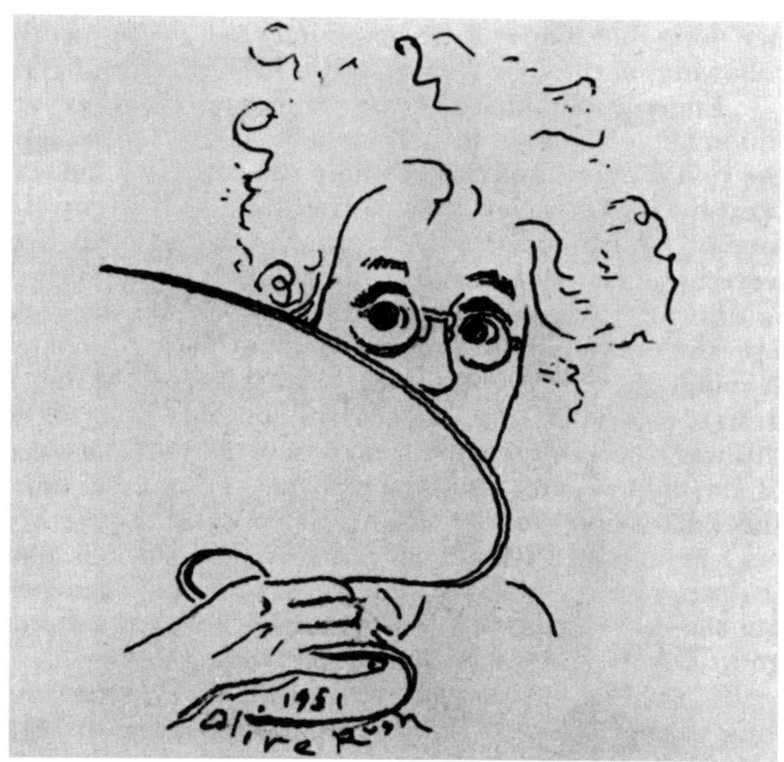

This pen-and-ink sketch of herself by Olive Rush hangs in the Quaker meeting house.

Her encouragement of young artists was unfailing. She especially loved and admired the American Indians and their art, and, in fact, when she was invited to paint murals at the Santa Fe Indian School, she refused to do so and suggested that the Indian students paint them instead. She got a group of students together to discuss the project with them, relying on them for the subject matter while she contented herself with giving them technical advice on fresco. "They were smart," she has said. "So smart, and painting was easy for them because they had never been told it was hard." Olive Rush also painted many murals herself, several of which are still cherished in the city.

One of the greatest influences on her work was Chinese painting, both in symbolism and the use of calligraphy. "I acknowledge the influence of the early Chinese, the Japanese, and El Greco," she once said. "They are my masters. They worked by the spirit, from and for the spirit. I am proud to belong to their line." Although these are "old" masters, Olive Rush was a part of the new and free movement which broke away from traditional form and subject matter. From the beginning, her work was "intuitive" rather than directly visual, an expression of an image rather than a scene. And she often spoke of the spiritual qualities in art: "To follow the inner light, that is the one great essential need at all times"; and "When you walk through a gallery it is easy to know which pictures are painted from an 'outer impulse' and which ones, as Kandinsky says, are 'produced by the stress of the inner need'!" To the end of her long life, Olive Rush experimented in her work, following, in the true Quaker spirit, her own inner light.

Eugenie Shonnard came to Santa Fe after an indomitable struggle to become a sculptor and bought the house on Hickox Street where she still lives. She was born in Yonkers, New York, a frail child with a sensitive love of nature and the rabbits, squirrels, and birds that were her pets. Her health made her shy, so she turned to drawing to express her love of the world. As she grew up, she was able to attend the New York School of Applied Design for Women. She planned to be a designer of wallpaper, book covers, and lace—but all of this was changed the day she accidentally picked up a piece of clay and began to mold and shape it. From that time, she knew that two-dimensional work would not satisfy her. Family and friends all tried to persuade her that sculpture was not for a hundred-pound semi-invalid girl, but she told them that all she wanted in the world was to go to Europe to study sculpture.

It was thought that she might not even survive the long voyage, but she knew that she would do it. In 1911, her mother and she sailed for France, where she studied under Bourdelle and the great sculptor Auguste Rodin. With her health much improved she made several trips to France and was soon recognized as an artist. A bronze rabbit of hers was bought by the Luxembourg Museum, and other works were commissioned in New York. She first visited New Mexico in 1925, and in 1927 moved to Santa Fe to stay.

The house her mother and she bought was on the edge of town then, with prairie and piñons just to the south. She had a horse named Peggy that she used to ride to town and hitch in the plaza. Later Peggy's stable became a studio, but the marks of her hoofs still scar the doors. The walls of the studio are foot-thick adobe; the ceiling with its four skylights is twenty feet high. Around the house and studio were a garden and an orchard of apricot trees. There were a well house and a root cellar with an earthen roof—the cellar is now a furnace room surrounded by carvings of birds and animals.

Miss Shonnard's first visit started her lifelong love and admiration for the Indian people. She has many close friends among them, including Maria Martinez, the famous potter of San Ildefonso, and is proud that she held Maria's son Popovi Da in her arms shortly after he was born. Her sculptures of her Indian friends are among her finest works.

Almost completely deaf from the age of twenty-seven, Miss Shonnard has turned to the senses of sight and touch to produce

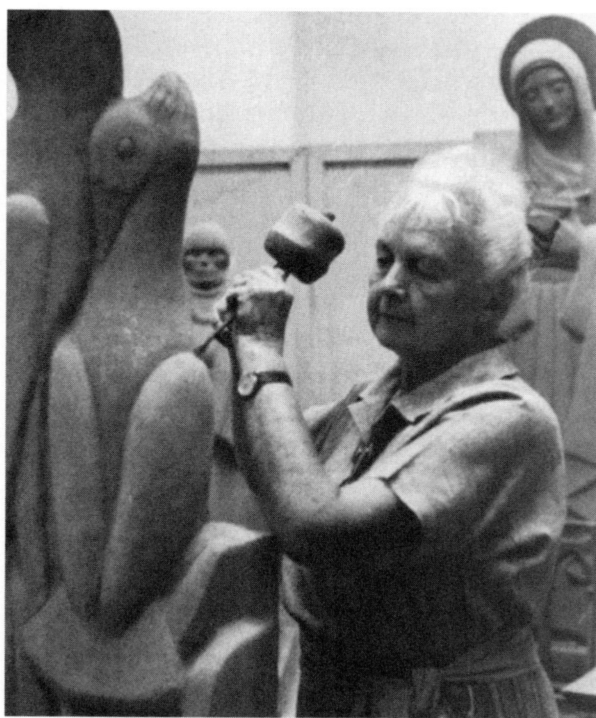

Eugenie Shonnard in her studio.

her powerful and spiritual works. The artist and art critic Alfred Morang has said of her work in his column "On the Arts" for a weekly Santa Fe newspaper:

> *Miss Shonnard is able to go beyond the physical appearance of the object and invest her emotional reactions with the most profound forms. Theories are not for her. She allows the subject to create the technical response and in that respect she parallels Picasso, whose various styles are in reality dictated by an inner response to plastic problems sensed within the phases of life which appeal to her. . . . Her emotional grasp of a primitive yet highly involved race is little short of amazing. To glance briefly at her technique of wood sculpture: she grasps the need of varied surfaces, that will in an impressionistic sense, cause light to function plastically. Her figures of Indians and animals are full of inimitable traits standing out in archaic simplicity of form.*

She herself has said, "God created form and color in this world. Also, he gave some of us talents for the use of these; therefore, we human beings must need them in our lives. There is no other answer. We artists must fulfill life's commission as artists."

Gustave Baumann, another prominent Santa Fe artist in the twenties and afterward, was born in Magdeburg, Germany, in 1881. He has said that his mother had a very endearing way of seeing visions of things that she wanted to happen—so one day when he was a small boy, she "saw" Gustave's Uncle Louis, who had moved to the United States, beckoning to her. She insisted that this meant the family was to join him, and join him they did.

Baumann grew up in Chicago and, as a young man, attended the Chicago Art Institute nights while working days in a commercial art studio. He joined the Palette and Chisel Club, where he met Walter Ufer, Victor Higgins, and Martin Hennings, all of whom were members of the Taos Society of Artists. They drank beer, drew from the model, and talked of what to do about

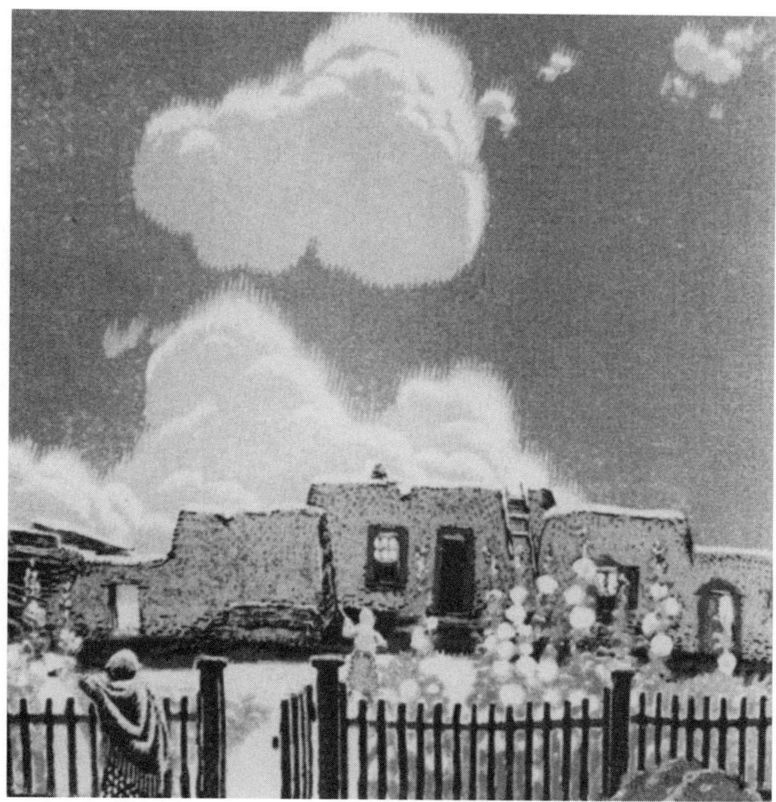

Gustave Baumann, Summer Clouds, *n.d. Woodblock print, 12 x 13 in. Museum of New Mexico.*

making a living from their art—other than by drawing shoes and buttonholes; Baumann's answer to the problem was a return to his native Germany. He had saved enough to go there and live for a year, so he went to Munich, a mecca for many art students at that time. He remarked once that he decided to study printmaking, and especially the making of woodcuts, because "I thought it would be easier than painting, until I found out differently." When his money gave out, he returned to Chicago and the commercial art world, with frequent trips to Brown County, Indiana.

"Art is a kind of tyrant," Baumann has said; "It pushes you around." It pushed him to New York and Connecticut before it sent him on a western trip to Taos, not in time to exhibit in the

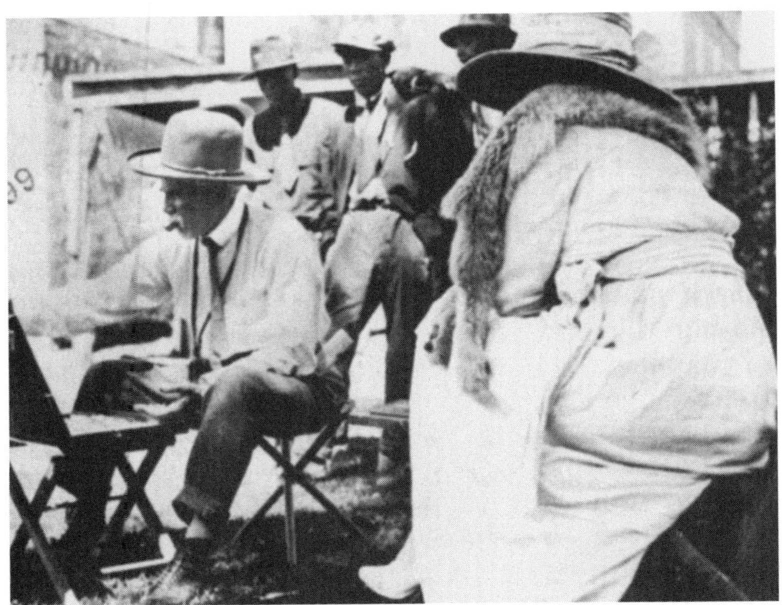

Julius Roshoven with an attentive audience on the patio of the Palace of the Governors.

opening show at the new museum in Santa Fe, but the next year, in 1918. Travelling on the same train westward with Baumann were another painter and his wife, the Julius Rolshovens. Nothing seems more improbable than that Rolshoven and his elegant wife could have settled happily into the way of life they were to encounter on this first trip to New Mexico. He was the son of a wealthy Detroit jeweller and a descendant of a family of medieval goldsmiths in Germany. With the encouragement of his cultivated family, Rolshoven had gone to Europe to study painting with Frank Duveneck in the 1870s.

It was the time of a great expatriot movement among American artists. John Singer Sargent, James Abbott McNeill Whistler, and Mary Cassatt were all living abroad, and academies in Paris and Munich were attracting many American students. It was also a very romantic time in art, and by the time Rolshoven, who was a superbly romantic painter, was thirty-one, he had established a formidable reputation in the major European art capitals. From Munich he went to Paris, then on to a study tour of Italy. By this time he had decided to make Italy

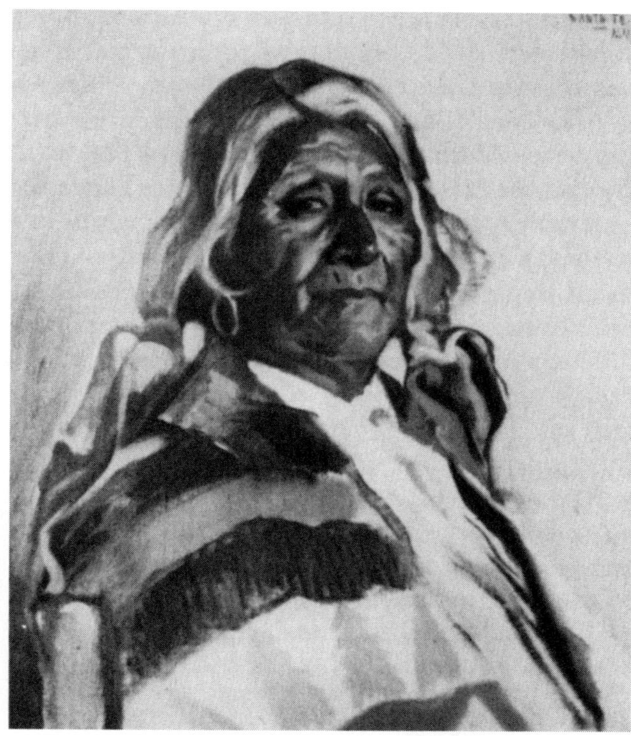

Julius Rolshoven, Santiago Naranjo, *n.d. Oil, 24 x 20 in. Museum of New Mexico.*

his permanent home. In 1907, he purchased the ancient "Castello del Diavolo" in Florence, and claimed it as his principal home until his death.

Rolshoven had always been interested in the American Southwest, however, and when he married Harriet Haynes Blazo they visited the area on their wedding trip. With Baumann they travelled to Lamy, then by the tiny two-car narrow-gauge to Santa Fe, and after a change to another narrow-gauge, on to Taos. Along the way they passed an Indian pueblo and stopped at Española (the town so loved by Fremont Ellis). Baumann later wrote in a catalog for a retrospective show of his work at the Fine Arts Museum:

> *Almost all the residents of this village were there to greet us as if it were the important event of the day. Cowhands and ranchers went this way and that, as if on important*

business, or rested themselves in a waiting buggy. Whatever was happening was all picture stuff if you chose to see it that way. There were no jittery taxi drivers ready to bite your head off if asked a civil question. I remember reboarding the train with considerable regret.

With train toots at cattle crossings, we entered the canyon of the Rio Grande, to stop at Embudo for lunch. We had been all morning going some forty miles, while now you can go all the way to Taos and back in less time.

It was nearing evening when the little train pulled to a halt at Taos junction, where the Rolshovens and Baumann were met by the wagon driver who was to take them to the hotel in town. Baumann's story of the event goes on:

The train gave a farewell toot when what I learned later was Long John Dunne made a belated appearance in weathered blue overalls and a tattered Stetson. A cud of tobacco gave his walrus mustache great mobility as he surveyed the scene, looking us over and then scratching his head as he counted the baggage, most of which was labeled "Rolshoven, Florence, Italy."

Then a voice accustomed to speaking to servants rang out, "I want all that baggage brought over with us because I have to dress for dinner tonight."

In spite of the difficulty of dressing for dinner, though, Rolshoven was fascinated with New Mexico and with Santa Fe and its plans for the new museum. His wife and he stayed for two years before returning to Florence at the end of the war. The University of New Mexico now owns a large collection of his paintings, many of which reflect the "noble savage" ideal of Indians.

Baumann loved Taos, although he has said, "Having seen something of sketching grounds in the East, wandering about in Taos streets and alleyways almost drove me frantic. There just was no limit and there was no need for imaginative

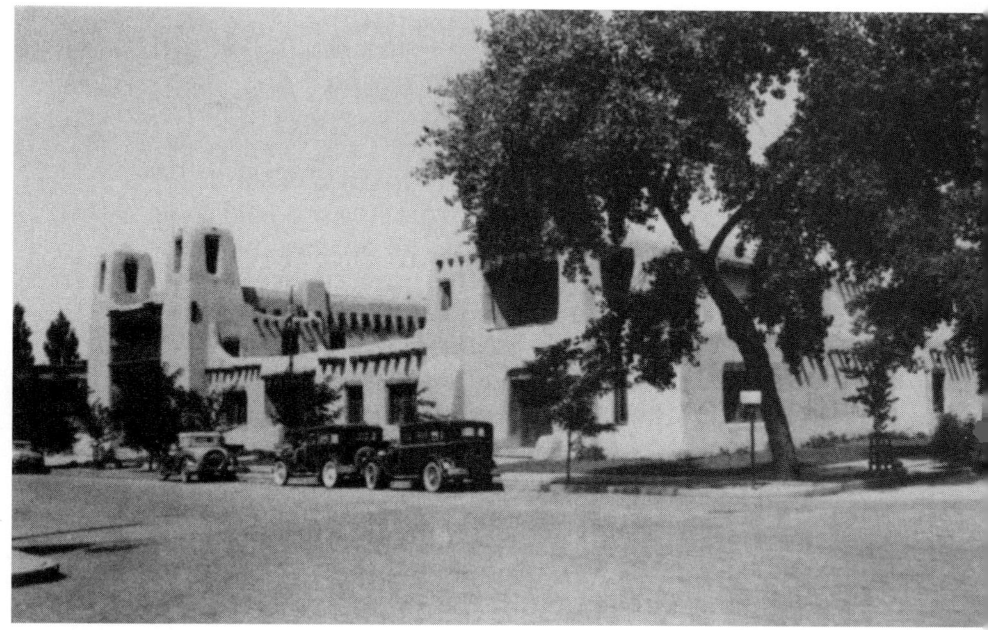
The Art Museum.

interpretations or of giving your versions of it; it was all there as is, with some leeway for your personal interpretations." Still, he wrote, "Seeing a mountain range from the distance always makes me wonder what is back of it. This particular range had a road through it that led to Santa Fe, if you were in no hurry to get there." And so he set out with some friends for Santa Fe, writing:

> *In those days there were three cars that stood up to the problem. One was that funny old Ford, then the Dodge and the Cadillac. We made it in a Ford after throwing a ceremonial kiss to Taos. The Ford rattled its way over roads and ditches, past little ranches with cows stopping their cud to see who was going by. The ranch looked as if the owners had left it to go away somewhere. . . . What took us over eight hours now can, if you are so minded, be done in one hour. It isn't the big rocks you see that make trouble, it's the little rocks you don't see.*

When bang went another tire, you stopped, jacked up the old Ford, and smeared a patch on the tire . . .

After passing through Velarde, Baumann recounts that the road became much easier until they came to a turnoff to Tesuque Pueblo:

We were within the city limits of Santa Fe, which had yet to learn about four-lane highways. We bumped through a long, sandy arroyo and there it was . . .

Unconsciously I gravitated to the plaza. It was a happy mixture of past and present with an incongruous obelisk sitting in the middle that made you wonder who was buried there. You could sit on comfortable benches shaded by a roof of trees and look around. While three sides of the plaza were preempted by stores the other side was occupied by a low building extending the entire length with a portal, that somehow overshadowed the three commercial sides and looked as if our Indians from Taos Pueblo might have had something to do with it. Could it be the art museum I had heard so much about? [It was the old Palace of the Governors; the Art Museum was across the street.] . . .

Seeing it [the Art Museum] for the first time was quite a revelation. It did not seem possible in what I had known in my earlier years as the Southwest, which was entirely filled with just Rocky Mountains and a town in the middle of them with a name that had two Qs in it; and now, of all things, to find a town named after a railroad with a full-fledged art museum.

Accustomed as I was to having art housed in those completely foreign Greek temples invariably alien to the surroundings, here was one equally strange, but somehow there was a certain feeling of rightness about it and I learned the meaning of the word indigenous, *but it took considerable readjusting to see it that way.*

Baumann wandered about the museum until he ran into Paul Walter, who was now the curator. Baumann recalled later:

Being of German ancestry we had something in common, although we said nothing about it, being just at the end of the first World War. It was a time when you had to be very careful. We exchanged notes and talked about the Taos artists' exhibitions and I divulged that I'd like to locate somewhere in New Mexico after straightening out my affairs in Chicago, adding that what I had seen of New Mexico made it a likely place to live and work out one's problems.

"So, I'll return as soon as I can, maybe next summer."

I still recall Paul saying, "Why don't you stay now?"

"I can't, Mr. Walter, I'm broke."

Then in his slight German accent he said, "Why don't you stay?" for the second time. "If you need the wherewithal, tell me how much and we'll go to the bank and get it." And so help me—we did.

I revised my schedule, was provided with working space in the basement of the museum, and from there on looked at life as worth living.

And so Santa Fe acquired one of its most interesting and articulate artists. He got a job working in the museum basement and making furniture for a studio with the help of the beloved Sam Huddleson, carpenter for the museum. Baumann later recalled:

The basement had a dirt floor where one could spit without Dr. Hewett noticing it, but you had to be careful of cigarette smoke. He was a devout tee-totaler. I even suspect he knew very little about art, but will please note, he with Frank Springer and the legal minded Col. Twitchell built the Art Museum which still functions. . . .

A museum basement is a distracting place to work; somebody is always looking for something or putting something away where it can't be found. With my furniture about completed, I transferred it to Canyon Road, sensing that some day Canyon Road would be the place art would gravitate to. Not being overly gregarious I moved away—built a studio of my own, when a nice Jane and love moved in on me, bringing with her all the surprises of a "happy sketching ground" that never changes.

This loving remark about Baumann's wife Jane leads one to tell a little about her and about how they met. Jane Henderson was a singer who had studied in Boston and New York and had sung opera in London when she was twenty-one years old. She had also toured Europe and acted in a Shakespeare company in Paris. Returning to her native home in Denver, she became deeply interested in the Indian people and their music. One fateful Christmas, she visited Santa Fe with a group of Denver friends and went with them to San Felipe to see the Christmas Eve dances which are held every year to honor the Christ Child. A long Catholic mass precedes the dancing, so Jane and her friends were taken to a small room to wait. It was unheated, and she was tired, so she lay down on the adobe *banco* (bench) along the wall, pulled her fur coat over herself, and went to sleep. Much later, Gus told her that he too had gone to the dances and had looked into the little room where he saw her sleeping. He said that she looked like a princess.

They did not meet on this visit, but a little later she decided to return to New Mexico and, following an invitation from one of the Indian families, to live in the pueblo of Santa Clara, where she could study Indian songs and chants. For six months, during winter weather, she lived there and absorbed the philosophy and meaning of the music. She lived in flannel shirts and riding pants and boots, and walked some miles each day to Española to pick up her mail. It was an experience she never forgot, and she still speaks of that time with great joy. During this visit, too, she met Baumann—awake this time!—and in 1925 she married him and

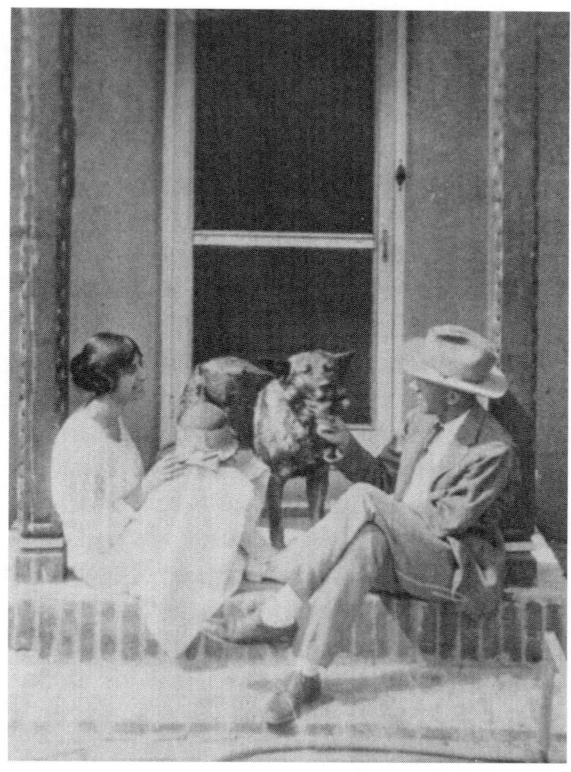

Jane and Gustave Baumann sitting on the front steps of their house.

moved into the house on Camino de las Animas which he had built in 1923.

Through all of their years in Santa Fe, the Baumanns were involved in the activities of the town, both funny and serious. Gus (with Will Shuster) was a cofounder of Zozobra, the Old Man Gloom of the Santa Fe Fiesta; the Baumanns loved and supported all musical events; and Gus took part with zest in artistic controversies, being a master at writing witty barbed letters to the newspaper. Jane, along with Olive Rush, was one of the organizers of Quaker meetings in the town. The Baumanns were friends of the Sloans, the Daveys, the Hendersons, the Van Stones, and Amelia and Martha White, generous patrons of the arts who had come to Santa Fe from New York.

Meanwhile, during the Depression, Baumann became "violently interested" in marionettes and, with help and advice from Tony Sarg (one of the most famous puppeteers in the United States) and Martin Stevens, he started carving and dressing the "little people." With Jane's acting and singing talents, and with a group of friends they trained, the Baumann marionettes became famous. They travelled all over the area performing plays, many of which members of the group made up themselves.

Baumann lived to a fine old age, working creatively almost to the end of his life. He always maintained a wicked glint of humor, but as an artist he was entirely serious and dedicated. Visitors loved to go to the Baumann house to see his paintings and woodcuts. Many visitors were Oriental artists, because Baumann worked in the true Japanese manner of making a separate block for each color, sometimes eight or nine for a single print.

The *Santa Fe New Mexican* once printed a few of Baumann's comments on life and art, and his own words seem to best express him as the dedicated artist he was: "I often wonder if other studios are burdened with such varied interests. . . . For me to paint after a siege of block-cutting is like having another baby which demands attention to its particular needs"; and "If you choose art as your way of life you accept a sacrifice in terms of worldly goods. But if you have the inclination inside you and don't accept that sacrifice, then you must make another sacrifice."

Amelia Elizabeth and Martha White, friends of the Baumanns, had set out from New York City to view a total solar eclipse in California in 1923, but stopped for a short visit with ranching friends in northeastern New Mexico. There the White sisters met the Frank Wilsons, who urged them to pay a visit to Santa Fe before going on west. The two sisters were so interested in the ancient city and its artists that they bought a piece of land before continuing on in their open Lincoln touring car to see the eclipse.

They purchased an acre and a half with a tiny house up the hill on Garcia Street and engaged William P. Henderson to alter and modernize the house for them that winter. They also asked Frank Wilson to try to acquire some adjoining land to go with it. The land he bought was half of the old Armenta Spanish land grant.

With the White sisters and Senator Bronson Cutting, Wilson formed the De Vargas Development Company with holdings reaching from Camino del Monte Sol to the Las Vegas Highway and south to Arroyo Chamiso—a sizable chunk of the southern part of the town. Henderson restored the old house and in time built a whole series of other buildings for Miss White in and around an arroyo on the land. During these building years, the Whites came to Santa Fe each summer, where they developed the strong and helpful relationships with the artists and other members of the community which made them loved citizens of Santa Fe.

They felt that the world should be made aware of the arts and crafts of the Indians, so they opened a shop on Madison Avenue in New York City, which was run by Dolly Sloan, to display their work. The Whites also worked with the Eastern Assn. on Indian Affairs to improve conditions for the Indians. Later, when they closed the Madison Avenue shop, they donated their collections to museums around the country.

The Whites' house on Garcia Street was a center for Santa Fe social life. Miss E. Catherine Rayne, Miss Amelia White's close friend and companion for many years, wrote of it:

> *Miss Martha wrote plays and musicals, many of which were produced at their home, named El Delirio. . . . This new home acquired a reputation for fabulous celebrations and parties, at which the "guests strolled the moonlit terraces amid the paper lanterns" or, as the case may be, conducted a Mayan "christening" of the irrigation/swimming pool, or masqueraded as foreign royalty and peasantry.*

Amelia White had a keen interest in archaeology and supported Sylvanus Morley's excavations in the Yucatan, travelling on muleback herself on some of his expeditions. Even when she was in her seventies, she travelled to Egypt and took a boat up the Nile to observe the artifacts which were to be covered by the Aswan Dam waters.

She also played the piano and harpsichord and helped start a Santa Fe Sinfonietta and Choral Society. Many young musicians were able to study through scholarships she provided. She presented the city of Santa Fe with its Animal Shelter as a memorial to her sister Martha, who died in 1938. She was also a founder of the Indian Arts Fund Collection; donated the land on which were built the Laboratory of Anthropology, the International Folk Art Museum, and the Museum of Navajo Ceremonial Art; and was a partner in the purchase of the old Sena Plaza. During World War II, she charged a small admission fee for exhibitions of art in her house and gave the money to the United Service Organizations. She converted a house on Garcia Street into a recreation center (known today as the Garcia Street Club), and gave piano lessons there herself. At her death at age ninety-four, she gave her house and land on Garcia Street to the School of American Research, where it has located its present headquarters. Not least importantly, she was a close and supportive friend of many Santa Fe artists, including Henderson, Baumann, Davey, and Sloan.

In the mid- and late twenties, Santa Fe was booming as an art center. While in 1917 there had been no art galleries other than the museum, by 1925 a gallery was established in Sena Plaza, and others soon followed. New groups of artists formed after the first one—the Cinco Pintores—and Santa Fe artists sent out exhibitions around the country. When the stock market crash suddenly ended the nation's days of prosperity, life in Santa Fe took on a somewhat sterner aspect, but the impact was not felt as rapidly or as hard in the adobe capital as elsewhere.

6
Depression Years

Santa Fe photographer Ernest Knee once said that in Santa Fe the twenties lasted into the thirties. It seems evident that the worldwide Depression did not hit as hard in Santa Fe as in other parts of the country because the area was largely rural. Life had always been rugged on the little ranchos, but there was an adobe house, room to graze a few animals, wood to burn, and food could be grown. Also, the state capital continued to supply jobs for a number of people. But for the artists, things were tougher than for many others. During hard times, people just don't have the money for luxuries like art. And by the thirties, Santa Fe had a large artist population.

To make ends meet during these years some of the Cinco Pintores rented out their houses on the Camino to visitors each summer while they homesteaded on government land to the northwest of town. John Sloan also bought a place in the same location, which he named Rancho Sin Agua (Ranch Without Water). In a letter to Shuster, written November 6, 1930, Sloan told of conditions in New York. The Sloans had just returned East after the usual summer visit to New Mexico. He wrote:

> *Business is pretty bad—without the teaching job at the League—but my private pupil has come back to me and that gives us some steady income. . . .*

> *We have not seen by the* S.F. New Mexican *any news of your return to the Camino but suppose that you have done so by this time—closing the homestead for the winter. We often think of the fun we had out there this summer—it surely is a spot of memories of gayety. . . . Things are really in a bad way in New York. Melancholy sights and bad news—bread lines, unemployed selling apples, to "keep the wolf away" at every street corner—100 and more racketeer shootings to the month—it's the jungle—wilds! And 13 months to elapse before the protest vote or "Revolution at the Ballot Box" takes effect!*

In spite of conditions in the East (or sometimes because of them), young artists kept following the dream of finding an adobe studio in Santa Fe and managing somehow. In 1928 two of them, Charles (Chuck) Barrows and Jim Morris, came to Santa Fe together. Morris said later that he got the idea from a painting of John Sloan's which he saw in New York. "At that time," Morris related in an interview for the *Santa Fe New Mexican*, "I was so sick of the green of the East. I was almost bilious from it. Green has always been a difficult color for me, difficult to work with." Sloan's painting was of Indian dancers, and the colors were golden brown and bronze—a welcome change for Morris, so he decided to go west.

His friend Chuck Barrows had been born in Washington, Pennsylvania, in 1903. He had studied at the Carnegie Technical Institute's College of Fine Arts and the Pennsylvania Academy of Fine Arts. Morris, four years older, had been a student at the Art Students League with a scholarship which Sloan had helped him obtain. The two started west in the classic Depression years way—hitchhiking and riding the rails from New York to Arkansas, where Jim's father lived. Mr. Morris was so horrified by their adventure that he gave the two fifty dollars to buy a car, a Model-T Ford. Consequently they arrived at the plaza in Santa Fe in more style than they had expected, but the trip almost finished the car's life. Aaron Copland, who was in Santa Fe that year, hired the two friends to drive him to Taos. They had made it

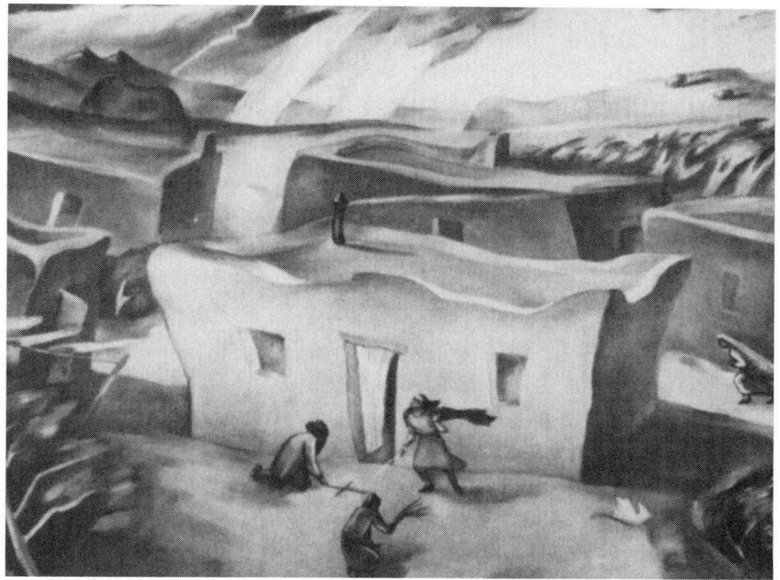

James S. Morris, Lightning, *late 1930s. Oil, 20 x 24 in. Museum of New Mexico. A painting done for the Federal Art Projects.*

almost to the top of the first long hill out of town when they had to roll back ingloriously. They sold the car.

Since they had no money for rent, they camped out on the Alameda, the parkway along the Santa Fe River. When Mrs. Ortiz saw how sparingly the two bought food, she offered them credit at the Ortiz grocery store. Then the wives of some of the artists in town arranged a show for them, and Morris and Barrows sold enough pictures to pay their bills with Mrs. Ortiz and have a bit remaining. Times might have been bad, but the Santa Feans were still welcoming newcomers and helping them to survive.

Their housing problem was solved when the two discovered a place for sale on Canyon Road. They convinced the real estate agent they could protect the empty property for three dollars a year. The next year, they persuaded him that since they had taken such good care of it, they should live there free of charge. He agreed, so they lived in the place for the next three years carrying on the helpful Santa Fe custom of bedding down any other young artist who came to town and needed a place to stay.

Anastacio Perea, presently the security officer at the Art Museum, tells fascinating stories of what life was like in Santa Fe when he was growing up in the thirties. He was born in the little town of Cerrillos, some seventeen miles south of Santa Fe. All of his life he has known the land and people of the area, the ranchers, and the craftsmen and artists. He relates that when he was a boy his family would hitch up the team and wagon at 5 o'clock in the morning and set out for Santa Fe. Along the way, the boys would ride for a while then jump off and run for a while. If they saw a rabbit, they turned into hunters on the spot. They would come into town by way of Cerrillos Road—now a major highway from Albuquerque with some of the heaviest traffic in the state, then a narrow peaceful dirt road. Almost up to the Santa Fe River it was still countryside, and even beyond the river there were no paved streets except for the brick one around the plaza. During the yearly fiesta, the whole length of the Alameda was a solid string of horses and wagons belonging to the folk who had come into town to celebrate.

Often on the way to town, Anastacio's family would stop off at the West ranch. The place belonged to an artist who has shown the Depression period, and the poor farmers and ranchers of the Southwest, more personally and honestly than almost anyone else. Harold E. West—Hal to all who knew him—was born in Honey Grove, Texas, in 1902, and attended a country schoolhouse in Indian Territory. He dropped out of high school in his first year, because he was more interested in drawing and sports than math. He finished out that year by attending an art school in Dallas, then went back and finished high school and set out to explore the country.

Meantime, Hal's sister Etna, a schoolteacher, had quit her job and decided to try her luck in the flourishing Taos art colony. But, as happened with so many, she made it as far as Santa Fe, and it was many months before she saw Taos. She later recalled that "there were no trains to Taos, just a stage line." She spent the first night in Santa Fe at the De Vargas Hotel. The next morning the manager of the hotel, Mrs. Sargent, decided that she should see Santa Fe, so she introduced Etna to the Shusters, who took over

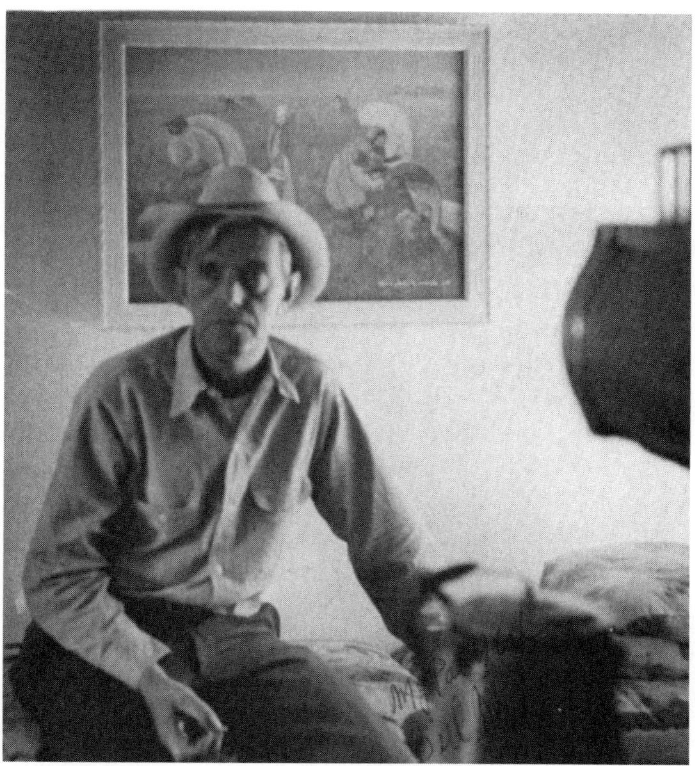

Harold E. West.

the job. "Shus and his wife," she said, "were wearing huge round sombreros and driving sort of a stripped down Model-T, and we were off." They stopped at the Gerald and Ina Cassidy house, where Shus explained "with a tinge of scorn" that they were successful Santa Fe artists and had a cook. "The exciting things in art," he said, "were happening on 'Telephone Hill' (the Camino del Monte Sol), where poor young artists were experimenting with new art forms and building their mud houses and studios on the slope of Sun Mountain." These artists were, of course, the Cinco Pintores, the Hendersons, Andrew Dasburg, and other friends. At the Cassidys', Etna met Wilbur Wiswall-—musician, playwright and writer, and, after a time, her husband. They were married at Olive Rush's house and went to Taos as part of their wedding trip.

With Etna living in Santa Fe, her three brothers soon came to visit. Hal, the first, arrived in 1926. He was much interested in art and quickly became friends with the Cassidys, the Shusters, and the Baumanns (whom he helped with their renowned puppet theatre). Gustave Baumann introduced Hal to printmaking, too, and gave him his first woodblocks. On this first visit to Santa Fe, Hal worked on the first house built on "starving hills," the area north of town where the governor's residence now stands.

Next, he decided to work his way to the East. He hitchhiked most of the way, arriving in New York in 1927. There he met Chuck Barrows and Jim Morris, who were already thinking of trying their luck in the West. Hal, the first of the trio to leave, stopped off along the way in Ohio to visit a farm belonging to the family of a Santa Fe friend. He renewed his acquaintance with their daughter, Mildred Van Sickle, whom he later married. The young couple stayed on in the Middle West for a while, Mildred teaching and Hal trying to find jobs in Chicago. Jobs, however, were nonexistent, so in 1930 Hal and Mildred headed west to Oklahoma, where their first son was born, and then on to Santa Fe.

From this time on, they lived on a series of ranches owned by other people, first in New Mexico, then back in Oklahoma, then in Ohio, where Hal left his family and headed back west alone in the desperate search for work. For a while, his brother and he picked cotton in Oklahoma, then they went back to Santa Fe where they opened a little shop that failed after a few months. Hal decided to try Oregon, but he got as far as Laramie, Wyoming, and then turned south to Denver.

The years of loneliness and wandering were not an unusual story during the terrible years of the Depression. All over the country young men were hitchhiking and looking for work. These were the years of the great migration of evicted farmers from the Middle West to California, too. But Hal turned back to Santa Fe once more, and in 1934 went to work for Preston McCrossen at McCrossen's Hand Woven Textiles Company. Hal's block-printing and silk-screening experience made him a valuable addition to the company. In December of that year, he was able to rent a house on Canyon Road and send for his

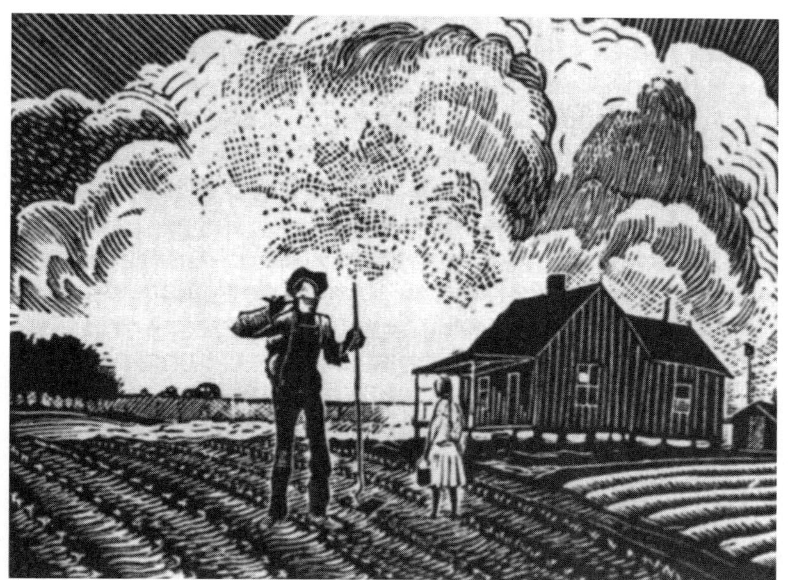

Harold E. West, Cotton Chopper, *1946. Linoleum block, 4 3/8 x 6 in. Museum of New Mexico.*

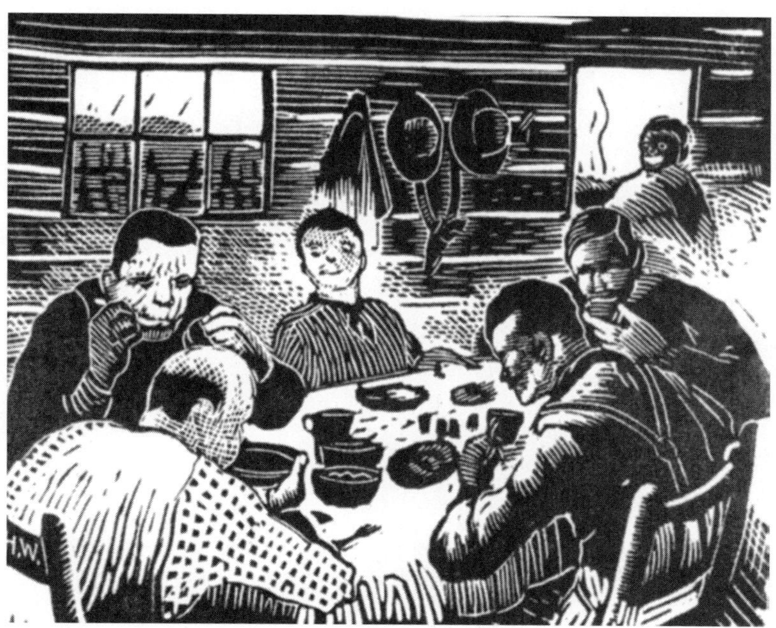

Harold E. West, Everything Tastes Good, *1940. Linoleum block, 4 x 5 in. Museum of New Mexico.*

family. When he met them at the train in Lamy, they had come home for good.

In the years that followed, the Wests started their own textile business, and in time moved south of town. Hal remembered his own lonely and hungry years, so their place became a regular stop for hungry young hitchhikers. In 1937, they moved to the Patania homestead, two miles off the highway to Albuquerque, and later Hal wrote a nostalgic poem-drawing of the years spent there:

1937 Four Year Camp 1940

Jack, Sarah, and Jerry started to school here—Archie and Phillip were borned here—Remember the Easter egg hunts, flower hunts, snake hunts? The play houses under the cedars, mocking birds, slick horses and horse shoe pitching—block prints, chocolate fudge and "in my den"—Chicken hawks, whooping coughs, and jumping rope?—and winter—sleading—traping—and chopping wood—rabbit hunts, not always good. Snow ice cream and mother's food. Remember the stories Mom often read And then that cold trip up to bed? and being snowed in many a day, until Uncle Gene brought food on a sleigh? Remember those long walks to the school bus?—It was always a thrill, when the setting sun shown on a lunch pail—Christmas! with ever-green and gifts that were good, happiness, company, plenty of food. We will all remember tho' the place is gone And so few of the memories can ever be drawn—Hal

Hal West worked under the Federal Art Projects, and in 1940 he was hired by the Museum of New Mexico as custodian at Puye, a prehistoric Indian site near Santa Clara Pueblo. He ran a gallery-museum there and had plenty of leisure time to work on his own art. During World War II he was able to buy the ranch, which still belongs to the family.

From this time on, Hal's painting assumed more and more importance in his life. His family was growing up, and his own health became very bad, so that he was no longer able to do heavy ranch work. In 1954, he moved to town and set up a studio on Canyon Road. It became a center for the Canyon Road art group. He had a place to pitch horseshoes at the side, and inside a big, black ranch-style stove which always supported a steaming coffeepot. Hal adored parties and seldom missed the opening of an art show. He was also one of the rare artists who never deprecated another artist's work, although he had a sincere and fierce dislike of nonrepresentational painting. When he died in 1968, Santa Fe lost a particularly individual and regional artist.

Meanwhile, the Art Museum, under the direction of Mrs. Mary R. Van Stone, continued its open-door policy. An article in *El Palacio*, on August 1930, told of plans for the Annual Exhibition of Artists and Sculptors of the Southwest, which was to coincide with the fiesta:

> *Plans for the annual exhibition are far advanced. Mrs. Mary R. Van Stone, curator of the art gallery, has mailed invitations to 73 artists asking them to participate.*
>
> *Each artist now working in the Southwest is assured of representation, and more than one work of each will be exhibited if space permits. For this reason, paintings over 12 square feet in area will be submitted to a jury. These invitations were mailed to the following artists: Santa Fe—F. C. Applegate, George W. Blodgett, Jozef Bakos, Henry Balink, Gustave Baumann, Harry Behn, Gerald Cassidy, Howard Coluzzi, Mrs. Fayette Curtis, Russell Cowles, Catherine C. Critcher, May Connell, Randall Davey, Andrew Dasburg, Allison Sommerville Dodge, Claire Dieman, John Dorman, Fremont Ellis, O. S. Emblem, Wm. Penhallow Henderson, Raymond Jonson, Dorothy Kent, Cyril Kay Scott, Datus Myers, Alice Clark Myers, Evaline Myers, Gladys Milligan, Willard Nash, Helen Needham, B.J.O. Nordfeldt, Guyrah Newkirk, Howard Ashman Patterson, Sheldon Parsons, Olive Rush, Charles S. Rawles, Warren E. Rollins, Albert H. Schmidt, Will Shuster, John Sloan, Norma Van Swearingen, Theodore*

Van Soelen, Dorothy Stewart, Eugenie Shonnard, Beulah Stevenson, Beulah Sutherland, Carlos Vierra, Dr. Charles Winchester, and Mrs. West.

Many of these names are familiar and have been discussed, but there are some new ones too. Some of the artists were interesting mainly as personalities; some made major contributions to the continuing artistic life of the town. George Winslow Blodgett was one of the latter. He did not intend to become an artist, and in fact started his career as a sculptor after nineteen years in the lumbering, heavy construction, and ranching businesses in the Cascade Mountains in Oregon. When Blodgett was thirty-eight years old he was told by a psychologist that he had creative ability and should try his hand at art. He went to New York and then to Paris to study, but his brief encounter with the art schools did not suit his temperament, so he worked on his own for the next two and one-half years. Then came a moment of revelation. He said that he was walking down his studio stairs one day when he suddenly envisioned a great hall of sculpture of the American Indian. Overcome by this idea he returned to America with a plan to complete a hundred or more life-sized studies in bronze of torsos, heads, and figures of the Indian people.

He came to Santa Fe in 1929 to work with the Pueblo people of the area, and lived there until his death from a heart attack in 1958. It is sad that his great dream was never realized, but before he died he had completed a number of his fine and highly realistic portraits. He once said of American art that "it must root in this [the Indian culture] or it cannot be a true American culture. This will be its basis, colored of course by later migrations from the old world, but this old world culture must be grafted upon the native, primitive arts to survive." It was this feeling which inspired his noble portraits of the Indian people. His works were purchased by various museums including the Metropolitan in New York, and the Museum of New Mexico is fortunate in having a group of the bronzes—all of well-known people from the area.

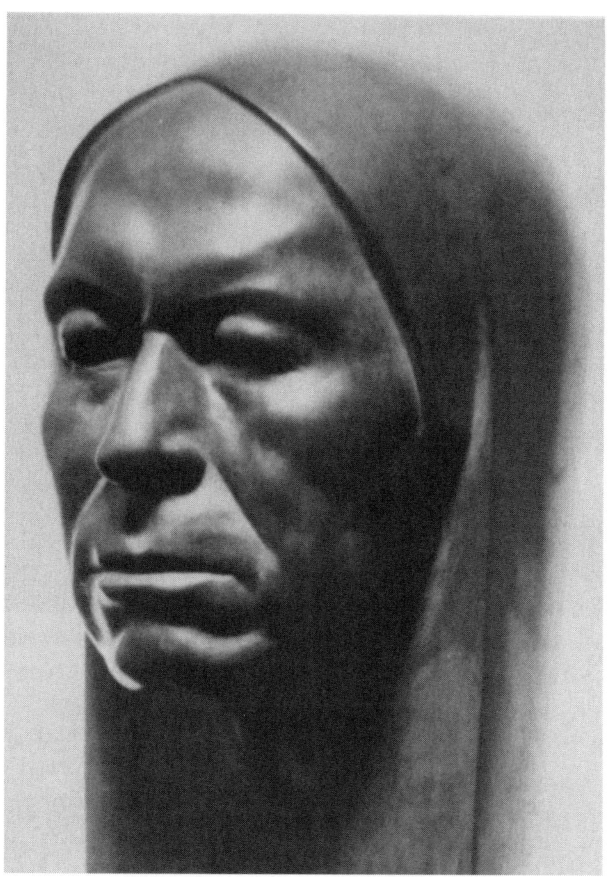

George Winslow Blodgett, José Montoya—San Juan, *n.d. Bronze, 17 1/2 in. high. Museum of New Mexico.*

Although not strictly a part of the Santa Fe art colony, there are two other indigenous artistic groups that should be mentioned: the Indian painters and the Spanish woodcarvers. Indians had long provided subject matter for artists in Santa Fe, but the Pueblo people (and later the Navajos, Hopis, and Apaches) were also creating beautiful watercolor paintings of their lives and ceremonies. The anthropologists had first encouraged the local Indians to paint, and soon afterward artists living in Santa Fe became aware of their rich talent. Among the early enthusiasts of Indian painting were William P. Henderson and his wife Alice

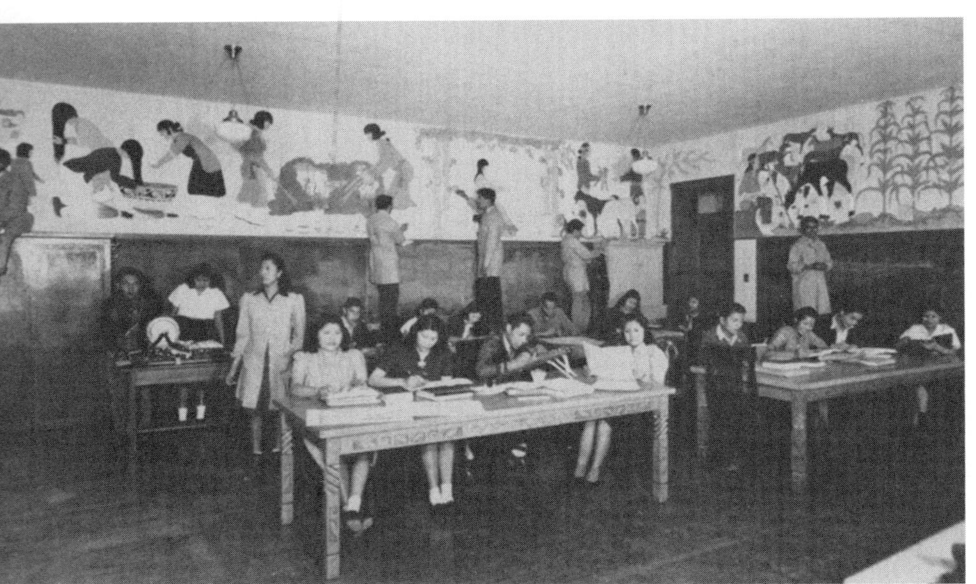

Student artists at the Santa Fe Indian School working on murals.

Corbin. Elizabeth De Huff, a writer whose husband had been hired as superintendent of the Santa Fe Indian School in 1918, also discovered the work being done by several students at the school and gave them help and understanding.

It was not until 1931, however, that the Indian School included art in its curriculum, and hired Dorothy Dunn to teach. She established the Studio, which flourished for the four years she was there. Many of her students achieved lasting fame, receiving materials and advice from this dedicated woman. As has been mentioned, Olive Rush also worked for a time showing a group of the Indian students the fresco process, and helping them paint a series of murals of their daily lives and beliefs for various rooms at the school.

Artists coming to the Santa Fe area were also quick to appreciate and collect the santos made by the Spanish villagers of northern New Mexico. These carvers, working in cottonwood, pine, or cedar, were following in a long tradition. Many present-day *santeros* are sixth- or seventh-generation carvers. Until recently, the religious figures were made entirely for use in their own homes or those of their neighbors. Now, they are sold, and are eagerly sought after by museums and private collectors.

One of the painters who collected santos was Cady Wells, who had come to New Mexico in 1927. At Jacona, near Santa Fe, he purchased and restored a house which has been called one of the outstanding examples of restoration of old New Mexican architecture. A highly cultivated and sophisticated artist, Wells was born in Sturbridge, Massachusetts, where his family was instrumental in the restoration of Old Sturbridge Village. He studied at Harvard and at the University of Arizona before settling at Jacona. He had also studied design in the East with Norman Bel Geddes, as well as music in Paris and Boston. In New Mexico he studied with Andrew Dasburg. Of his work, a critic for the *New York Times* said:

> *Cady Wells is an example of the major tendency in recent abstraction. Inspired perhaps by some of the Indian designs of the Southwest, Wells has created a kind of elusive, vibrant hieroglyph which registers and abstracts impressions of landscapes and ritualistic objects with the delicacy of a seismograph. Despite a certain repetitiveness, and their formidable esotericism, it is difficult to resist being inveigled into a journey of enchanted discovery in these curious inner landscapes.*

Other artists were also much interested in Spanish Colonial arts. Marsden Hartley, for example, who was in Santa Fe in 1916–1917, had painted his great *El Santo*. But the gift of Cady Wells's santo collection to the Museum of International Folk Art insured that Santa Fe would remain and grow as a center for the study and appreciation of this deeply moving art form. Wells gave his collection with the stipulation that E. Boyd, artist and fellow scholar, would be the curator of Spanish Colonial Arts—a position which she filled with great eminence for the rest of her life.

In 1933, with the Depression at its worst, the United States government started the unique series of programs which were to have a tremendous effect on the art and artists of the country. Some of the projects were based on the financial need of the artists, while in others the works were chosen through competitions or other selection processes. The programs were especially noteworthy in New Mexico, since they included work by artists of all three major cultures.

The first of these programs was the Public Works of Art Project, set up under an advisory committee to the Treasury Department, with funds allocated through the Civil Works Administration. The entire country was divided into sixteen regions, with New Mexico and Arizona making up Region 13. Each region established its own committee to administer the program in its area; Region 13's committee consisted of Jesse L. Nusbaum as director, Kenneth Chapman, secretary; Gustave Baumann, area coordinator; and Bronson Cutting, John G. Meem, Mary Austin, and Caroline Thompson, committee members.

Since Jesse Nusbaum was an anthropologist and a highly regarded photographer but not an artist, he asked Baumann to act as coordinator, to appraise the artistic value of the work produced. Jane Baumann relates that at first Gus did not want to take part in such a project. After thinking it over, however, he told her that he had always felt that the government should do more for the arts, so when they were trying to do so he had a moral obligation to help. The comments in his reports were always blunt and honest, and sometimes extremely outspoken: "A good painter of very slow perception," "Considered himself underpaid—dropped early," "Prolific worker—died in Harness" (this was Cassidy, who died in 1934), "Anything to escape female responsibility. . . . If only he painted as well as he talked." Of Raymond Jonson, he wrote, "Very meticulous. Worked on Library of N. M. University. Major project, more than ephemeral value." Of a different painter, he said, "Paintings breathed same old atmosphere"; of another, "Ability as painter effaced by drink."

During the Public Works of Art Project days, artist Datus Myers was the coordinator in charge of Indian artists, and later in charge of all artists in New Mexico. Myers had come to New Mexico in the summer of 1923 with his wife and daughter to spend some time painting in Taos and Santa Fe. A studio was made available to him in the Palace of the Governors, and he enjoyed his Santa Fe summer so much that after several visits to both Taos and

Santa Fe, his wife and he bought property on the Camino del Monte Sol, where they built a large and beautiful home.

Myers was born in Oregon in 1879, and studied art at the Chouinard School of Art in Los Angeles and later at the Chicago Art Institute, paying his way with money he earned running the family's farm in Oregon. In Chicago he studied sculpture as well as painting and won a series of prizes which enabled him to travel to Europe. Back in Chicago, he became a part of the active art colony and married Alice Clark, a fellow student at the Institute and later one of the first women architects in the country. After they discovered Santa Fe, and found Chicago friends such as B.J.O. Nordfeldt living there, they stayed in the town for twenty-eight years, Myers painting and doing research in Oriental, Egyptian, and American Indian art. After the Federal Art Project days, Myers taught art at the Arsuna School of Fine Arts in the city. Myers's New Mexico paintings depict the Indians and landscape; he also did charcoal and pencil portraits of many other painters and writers. The last few years of his life were spent in northern California, but he is fondly remembered for the important part he played in the Santa Fe art community.

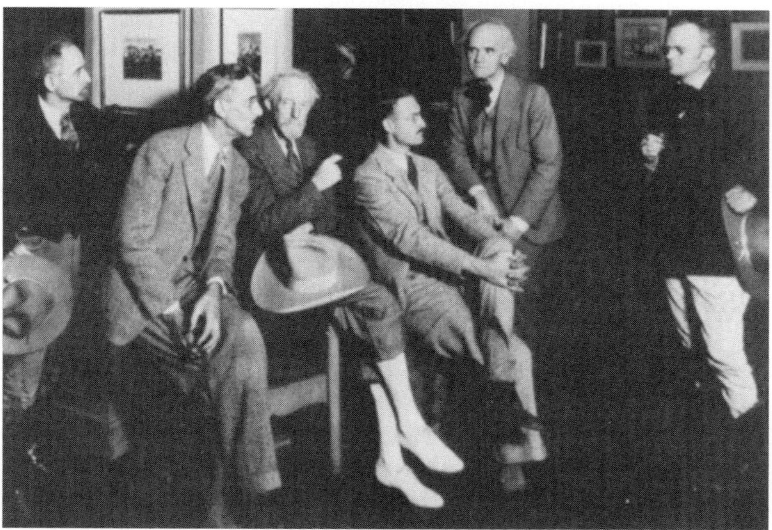

A distinguished group of artists in a gallery in La Fonda, the Harvey hotel on the plaza, 1933. Left to right: Carlos Vierra, Datus Myers, Sheldon Parsons, Theodore Van Soelen, Gerald Cassidy, Will Shuster.

In spite of some failures, the Public Works of Art Project, the Treasury Relief Art Project, and the Works Progress Administration (WPA) programs resulted in many fine works, often by important artists. Public buildings in the state were greatly enriched by them. An example of this is the fine series of murals by William P. Henderson which are to be seen in the Federal Courthouse in Santa Fe. Other notable murals are the group done by Peter Hurd in the old Post Office in Alamogordo, Olive Rush's frescos at New Mexico State University in Las Cruces, and those by Theodore Van Soelen in the Grant County Courthouse in Silver City.

Altogether, Region 13 received works by ninety-seven artists, fifty-one of them from New Mexico. Eight hundred and sixty-six works were completed in the region—murals, easel paintings, watercolors, sketches, etchings, lithographs, sculpture, block prints, lighting fixtures, wood carvings, and enlarged Indian designs. After the start of World War II, the WPA art program was changed into the Graphic Section of the War Services Program, and the whole program was dropped in 1943. However, this great experiment by the government, as many of the artists have said, enabled them to survive the Depression in New Mexico.

In 1935, Russell Vernon Hunter was appointed state director of the Federal Art Program in New Mexico, a post he was to fill for seven years until the projects were ended by the war. Hunter's family had moved from Illinois to eastern New Mexico early in his childhood, and he grew up with a deep love and understanding of the state and its people. In a tribute in the *Santa Fe New Mexican* written after Hunter's death in 1955, Georgia O'Keeffe spoke of her regard for him:

> *Our friendship started with a mutual love and wonder for the plains. The plains that stretch off flat like a table top on all sides in the Texas Panhandle—wide, wonderful and at times terrifying like the ocean. He had grown up on the plains and knew firsthand much that I hadn't known and he pictured it to me very vividly—particularly in his letters.*

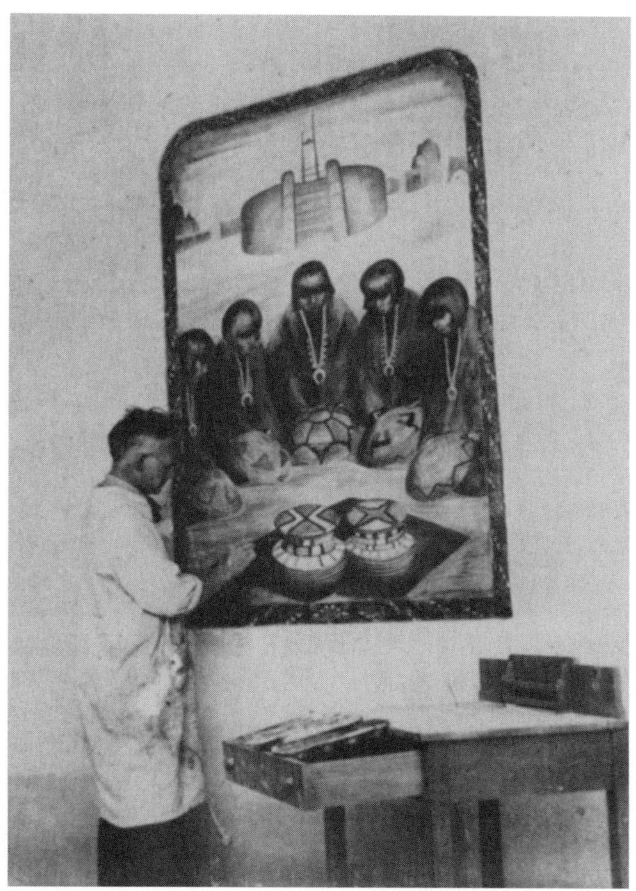

Will Shuster painting one of the frescoes for the patio of the Fine Arts Museum which were done under the Federal Art Projects in 1934.

We both knew a great deal about the Texas winds and dust storms that turned over a few houses in Amarillo every good windy day before the town was full of trees.

That wind was really something to know about.

We had much talk about painting. We agreed and disagreed. I never saw many of his paintings but one of cattle with a feel of the plains is very vivid to me—so vivid that if he only painted that one it is something done.

One of the last times I saw him a couple of years ago, he remarked, "I am not painting, but when I have something to say I will paint—too many paint when they have nothing to say." That was like him.

During the years he served as WPA art director, Hunter's great interest in religious folk art in New Mexico led him to write the Spanish Colonial Arts section of the *New Mexico Guide* and to supervise publication of the portfolio *Spanish Colonial Design in New Mexico*. When the war ended the art projects, Hunter became regional director of the United Service Organizations, and in 1948 he became administrative director of the Dallas Museum of Fine Arts. In 1952, he was named director of the Roswell Museum, which had been built as a Federal Art Center under his administration of the State WPA Art Program, a post which he held until his death in 1955.

Alfred Morang, writer, musician, painter, and one of Santa Fe's most colorful personalities, came to New Mexico in 1937. His wife, Dorothy, and he made the long trip from the East Coast by bus—she has said that they clung together in terror as the bus made its way over the frightening Raton Pass and down the

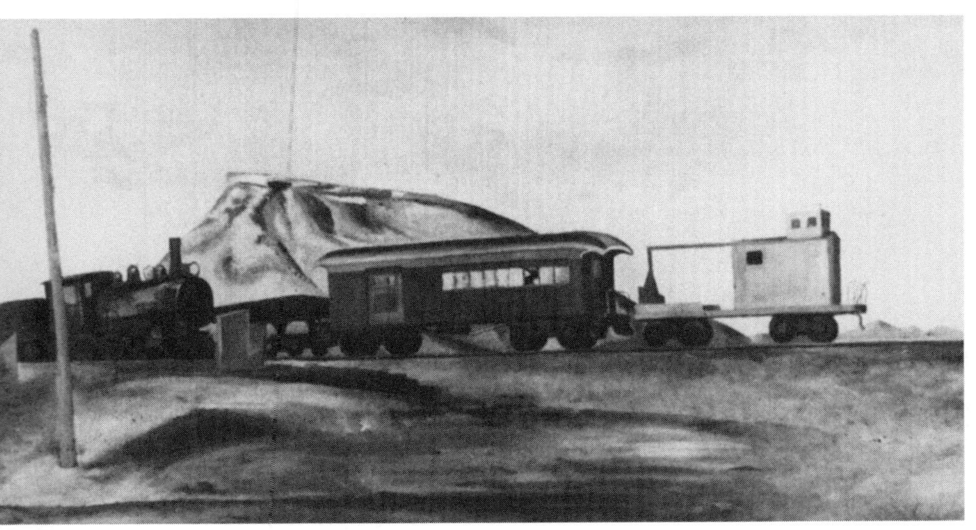

Russell Vernon Hunter, The Chili Line (also called The Narrow Gauge), *n.d. Oil, 24 x 39 in. Museum of New Mexico.*

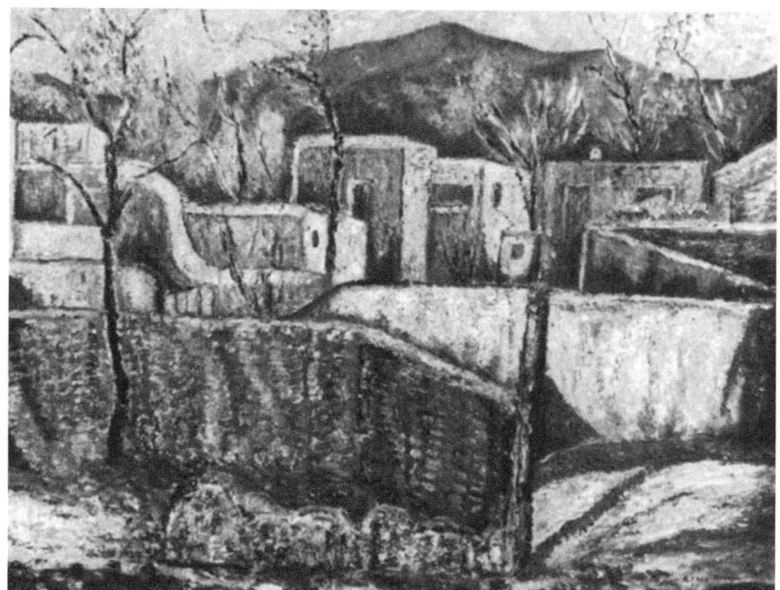

Alfred Morang, Santa Fe Houses, *1938. Oil, 20 x 24 in. Museum of New Mexico.*

mountains to Santa Fe. Born in Maine, Alfred was considered a prodigy on the violin as a child, and as he grew up he played in orchestras and dance bands. Dorothy, also born in Maine, was a graduate of the New England Conservatory of Music. While in the East, Alfred had had considerable success as a writer, and the Morangs had close friendships with many well-known writers, including Erskine Caldwell. Both were also deeply interested in painting.

Upon their arrival in Santa Fe, they moved into a studio in Placita Rafaela, which soon became famous for the open-house meetings the artists held there. In the *New Mexican* (previously the *Santa Fe New Mexican*) for May 5, 1955, Lorraine Carr wrote: "All of the art group gathered for wine, good talk, and music. Perhaps there is not a person in the colony at Santa Fe that has not visited the old studio. We recall that often the cats filled the chairs and the guests might have to lean against the wall, but it was a place where artists gathered." Santa Fe also listened to Morang's radio program on art, which continued for over fifteen years. For years, too, he wrote a column called "Art

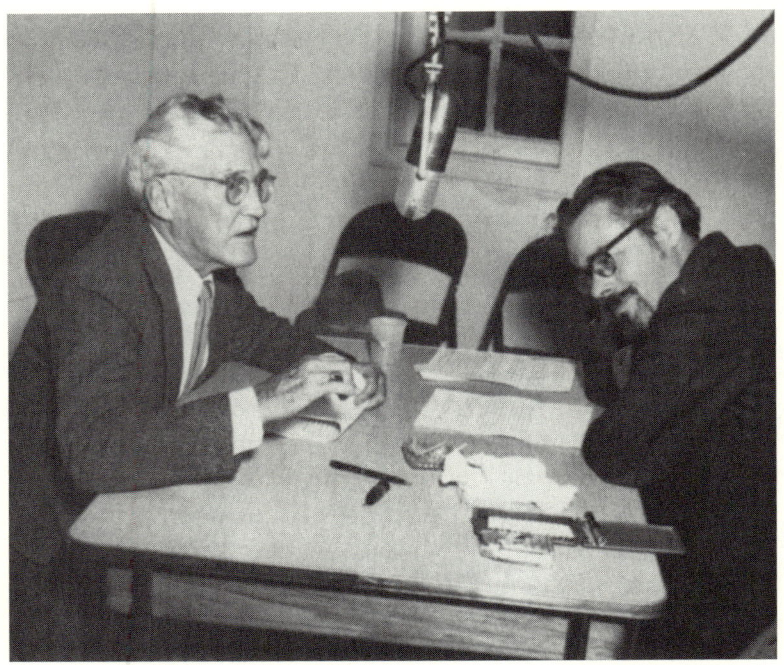

John Sloan and Alfred Morang on radio station KVSF, August 1947.

in the News" for a weekly newspaper in Santa Fe. In addition, he established the Morang School of Art in Santa Fe shortly after the war, and had a great influence on the many young artists who studied with him there, as well as on those who read his book *Adventure in Drawing*.

Alfred Morang's appearance fulfilled everyone's idea of the typical bohemian artist. He was slight in build with long hair, a mustache and beard, and a flamboyant, swaggering air. The surface appearance, however, covered a brilliant intellect and a tireless passion for art. His greatest heroes were the French Impressionists, but there is much of his friend John Sloan, too, in his etchings, many of which picture barroom scenes and "ladies of the evening," as he called them. When he died in a fire in his little adobe house on Canyon Road, Santa Fe had lost a man whom Dr. Reginald Fisher, then director of the Art Museum, called an "inventive, searching, daring, self-expressing creature . . . the Premier of the Santa Fe Bohemian Colony."

Dorothy Morang's interests in art developed in a considerably different direction from Alfred's. She became deeply interested in the Transcendental group and studied with Raymond Jonson and with Emil Bisttram for a time. Her musical training is clearly to be seen in her abstract paintings, collages, and pastels, with their harmonies of color and rhythmic changes of line and form. She worked under the WPA, later for the Office of War Records in the museum, and after the war, as a curator at the Art Museum until her retirement.

In 1937, the Art Museum celebrated its twentieth anniversary. They had been remarkable years, with a small but intensely interested group determining to help the town become an intellectual and cultural center—carrying on the exciting archaeological work to be done in the area; building the "New" Art Museum, even during the war; bringing musicians, writers, and photographers, as well as artists, to the town; and encouraging and promoting the arts and crafts of the Indian and Spanish people.

An important part of the museum's original idea, as conceived by the founders, was its open door policy. In the foreword to the catalog of the 1937 Twentieth Anniversary Exhibition Dr. Edgar L. Hewett, still the director of the museum, made a statement that sums up those years:

> *It is a good time for artists and public to take stock. . . . An "open door policy" was adopted and has been consistently adhered to. Its alcoves have been open to the most eminent painter or sculptor, to the unknown beginner . . . all on equal terms. There has been no jury, no favoritism for any theory or "school" of art. The director's idea was to provide all the facilities possible within our means, then keep out of the way and give art a fair field.*
>
> *The wisdom or unwisdom of the policy is open for discussion in the light of twenty years' trial. It is based on our theory that freedom is essential to efficiency in art, science, and public affairs; that intolerance is a blight on the human spirit. We are ready to modify it if*

convincing reasons are advanced. We are broadening the scope of the gallery's activities. We are now enabled to include music, and are offering a free concert every Sunday afternoon: pipe organ, piano, violin, flute, and voice, represented by capable artists. We would like to do more for sculpture; would like to include drama—but that calls for a museum theater. We believe firmly in the integration of the arts, of all the agencies that bring beauty and harmony into the lives of men.

We miss from this anniversary exhibition men whose endeavors enriched Southwestern art and life: Robert Henri, Donald Beauregard, George Bellows, Walter Ufer, Julius Rolshoven, Irving Couse, Herbert Dunton, Bert Harwood, Gerald Cassidy. Fortunately they are well represented in our permanent collections. We are watching eagerly for the strong new artists to carry the torch to farther horizons.

Suggestions as to the future policies of this gallery, from artists and public, will be greatly appreciated and given earnest consideration.

The catalog listed sixty-eight artists from Santa Fe compared with the forty-eight shown in the 1930 catalog, so the Santa Fe group had continued to grow during the Depression era. Some of the names included are artists who live in Santa Fe today, such as Betty Binkley, Fremont Ellis, Jozef Bakos, Louis Ewing, Paul Lantz, Bill Lumpkins, Helmuth Naumer, Eliseo Rodriguez, Myrtle Stedman, Brooks Willis, Yolanda Belloli, and Dorothy Morang.

Although Dr. Hewett had listed the names of some friends who had died, and although many people were now watching Europe with anger and dread, there was still time in Santa Fe for another of the joyful events which the artists loved so much. In 1939, the World's Fair had opened with much fanfare in New York, and so in July of the same year the artists provided their town with a Santa Fe World's Fair. Among the "old

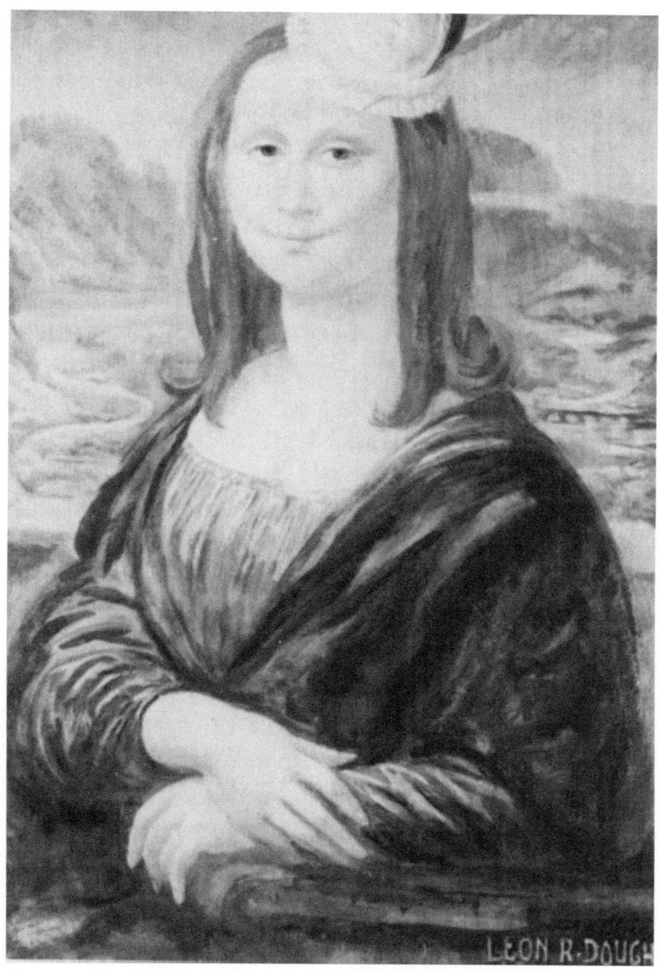

John Sloan [Leon R. Dough], Mon'l Lease Her.

mistress-pieces" listed were a portrait of Jozef Bakos "painted in Buffalo by the old master of the stein, Peter DeHooch." There was a scene from the first fiesta in Santa Fe, painted by "an early American itinerant artist who passed through and—out." "Mon'l Lease-er," said the sponsors of the show, "could be but one famous lady, even with the doll's hat of 1939. There is great concern over the appearance of this well-known and beloved picture, but the Art Committee is sure that it was John Sloan who did this original and the one in the Louvre is only a sickening copy." The exhibition showed, again, that while

Santa Feans take art very seriously, they have never been able to take themselves too much that way.

Very soon the peaceful days were to end. The Depression was receding and—although Los Alamos was still a closely guarded secret—the Atomic Age was about to be ushered in. Once again, the artists and other young men and women would go to war. Santa Fe's early golden age was ending, but nevertheless the years after the war were to bring new vitality to the mountain colony.

7
Serenity in Times of Change

When Santa Fe servicemen returned from the war, they found that many changes had taken place at home. The population of the state had exploded during World War II; Albuquerque became a big city, and Santa Fe was no longer a village. Although there was still no railroad connection with the outer world closer than Lamy, twenty miles away, modern highways, faster cars, and especially airplanes were breaking Santa Fe's physical isolation once and for all. More and faster means of communication too—particularly television—would make it harder to be regional. In many ways, neither America nor Santa Fe would ever be the same again.

At the conclusion of the years of war the federal government offered a service to returning young men and women that had a tremendous effect on the country's art and artists. G.I. benefits and a number of other grants and loans allowed many thousands to acquire college educations. Consequently, the postwar generation of artists all over the country received a broader, more art history–directed training than had their predecessors. For the first time, New Mexico produced a crop of locally trained young artists—products of the University of New Mexico and a proliferation of other art schools in the state—so that the Santa Fe art colony was no longer so dominated by artists trained in other places. But art schools everywhere in the country were strongly influenced by the work being done in the big cities, primarily abstract and nonobjective painting in the fifties followed by the rapid succession of intellectualized styles—optical art, pop art, computer art, minimal art—in the sixties.

A great deal of romantic, objective painting—such as southwestern landscapes and cowboy scenes—was still done in Santa Fe in the fifties and sixties, as it is to this day. But in the fifties many local artists were doing nonobjective work which did not depend on a particular environment for inspiration. The romantic storytelling art of the early Santa Fe painters was somewhat looked down on by many in those years, as was the later regional art of the thirties.

By the early fifties, there was a much larger group of artists working in New Mexico than ever before—in fact, so great a number that in 1951 the Art Museum announced that its annual show would have a jury for the first time. This prompted a telegram to Will Shuster from that great opponent of the jury system, John Sloan. "Dear Shus," it read:

> *I have just heard that S.F. Art Museum is having its first Juried Ex. - STOP! This means there will be no more distinction about the Annual Ex. STOP. The famous Open Door Annual of Santa Fe will be no more. STOP. Robert Henri and Edgar Hewitt will "turn in their graves" muttering - STOP. And now watch the miserable, puny, stinking, pallid efforts to show twentieth class imitations of the current fashions. OH STOP! Surely the Hanging Committee always managed to indicate those works which, in their opinion, were inferior. But all works were hung. "They" probably say, "There is no room" – "number of artists increases." STOP. Why not hang two or 3 lines? All great exhibitions in the 80s and 90s had 3 or 4 lines. They didn't need Interior Decorators to hang exhibitions, which are of course temporary - STOP. The "Open Door" might have let in Publicity, Honesty, Equity. The jury will cause all these to - STOP. I, who am about to be Opera . . . Wednesday Salute thee with love. John Sloan—Hanover, N.H.*

The operation which Sloan half refers to was performed, and a few days later he died.

It must have seemed to some at the time that Santa Fe was to become a memory as an adventure in art and in living—but then the picture shifted again. It is easy enough to look back through time in the mind's eye and see the little figures building their own adobes, marching happily in the fiesta parades, painting the dusty land and its people. It is easy to pick the interesting and amusing quotes *knowing* which artists have remained important and influential—and to sense a pervading atmosphere when an era falls into place as a distant view—but it's harder, of course, to see the pattern of our own time.

At least we know that Santa Fe did not become the memory of an art center. In the sixties, when many people became concerned with the environment and wanted to move closer to the earth again, they turned naturally to the Southwest, where the earth is so overwhelmingly present. Many artists, along with other young people, in revolt against highly structured and complicated urban ways of life, came to New Mexico to retreat into a simpler style of rural or semi-rural living, either solitary or in communes. This sort of experiment was not entirely new to Santa Fe, of course, although the magnitude of the migration sometimes felt overwhelming to established residents. Homemade tipis and irregularly shaped sculpted adobe houses began to crowd the hills around Santa Fe.

Many newcomers brought with them their interest in consciousness-raising drugs and disciplines. From their experiences a new kind of representational art had emerged—a Super-Realism that is highly skilled technically, highly derivative stylistically, and in many cases highly romantic in subject matter, with a great borrowing of images and materials from the Southwestern Indian cultures. The Indians were generally admired by them, as they seemed to represent everything these artists were looking for—a deeply spiritual, simple but ritualized way of life which had never left the earth.

An event of great importance to Indian art itself was the opening of the Institute of American Indian Arts in 1962, in

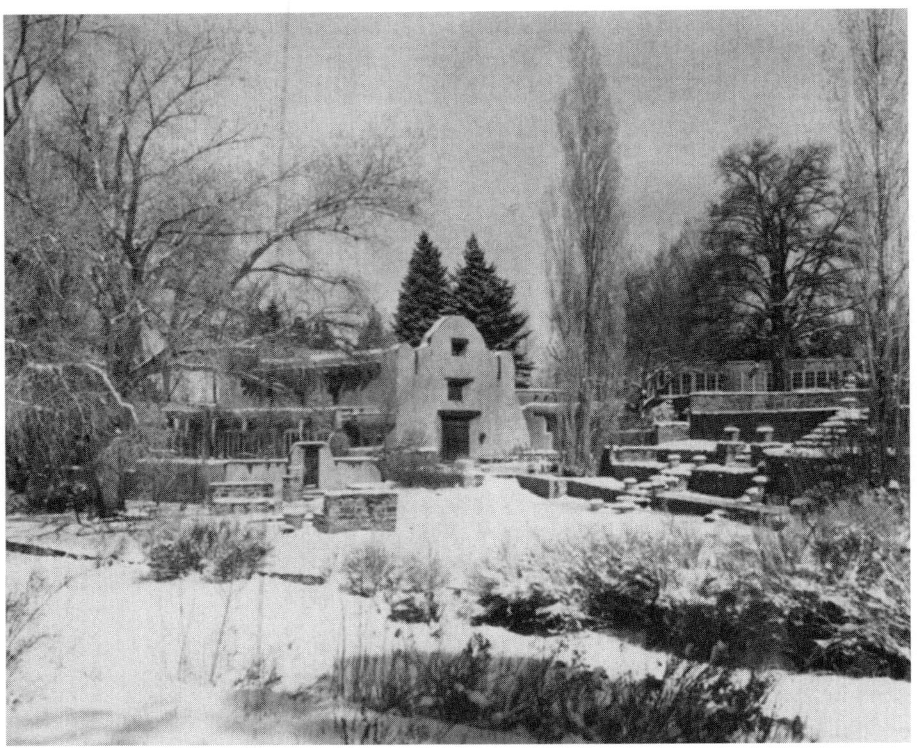

The Amelia White residence in the 1970s.

place of the old Santa Fe Indian School. The Institute, which operates as a training place for high school and college-level students from all Native American tribes in all of the arts, emphasizes the students' realization of their own tribal backgrounds while they work in great artistic freedom. A new, sophisticated generation of Indian artists is producing major works of American art in a variety of styles.

In recent years, too, the collectors and critics have looked again at the art created in Santa Fe in the early years of the century. They are far enough away from it now to see that some artists had powerful statements to make, while others had only pleasing ways. Art galleries have proliferated in the old town, with many concentrating on early work. Santa Fe has gained a large population of well-to-do, cultured, retired and part-time residents who patronize all the arts. The town doubles in size with opera and concert lovers and other visitors each summer,

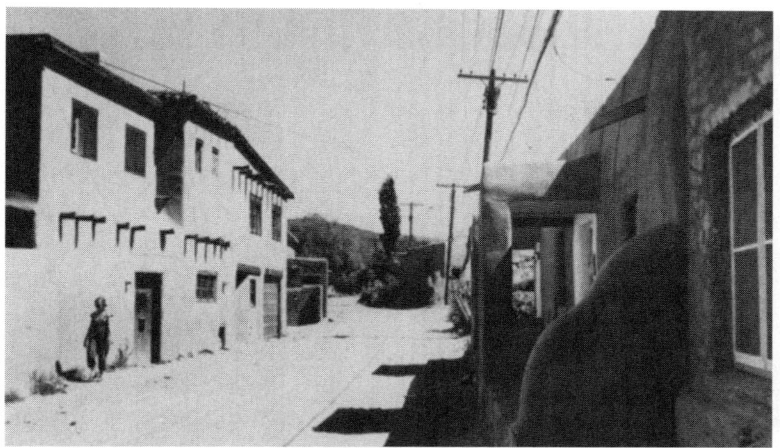

Canyon Road, facing east.

and every September the fiesta, started so long ago as a religious memorial and later expanded into a town-sized party by the artists, draws great crowds of visitors. Through all of the changes, the Fine Art Museum has stood at the corner of the plaza, with Edgar L. Hewett as its director until his death in 1946. Its policies have changed to reflect the times, but it has remained a focal point for the artistic community.

Somehow, in spite of a swelling and shifting population, Santa Fe has managed to remain its unique self—not just an artists' colony within a growing American city, but genuinely, one might say, eccentric throughout. Where else does the average person feel the confidence to build his own house, from the adobes on up? Where else can a person drive his car through flash flood conditions each spring because some residents oppose the paving of historic streets? See millionaires living next to laborers (one as likely to have a Ph.D. as the other)? Perhaps meet at an all-night grocery store at three in the morning the Italian painter who ran his dog for mayor, turbaned members of a local religious sect, friends who farm in a tiny Spanish village to the north, and a local stockbroker? They all have time to stop and talk to each other.

These kinds of things are precisely what some people don't like about Santa Fe. But artists like the easy tolerance of the place—the feeling that they can experiment, in their lives and

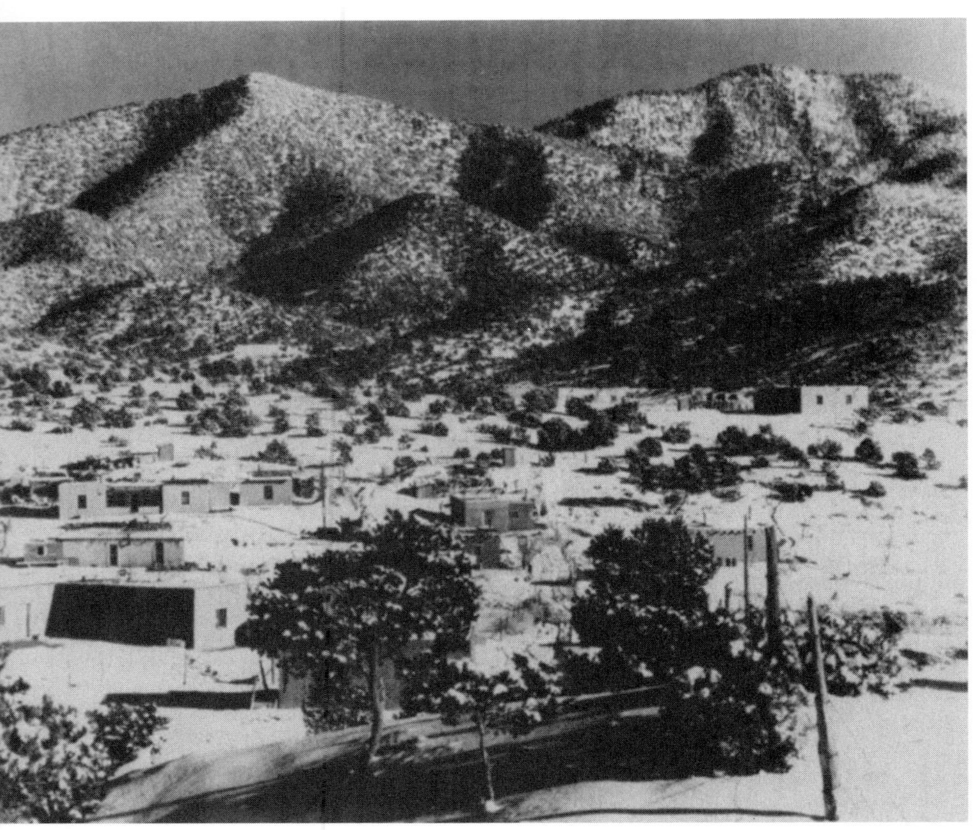

Santa Fe landscape.

in their work, and still not be "on the fringes" of society. Santa Fe has never been an art colony in the narrow sense of the word, a group of artists living closely together, influencing each others' work so much that a local style of painting emerges. Instead, it has been a real town, where artists can withdraw into their own work, or mingle with other artists, or take part in the general political, social, and economic life of Santa Fe to the extent they desire.

And somehow the place can simultaneously incorporate novelty, hold on to its heritage, and still remain serene and unified. The residents of Santa Fe have always, through the centuries, valued the beauty of the place. That sort of thing is contagious—and of course the artists have had a great deal to do with it—but much of the credit must finally go to the land itself. There is such a grandeur and simplicity in the landforms, such a subtle richness of textures and a clarity of light, that it would be hard not to see. It seems to give people the feeling that they're a part of things—there's a natural progression from the town, which is still small enough to be known intimately, to the rounded hills, human in scale, that surround it, to the larger mountains that protect the hills, to—quite suddenly—the stars, that are infinitely distant and yet—surprisingly close. It's no wonder that nearly every person one meets in Santa Fe either writes or dances or sculpts or paints—or plans to try.

Photographic Credits

Photographs furnished by the Museum of New Mexico photo archives are designated MNM.

xii David Noble
2 MNM
3 MNM
5 MNM
7 MNM
7 MNM
8 MNM
9 MNM
10 MNM; photo, Jesse Nusbaum
11 MNM
12 Courtesy Ernest Knee
14 MNM
16 MNM
17t Roswell Museum & Art Center, permanent collections
17b MNM
18 MNM
19 MNM
21 MNM
22 MNM
23 Courtesy Springer-Davis family
24 MNM
26t MNM
26b MNM
27 MNM
29 MNM
30 MNM
34 MNM
35 MNM; photo, Ina S. Cassidy
37 MNM
39t Courtesy Mrs. Edgar L. Rossin
39b MNM; photo, T. H. Parkhurst
40 MNM
41 MNM
42 MNM
43 David Noble
44 MNM
46 MNM; photo, Jesse Nusbaum
46 MNM
49 MNM
57 MNM
60t MNM
60b MNM; photo, T. H. Parkhurst
62 David Noble
64 Courtesy Mrs. Gene Jones
65 MNM
67 Courtesy Mrs. Edgar L. Rossin
68 MNM
69 MNM
71 MNM
72 MNM
74 Collections School of American Research; photo, T. H Parkhurst
77 MNM
79 MNM
80 Courtesy Laura Gilpin
82 Courtesy Fremont Ellis
83 MNM
83 MNM
84 MNM
101 MNM
103 MNM
105 MNM
107 MNM
108t MNM
108b MNM
110 MNM
111–12 Courtesy Stephen R.Arias, El Nido Restaurant, Tesuque, N.M.; photo, David Noble
113 MNM
114 MNM
115 MNM
116 Courtesy Alfred Dasburg
117 MNM; photo, T. H. Parkhurst
120 MNM
122 MNM
123 Collections School of American Research; photo, T. H. Parkhurst
125 Courtesy Raymond Jonson
126 MNM
128 MNM
129 Courtesy Mrs. Sylvia Loomis, Executor of the Olive Rush Trust
131 MNM
133 MNM
134 MNM
135 MNM
137 MNM; photo, T. H. Parkhurst
141 Courtesy Ann Baumann
147 MNM
149 Courtesy Harold E. West family
151t MNM
151b Courtesy Harold E. West family
155 MNM
156 Courtesy Ernest Knee
159 MNM
161 MNM
162 MNM
163 MNM
164 Courtesy Art Taylor
167 Courtesy Ernest Knee
172 David Noble
173 MNM
174 MNM

Index

Photos are noted in bold.
Works of art are noted by an asterisk.